Web Marketing For Dummies

W9-DEG-859

Cheat Sheet

Web Site Secrets for Marketing Success

Here are some quick tips to optimize your site for marketing effectiveness:

- Attract attention with your home page and headline.
- Maintain interest with text that's about "you," not about "me."
- Build desire with frequently updated content.
- Include many *calls to action.*
- Make your site easy to use and navigate.
- Post your phone number and street address on every page.
- Collect e-mail addresses to communicate with prospects and customers.
- Test your site before launching it.
- Use results of your traffic and sales statistics to improve your site.

What Every Successful Web Site Must Do

You should see increased sales once your site accomplishes these goals:

- Draw new visitors to your site.
- Keep them there for several pages.
- Bring them back for repeat visits.
- Answer "What's in it for me?"

Ways to Attract Repeat Visits

If you can entice visitors to return to your site, you're halfway to success. Consider one or more of these techniques:

- Chat rooms, message boards, blogs, and wikis
- Guest books or social networking pages
- Free postcards, screensavers, music downloads, or other offers
- Games and contests
- Coupons, discounts, or free shipping
- Online events

The Search Engines That Matter

Submitting your site for free to these four search engines will cover about 90% of the natural search market:

- **Google:** www.google.com/addurl/?continue=/addurl
- **Yahoo!:** http://search.yahoo.com/info/submit.html
- **MSN:** http://search.msn.com/docs/submit.aspx?FORM=WSDD2
- **dmoz (Open Directory Project):** www.dmoz.org/add.html

Useful Market Research Sites

It's easy to research your target market online with these sites:

- **ClickZ:** www.clickz.com
- **Internet.com:** www.internet.com
- **MarketingProfs:** www.marketingprofs.com
- **MarketingSherpa:** www.marketingsherpa.com
- **Web Marketing Today:** www.wilsonweb.com

For Dummies: Bestselling Book Series for Beginners

Web Marketing For Dummies®

Cheat Sheet

Web Marketing Glossary

It always helps to know the jargon when you journey to a new country:

- **above the fold:** Content and/or ads that appear on a page before a viewer needs to scroll.

- **AIDA (attention, interest, desire, action):** The direct marketing acronym for steps to purchase.

- **B2B (business to business):** Companies and sites that market to other businesses.

- **B2C (business to consumer):** Companies and sites that market to individual customers.

- **banner ad:** A graphic ad that links to the advertiser's site.

- **break-even point:** The dollar amount or number of sales needed for net revenue to cover Web site costs; a subset of the overall breakeven calculation.

- **call to action:** A marketing technique that asks prospects to take a specific action to move toward a sale.

- **cookie:** Identifying code downloaded to a user's machine to recognize repeat visitors or track online activity.

- **conversion rate:** The percent of site visitors who take a particular action or make a purchase, often called *converting browsers to buyers.*

- **CPC (cost per click):** Amount actually paid for a click-through to a site from an ad.

- **CPM (cost per thousand):** The advertising cost to reach 1,000 viewers or listeners; allows comparison among various advertising methods.

- **CTR (click-through rate):** The percent of people viewing an ad who click on it.

- **PPC (pay per click):** Payment method for online ads in which advertisers pay for each click-through, rather than by number of impressions or flat rate (*see* CPM).

- **ROI (return on investment):** The amount of money earned (or lost) as a percent of the amount invested, usually stated for a period of a year; can compute for a Web site, an ad campaign, or an entire business.

- **SEO (search engine optimization):** The process of making a Web site search-engine-friendly to improve ranking in search results.

- **SEM (search engine marketing):** The combination of SEO with paid search marketing through PPC, paid inclusion, or paid appearance.

- **URL (uniform resource locator):** Address designating the location of information on the Web; includes a registered domain name.

Wiley, the Wiley Publishing logo, For Dummies, the Dummies Man logo, the For Dummies Bestselling Book Series logo and all related trade dress are trademarks or registered trademarks of John Wiley & Sons, Inc. and/or its affiliates. All other trademarks are property of their respective owners. Copyright © 2007 Wiley Publishing, Inc. All rights reserved. Item 4982-2. For more information about Wiley Publishing, call 1-800-762-2974.

For Dummies: Bestselling Book Series for Beginners

Web Marketing
FOR
DUMMIES®

Web Marketing

FOR

DUMMIES®

by Jan Zimmerman

Wiley Publishing, Inc.

Web Marketing For Dummies®

Published by
Wiley Publishing, Inc.
111 River Street
Hoboken, NJ 07030-5774
www.wiley.com

Copyright © 2007 by Wiley Publishing, Inc., Indianapolis, Indiana

Published by Wiley Publishing, Inc., Indianapolis, Indiana

Published simultaneously in Canada

No part of this publication may be reproduced, stored in a retrieval system or transmitted in any form or by any means, electronic, mechanical, photocopying, recording, scanning or otherwise, except as permitted under Sections 107 or 108 of the 1976 United States Copyright Act, without either the prior written permission of the Publisher, or authorization through payment of the appropriate per-copy fee to the Copyright Clearance Center, 222 Rosewood Drive, Danvers, MA 01923, (978) 750-8400, fax (978) 646-8600. Requests to the Publisher for permission should be addressed to the Legal Department, Wiley Publishing, Inc., 10475 Crosspoint Blvd., Indianapolis, IN 46256, (317) 572-3447, fax (317) 572-4355, or online at http://www.wiley.com/go/permissions.

Trademarks: Wiley, the Wiley Publishing logo, For Dummies, the Dummies Man logo, A Reference for the Rest of Us!, The Dummies Way, Dummies Daily, The Fun and Easy Way, Dummies.com, and related trade dress are trademarks or registered trademarks of John Wiley & Sons, Inc. and/or its affiliates in the United States and other countries, and may not be used without written permission. All other trademarks are the property of their respective owners. Wiley Publishing, Inc., is not associated with any product or vendor mentioned in this book.

LIMIT OF LIABILITY/DISCLAIMER OF WARRANTY: THE PUBLISHER AND THE AUTHOR MAKE NO REPRESENTATIONS OR WARRANTIES WITH RESPECT TO THE ACCURACY OR COMPLETENESS OF THE CONTENTS OF THIS WORK AND SPECIFICALLY DISCLAIM ALL WARRANTIES, INCLUDING WITHOUT LIMITATION WARRANTIES OF FITNESS FOR A PARTICULAR PURPOSE. NO WARRANTY MAY BE CREATED OR EXTENDED BY SALES OR PROMOTIONAL MATERIALS. THE ADVICE AND STRATEGIES CONTAINED HEREIN MAY NOT BE SUITABLE FOR EVERY SITUATION. THIS WORK IS SOLD WITH THE UNDERSTANDING THAT THE PUBLISHER IS NOT ENGAGED IN RENDERING LEGAL, ACCOUNTING, OR OTHER PROFESSIONAL SERVICES. IF PROFESSIONAL ASSISTANCE IS REQUIRED, THE SERVICES OF A COMPETENT PROFESSIONAL PERSON SHOULD BE SOUGHT. NEITHER THE PUBLISHER NOR THE AUTHOR SHALL BE LIABLE FOR DAMAGES ARISING HEREFROM. THE FACT THAT AN ORGANIZATION OR WEBSITE IS REFERRED TO IN THIS WORK AS A CITATION AND/OR A POTENTIAL SOURCE OF FURTHER INFORMATION DOES NOT MEAN THAT THE AUTHOR OR THE PUBLISHER ENDORSES THE INFORMATION THE ORGANIZATION OR WEBSITE MAY PROVIDE OR RECOMMENDATIONS IT MAY MAKE. FURTHER, READERS SHOULD BE AWARE THAT INTERNET WEBSITES LISTED IN THIS WORK MAY HAVE CHANGED OR DISAPPEARED BETWEEN WHEN THIS WORK WAS WRITTEN AND WHEN IT IS READ.

For general information on our other products and services, please contact our Customer Care Department within the U.S. at 800-762-2974, outside the U.S. at 317-572-3993, or fax 317-572-4002.

For technical support, please visit www.wiley.com/techsupport.

Wiley also publishes its books in a variety of electronic formats. Some content that appears in print may not be available in electronic books.

Library of Congress Control Number: 2006936827

ISBN: 978-0-470-04982-2

Manufactured in the United States of America

10 9 8 7 6 5 4 3

1B/SQ/RS/QW/IN

About the Author

Jan Zimmerman has found marketing to be the most creative challenge of owning a business for the nearly 30 years she has spent as an entrepreneur.

Since 1994, she has owned Sandia Consulting Group and Watermelon Mountain Web Marketing in Albuquerque, New Mexico. (*Sandia* is Spanish for *watermelon*.) Her previous companies provided a range of services including video production, grant writing, and linguistic engineering R&D.

Jan's Web marketing clients at Watermelon Mountain are a living laboratory for experimenting with the best techniques for Web success in site design, content development, word-of-Web marketing, search engine optimization, and offline integration.

Ranging from hospitality and tourism to retail stores, B2B suppliers, trade associations, and service companies, her clients have unique marketing needs but share similar business concerns and online challenges. Her consulting practice keeps Jan aware of the real-world issues facing small-business owners and provides the basis for her pragmatic marketing advice.

Throughout her business career, Jan has been a prolific writer. She has written four editions of another book about marketing on the Internet, as well as the books *Doing Business with Government Using EDI* and *Mainstreaming Sustainable Architecture*. Her concern about the impact of technological development on women's needs led to her book *Once Upon the Future* and an anthology, *The Technological Woman*.

The writer of numerous articles and a frequent speaker on Web marketing topics, Jan has long been fascinated by the intersection of business, technology, and human beings. In her spare time, she crews for a hot air balloon as a way to get her feet off the ground.

Jan can be reached at books@watermelonweb.com or www.watermelonweb.com.

Dedication

In Loving Memory

Aunt Ceil

For lessons taught and laughter shared

Author's Acknowledgments

The idea of a writer, locked in a cell alone with her computer and literary agony, is a myth — at least for nonfiction. This book could not have been written without a cast of dozens, especially researcher Diane Martin, who did a mammoth job of organizing information.

She provided background files, compiled sites for the many tables in this book, and rooted out arcane online facts, often at the last minute. Working on my truly crazy schedule, Diane checked thousands of links and reviewed hundreds of sites for screen shots. Not many people are asked to search the Web for a good site index. Diane interviewed companies for the Real World stories with genuine interest and skill. Finding those companies — and clearing copyrights for them — required endless calls and e-mail.

The staff at Watermelon Mountain Web Marketing supplemented her efforts, drawing on their extensive knowledge of the Internet to suggest sites or ways to locate information. My particular thanks to Tenley Zumwalt, Sandy Flowers, and Shawna Araiza, for helping with research, Photoshop, and those endless copyright clearances. I owe my staff a great debt for taking on extra work to allow me to write — not to mention their patience and computer support and ignoring my frustration with PCs. I promise to buy myself a new Mac, guys.

As always, my family, friends, and pets earn extra hugs for their constant support and encouragement. I'm lucky to have friends who accept that I could not always be there for them but are there for me — friends like Diane Johnson, who made copyright clearance calls on her vacation visit. The garden, alas, is not so forgiving.

Special thanks to all my clients, who have taught me so much and given me the opportunity to put into practice what I preach.

I'd also like to thank Kim Darosett, project editor at Wiley, for her flexibility and patience with an author who sometimes can't remember an answer from one chapter to the next, and copy editor Heidi Unger. Together, they have made this book much better than it started out. My thanks also to technical editor Paul Chaney for his careful checking of links and knowledge of Web details, and to all the other staff at Wiley — from the art department to legal — who have provided support. If errors remain, I am certain they are all mine. My appreciation goes to senior acquisitions editor Steve Hayes, for making this project possible, and to my agent, Margot Hutchison of Waterside.

I don't know how this superwoman has worked through the past several years as her young son struggles with cancer. Margot and her extraordinary family teach us all a lesson about what's important in life. If you enjoyed this book, please consider donating to Alex's Lemonade Stand in honor of Sam Hutchison at www.alexslemonade.org/donate_now.php. Thank you in advance, dear readers.

Publisher's Acknowledgments

We're proud of this book; please send us your comments through our online registration form located at www.dummies.com/register/.

Some of the people who helped bring this book to market include the following:

Acquisitions, Editorial, and Media Development

Project Editor: Kim Darosett

Senior Acquisitions Editor: Steve Hayes

Copy Editor: Heidi Unger

Technical Editor: Paul Chaney

Editorial Manager: Leah Cameron

Media Development Specialists: Angela Denny, Kate Jenkins, Steven Kudirka, Kit Malone

Media Development Coordinator: Laura Atkinson

Media Project Supervisor: Laura Moss

Media Development Manager: Laura VanWinkle

Editorial Assistant: Amanda Foxworth

Sr. Editorial Assistant: Cherie Case

Cartoons: Rich Tennant (www.the5thwave.com)

Composition Services

Project Coordinator: Jennifer Theriot

Layout and Graphics: Lavonne Cook, Denny Hager, Barbara Moore, Laura Pence

Proofreaders: John Greenough, Jessica Kramer, Techbooks

Indexer: Techbooks

Anniversary Logo Design: Richard Pacifico

Publishing and Editorial for Technology Dummies

Richard Swadley, Vice President and Executive Group Publisher

Andy Cummings, Vice President and Publisher

Mary Bednarek, Executive Acquisitions Director

Mary C. Corder, Editorial Director

Publishing for Consumer Dummies

Diane Graves Steele, Vice President and Publisher

Joyce Pepple, Acquisitions Director

Composition Services

Gerry Fahey, Vice President of Production Services

Debbie Stailey, Director of Composition Services

Contents at a Glance

Table of Contents

Introduction

- -

*I*t looks so simple on TV. Launch Web site, count money. If only real life were that easy! Alas, with billions of Web sites competing for attention, it's not simple at all.

On the other hand, marketing online isn't rocket science. This book charts a practical course of action to put your business Web site to work, adding profits to your bottom line. Whether you're just beginning to develop an online presence or you've been online for years and are anxious to build traffic, this book will help you drive prospects to your site and convert them into customers.

Web Marketing For Dummies leverages your offline knowledge of marketing into mastery of the Web. Because I've written this for owners of small businesses, where cash is king, I suggest dozens of free to low-cost guerrilla marketing ideas that you can try online.

There is no simple formula that says shoe companies should use this Web marketing method and architects should use that one. I urge you to keep a picture of your customers or clients in mind as you read this book. If you always ask yourself whether a particular method would appeal to your target market, you'll make the right decisions. Answer your customers' question, "What's in it for me?" and your Web marketing plan will work magic for you.

About This Book

This book is a reference guide to Web marketing. It's written like good Web copy: short sentences, short paragraphs, short chapters, with lots of bullets and tables so you can find information quickly.

Please look at the pretty pictures. Not only do they save you 1,000 words of reading, they're good examples of what you're trying to accomplish.

Dip into a chapter when you confront a particular problem with Web marketing to find the information you need right then and there. The rest will wait.

This book is intended for business people, not techies. Where there is technical information, I suggest you share that tip with your Web developer. Let him or her worry about Apache Mod Rewrites for search-engine-friendly URLs. You worry about your business.

Conventions Used in This Book

Doing something the same way over and over again can be boring, but consistency makes stuff easier to understand. In this book, those consistent elements are *conventions*. There are only a few:

- ✔ When URLs (Web addresses) appear within a paragraph, caption, or table, they look like this: www.dummies.com.
- ✔ New terms appear in *italics* the first time they're used, courtesy of the copy editor.
- ✔ Anything you have to type is in **bold**, but frankly, I don't think you have to type a single thing in this book. Mostly, you just have to think.

Fortunately, Web marketing is platform- and operating-system-independent. It doesn't matter whether you're on a Mac with OS X or a PC running Windows XP, but I do recommend a high-speed Internet connection. You can no longer realistically monitor your Web site, upload content, review statistics, or research your market at turtle speed (dialup).

What You Don't Have to Read

You don't have to read anything that seems irrelevant to your business! You can scoot past the text following a Technical Stuff icon because that's really for your developer. You can bypass the Real World stories in sidebars, though you might enjoy reading the experiences of actual business owners who tried the marketing techniques under discussion. Sometimes, they divulge a helpful insider secret or two.

Chapter 5, which discusses building and merchandising an online store, applies only if you plan to sell online. If that doesn't apply to you, skip that one. If you're just getting started or have a very limited budget, you might want to postpone reading Part IV, Spending Online Marketing Dollars. Instead, stick with the affordable, basic techniques described in Part III until your site generates revenue or produces solid leads.

Foolish Assumptions

In my head, I've constructed a picture of you, the reader. I assume you (or your designated staff member) already

- ✔ Have a computer with high-speed Internet access.
- ✔ Are (or soon will be) an owner or a department manager in a small-to-mid-size business.
- ✔ Have or plan to write a business plan.
- ✔ Frequently use standard applications such as Word and Excel, e-mail, and browsers.
- ✔ Are comfortable searching the Web by using keywords and search engines.
- ✔ Can write and do basic arithmetic, especially when dollar signs are involved.
- ✔ Know your business and target markets.
- ✔ Have a passion for your business and a commitment to providing excellent customer service.

If my assumptions are incorrect, you'll probably find this book either too easy or too hard to read. On the other hand, if my description is accurate, this book is just right for you.

How This Book Is Organized

I divided this book into parts that follow a chronological development process, from business planning and market research, through the design of a marketing-effective Web site and online store, to online promotion that pushes qualified traffic.

For information on a specific topic, check the headings in the Table of Contents or look at the Index.

By design, this book enables you to get as much (or as little) information as you need at any particular moment. If you're starting from scratch, you might want to start with Part I. If you already have a successful Web site and want to increase traffic, start with Part III.

Part I: Getting Going with Online Marketing

Unless you have endless wealth and infinite time, you need some idea of what you're trying to accomplish online before you start. This section stresses the importance of Web planning as it intersects with all aspects of your business, including the financial ones. Stocked with useful planning forms and checklists, this part shows how to plan for success from the beginning.

Part II: Building a Marketing-Effective Web Site

Profitable business Web sites don't happen by accident. From a marketing perspective, a successful site attracts visitors, keeps them on the site, and brings them back for repeat visits. This section addresses building a marketing-effective Web site and online store, as well as implementing marketing ideas right on your site. Onsite marketing methods, including viral techniques, are usually either free or inexpensive, making them especially attractive for businesses getting started online.

Part III: Exploring Online Marketing Basics

The core of this book, Part III covers the absolutely essential components of online marketing: word-of-Web techniques, link campaigns, e-mail marketing, natural search engine optimization, and integration with offline techniques. While some of the methods in this section are time consuming, they don't require deep pockets.

Part IV: Spending Online Marketing Dollars

Use with caution: The advertising and marketing techniques in this part cost real moolah. Pay per click and banner advertising can both escalate to expensive media buys. Marketing techniques that use advanced technology and multimedia are expensive to produce.

Part V: Maximizing Your Web Success

A book about Web marketing would be incomplete without discussing Web analytics and sketching the overall environment in which Web marketing occurs. From legal and tax issues to a review of basic business concerns, this part will help you maximize the return on your Web investment.

Part VI: The Part of Tens

Like all *For Dummies* books, this one has a Part of Tens. These chapters list ten free ways to kick off your Web marketing campaign, ten of the most common Web marketing mistakes, and ten tips to rejuvenate a tired site. Turn to the Part of Tens for good ideas again and again.

Icons Used in This Book

To make your experience easier, I use various icons in the margins to indicate particular points of interest.

Whenever I provide a hint that makes an aspect of Web marketing easier, I mark it with the Tip icon — it's my way of sharing what I've figured out the hard way — so that you don't have to. Of course, if you prefer to get your education through the school of hard knocks, be my guest.

This icon is simply a friendly reminder. There are more details in this book than any normal person can remember. Use this icon to help you remember basic principles of Web marketing. Look up all the rest when you need it!

Ouch! This icon is the equivalent of an exclamation point. Heed these warnings to avoid potential pitfalls.

Sometimes I feel obligated to give developers some technical information; they don't always know as much as they think they do. I mark that stuff with this geeky guy so you know it's information to share, not necessarily to understand.

No one can do a Web site alone. It helps to know who can provide assistance. This icon suggests what type of professional to call. No names, but at least you have a search term to use! For a business Web site, I don't recommend using amateurs or helpful friends and relatives, unless they're already professionals in the field.

This icon designates a real-world story about a company that's tried the technique under discussion. Real-world stories are fun to read and contain useful tips from actual business people.

Where to Go from Here

You'll find helpful features on the companion Web site for this book at www. dummies.com/go/webmarketing.

From the site, you can download copies of the planning forms and checklists that appear throughout the book — and a few extra ones. Use them to develop your own Web marketing plans, or to track and analyze what you've done. For convenience, you can use the live links to key resource sites to stay up-to-date, subscribe to blogs or newsletters, or simply find out more than fits between any two covers.

If you find errors in the book, or have suggestions for future editions, please email me at books@watermelonweb.com.

Part I
Getting Going with Online Marketing

The 5th Wave   By Rich Tennant

"You know, it dawned on me last night why we aren't getting any hits on our Web site."

In this part . . .

Unless you're Mr. or Ms. Moneybags, know what you're doing before you start spending money and time with online marketing. This section stresses the importance of Web planning as it intersects with all aspects of your business, including the financial ones.

Chapter 1 puts Web marketing in the context of overall marketing. You discover that what you already know about marketing is true, such as the importance of return on investment (ROI). At the same time, Web marketing confronts you with new techniques and terms, such as the *conversion funnel,* which measures what percent of site browsers convert to buyers.

It's easy to get so enthralled by Web technology that you lose site of your business goals. Take advantage of basic planning tools in Chapter 2 to maintain a focus on your bottom line, even as your marketing world grows more complex. A quick review of basic business and marketing principles demystifies Web marketing and positions you at the starting line.

Before you create — or redesign — your Web site for success, come to terms with your own limitations. Except for genius-types who work 48-hour days, everyone needs help. In Chapter 3, you find out how to select good professional help or how to take advantage of online tools to get going.

Chapter 1

Taking Your Marketing to the Web

*1*s it hypnosis? Seduction? Simple amnesia? Don't let dot-com technobabble dazzle you into forgetting every business lesson you learned the hard way. You know there are no magic marketing bullets offline; there aren't any online either. You know that you build a customer list slowly, experimenting with a variety of techniques until word-of-mouth marketing kicks in. You want to be successful online? Then approach the Web the same way you approach your offline business — with an awareness of business fundamentals, a combination of marketing techniques, and an indelible focus on your customers:

✔ **You must have the business fundamentals right before you can have a truly successful Web site.** Many sites flounder on straightforward business issues of cost, merchandising, back-office support, and customer service. Too many confuse revenues with profits, only to discover in quarterly financials that their sites are sinking into the Red Sea.

✔ **Successful Web marketing requires a combination of methods.** Nowhere in this book do you read that the solution to all your Web woes lies in content, search engine optimization, link campaigns, pay per click ads, banners, e-mail newsletters, or any one online or offline marketing technique. Many are necessary, but none alone is sufficient to bring in all the traffic you need. Instead, you must select judiciously from an extensive marketing menu: a little appetizer, a nice side dish, maybe an entree that takes the most of your Web marketing dollars and efforts. Oh, don't forget dessert.

✔ **The customer is the measure of all things Web, from site design to marketing.** Don't let technology or personal inclination distract you from a focus on what the customer wants. And don't get carried away with what Web technology can do.

From those principles, you can see that Web marketing fits within the definition of marketing you're already familiar with. When they're well implemented, online techniques might offer a more cost-effective marketing mix, greater flexibility, or easier expansion to new markets than offline techniques. With this book as your reference guide, you can master these new tools, adding a sense of adventure, as well as profits, to your bottom line.

Rearranging Your Marketing Mix

If you're already in business, you know you have to spend money to make money. You may need to redistribute your marketing budget to free up funds for marketing online. Here's a method to elevate your marketing analysis from guesswork to grand plan. First, make a four-column list organized as follows:

- ✔ The first column lists all the marketing techniques you currently use.
- ✔ The second column lists the target market you reach with that technique.
- ✔ The third column lists how many new customers you think that technique brings in.
- ✔ The fourth column lists how much you spend per year on that technique.

If you've been in business for a while, you might have forgotten some of your recurring marketing investments. Here are a few examples to spark your memory: a Yellow Pages listing, signs, business cards and letterhead, logo design, a listing in a local business club directory, T-shirts for the girls' soccer team, newspapers or other print ads, direct mail, local fliers, word of mouth, radio spots, billboards, and so on.

If you don't have extra money to invest in developing and promoting a Web presence, decide which existing methods you can cut in favor of more cost-effective online marketing. If you duplicate your reach at lower cost online, you can put the difference into your Web site.

What you already know about marketing is true. Profit from your own success. Unless you're starting a new business online, your new customers are going to look an awful lot like your old ones. You already know how to sell to them, what they need, and what appeals to their emotions.

Reaching your current audience online

If you haven't done so in a while, write a paragraph describing your current customers: age, gender, income level, education, geographical region, or job title (if you sell business to business). What else do they buy? What do they like to read? It's easy to research your markets online. If you need to, segment your customers into different groups that share the same characteristics.

When you design your site and implement your Web marketing campaign, use these profiles to decide what to do and where to spend.

Finding new customers

If you intend to use the Web to find new customers, decide whether you're simply expanding your geographical reach; going after a new consumer demographic or vertical industry segment for existing products, or selling new products and services to completely new audiences.

All the guerrilla marketing aphorisms apply online. Rifles, not shotguns! Target one narrow market at a time, make money, and reinvest it by going after another market. Don't spread your marketing money around like bees spread pollen — a little here, a little there. That will dilute your marketing dollars and reduce the likelihood of gaining new customers.

Write up the same type of profile for your new target audience(s) that you write up for your existing ones. As you read through the marketing chapters of this book, match the profiles of your target markets to a given technique to find a good fit.

Discovering the long tail of opportunity

You might hear the phrase the long tail to describe the market model used by successful Web sites. The long tail, shown in the graph in Figure 1-1, describes a situation in which a lot of low-frequency events (think sales for various products) add up to more than a few, high-frequency events. The low-frequency events tail off, but added together they make up more than half the total.

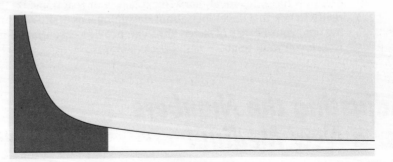

Figure 1-1:
A graph of the *long tail* for Sales versus Products.

Sales

Products

This theory suggests that the reach of the Web is so vast that you can have a profitable business selling many items to a few people rather than spending a humongous marketing budget to sell a few items to many people. It works for Amazon.com, Netflix, iTunes, and eBay. Why not for you? The trick is that those few people need to find your products in the vastness of cyberspace, or you have to find them.

Of course, that's Web marketing, which is what this book is all about. If you're curious, read more about the long tail at http://en.wikipedia.org/wiki/Long_tail, or in Chris Anderson's book *The Long Tail: Why the Future of Business is Selling Less of More* (Hyperion).

Understanding Web Marketing Essentials

While this book is full of the endless details that make up a successful Web marketing campaign, you need to keep only three, overarching points in mind. If you measure everything you do against these criteria, you'll come out fine:

- ✔ Do your plans fit with the needs and interests of your target audience?
- ✔ Do your plans make financial sense?
- ✔ Are your plans within your capabilities to execute?

Right this very minute, create two new folders in your bookmarks, one for sites you love and another for sites you hate. Better yet, set up an account at del.icio.us (http://del.icio.us), which allows you to gather all your bookmarks in one, convenient, online account, accessible anywhere. With one click, you can *tag* (bookmark) any site you see for future reference.

Whatever your online activities, make a habit of tagging or bookmarking the sites that appeal to you and the ones you can't stand. Don't worry if you don't yet have the vocabulary to explain your reactions. By the time you're ready to talk to a developer about designing a new site or upgrading an existing one, your library of saved sites can provide essential information about where you want to go.

Adjusting the Numbers for a New Medium

For you, as a business owner or manager, the Web is a new means to meet your goals, not an end itself. You can hire professionals to take care of the technical and marketing details, but no one knows — or cares — as much about your business and your audience as you do.

The Web offers an unprecedented opportunity to reach very narrow, niche markets with customized, sometimes individualized, products and services. Think imaginatively about the big picture. What are your long-term strategies for growing your business? Can you take advantage of Web technology to help your company prosper by

✔ Supporting your current customers more cost-effectively

✔ Expanding to new markets

✔ Expanding your list of products or services

Rid yourself of one myth right now. The truth is that marketing on the Web is not free. You can spend a lot of money, a lot of time, or some combination of the two, but you can't get away without an investment of some sort. Before you go online, think hard about the numbers. As a good businessperson, consider these key benchmarks, which are described in the sections that follow:

✔ The cost of customer acquisition

✔ The break-even point

✔ Return on investment (ROI)

Don't call a Web developer about money! If you're not sure how to compute these numbers, ask your bookkeeper or CPA for help. Or go to one of the many Small Business Development Centers around the country for free assistance. (Go to `http://sba.gov/sbdc/sbdcnear.html` to find a center in your area.)

Estimating the cost of customer acquisition

Can you acquire customers for less than the average $20–$30 cost of finding a new retail customer offline? Maybe, but it depends on what you're selling. Generally, the more expensive your product or service, the more you must spend to acquire a new customer.

The cost of lead acquisition equals your marketing cost divided by the number of customer leads that the activity generates:

```
cost of lead acquisition = marketing cost ÷ # of leads
```

If you spend $100 for pay per click ads on Google to get 20 people to your site, your cost is $100 divided by 20, or $5 per lead. If only two of those 20 people buy, your cost of customer acquisition is actually $50. That's fine if they each spend $250 on your site, but what if they spend only $25? You can compute acquisition cost for any single marketing campaign or technique or across an entire year's worth of marketing expenditures.

The average cost of acquiring a new customer approximately equals the profit derived from an average customer's purchases in the first year. In other words, you might not make a profit on your customers unless they spend more than the average or you retain them for more than a year. Yes, indeed, it's a cold, cruel world. However, if you take advantage of the many free and low-cost techniques in this book, you can reduce your dollar cost of customer acquisition and stand a better chance of making a profit.

It takes three times as much money to acquire a new customer as it does to keep an existing one.

Computing your break-even point

Break-even is the number of sales at which revenues equal total costs. After you reach break-even, sales start to contribute to profits. To calculate the break-even point for your Web site, subtract your *cost of goods* for a product (or cost of delivering services) from your revenues for that product, which yields the *gross margin:*

```
revenues - cost of goods = gross margin
```

Now, total the *fixed costs* (charges that are the same each month, regardless of how much business you do) for your Web site, such as monthly developer's fees, hosting, charges for your Internet service provider (ISP), overhead, and in-house labor. Finally, divide your *fixed costs* by your *gross margin*. That tells you how many sales you must make to pay for your basic Web expenses.

```
fixed costs ÷ gross margin = break-even point
```

Costs of sales are expenses that vary with the amount sold, such as shipping and handling, commissions, or credit card fees. For more accuracy, you can subtract these from your revenues as well. Divide the result into your fixed costs to get the break-even point.

Figuring out whether you'll make money online

Return on investment (ROI) looks at the rate at which you recover your investment in site development or marketing. Often you calculate ROI for a period of a year. To calculate ROI, simply divide profits (not revenue) by the amount of money invested to get a percentage rate of return:

```
profits ÷ investment = rate of return
```

You can also express ROI by how long it will take to earn back your investment. An annual 50 percent ROI means it will take two years to recover your investment. As with acquisition costs, you can compute ROI for your original investment in site development, for any single marketing campaign or technique, or across an entire year's worth of Web expenses.

Don't spend more on marketing than you can make back. Losing money on every sale is not a good business plan.

Now, go have some fun and make some money online!

Chapter 2

Planning for Web Marketing

*I*t's easy to get so involved with the Web that you lose sight of your business goals. In this chapter, I show you how a few, simple, planning tools can help you track the big picture while maximizing the contribution of your Web site to your bottom line.

If you mastered marketing principles in business school long ago, this chapter connects cybermarketing to your memories of business plans, the four Ps of marketing (product, price, placement, and promotion), and Maslow's Triangle. If your marketing knowledge comes from the school of hard knocks or if you're new to business, these conceptual marketing tools enable you to allocate marketing dollars in a new environment.

As you go through the planning process, I suggest that you summarize your decisions on the forms in this chapter. Refer to them whenever you're uncertain about a Web marketing decision. These forms also make it easier to convey your site goals and objectives consistently to developers, graphic designers, other service providers, and employees. For your convenience, you can download full-page versions of these forms from the book's companion Web site at www.dummies.com/go/webmarketing.

Preparing an Online Business Plan

If you're starting a new business of any type, you need to write a business plan. If you're adding online sales to an existing operation, dust off and update your current business plan as well. Opening an online store is like opening a new storefront in another city; it requires just as much planning. Even if you're only launching or revamping a Web site, I suggest writing a shortened version of the business plan outlined in the following list.

Most business plans include some variation of the following sections:

- Summary
- Description of Business (type of business and goals)
- Description of Product or Service
- Competition (online and offline)
- Marketing (target market, need, objectives, methods, promotion)
- Sales Plan (pricing, distribution channels, order fulfillment)
- Operations (facilities, staffing, inventory)
- Management (key players and board)
- Financial Data (financing, financial projections, legal issues)

The SBA (Small Business Administration) site includes free online business advice for start-ups at www.sba.gov/starting_business/index.html, or search the Web for sample business plans at sites like Bplans.com (www.bplans.com/sp/businessplans.cfm).

Going into detail about the process of writing a business plan is beyond the scope of this book. If you need assistance, business attorneys or accountants can help you get started and are familiar with local business organizations. For free help, check out the business program at the closest community college or university or locate a nearby small business support office at one of the following sites:

- Small Business Development Center (SBDC) www.sba.gov/sbdc/sbdcnear.html
- Small Business Administration (SBA) http://sba.gov
- Service Corps of Retired Executives (SCORE) www.score.org/findscore/index.html

To get a good handle on the basics, you might want to read *Starting an Online Business For Dummies,* 4th Edition, by Greg Holden (Wiley Publishing) or *Business Plans Kit For Dummies,* 2nd Edition, by Steven D. Peterson, Peter E. Jaret, and Barbara Findlay Schenck (Wiley Publishing).

Web sites don't solve business problems; they create new challenges. If your business is experiencing any problems, fix them first! Any difficulties with computer infrastructure, record-keeping, manufacturing, supply chains, customer service, order fulfillment, staffing, cost controls, training, or pricing are only magnified when you go online.

Planning to Fit Your Business Goals

Before you state the goals for your Web site, you must be clear about the goals for your business. Your answers to a few basic questions establish the marketing framework for your site. Answer the questions in the Business Profile section of the Web Site Planning Form in Figure 2-1. These questions apply equally to businesses of any size and to not-for-profit organizations, educational institutions, and governments.

Here are a few examples of business profile questions:

- ✔ Are you a new company or an existing one with an established customer/client base?
- ✔ Do you have an existing brick-and-mortar store or office?
- ✔ Do you have an existing Web site and Web presence?
- ✔ Do you sell goods or services?
- ✔ Do you market to individuals (which is called *B2C* for *business-to-consumer*) or to other businesses (which is called *B2B* for *business-to-business*)?
- ✔ Who are your customers or clients (generally referred to as your *target markets*)?
- ✔ Do you sell — or want to sell — locally, regionally, nationally, or internationally?

Answer the other questions of the Business Profile section of the form to get an overall idea of what your business looks like.

Your Web site is the tail, and your business is the dog. Let business needs drive your Web plans, not the other way around.

Web Site Planning Form

For Web Site (URL): ~~www. barnnefe~~ www. barnerd. com

Prepared by:_____ **Date:**_____

Web Producer/coordinator:_____

 Contact Info:_____

 Producer/coordinator:_____

 Contact Info:_____

Business Profile:

Is the Web site for a new or established company?
- ● New company
- ○ Existing company, in business _____ years.

Does the company have an existing brick-and-mortar operation?
- ○ Yes
- ● No

Does the company have an existing Web site or Web presence?
- ○ Yes
- ○ No

Does the company have an existing logo?
- ○ Yes
- ● No

What type of business is the Web site for?
- ☐ Manufacturer
- ☐ Distributor
- ☐ Retailer
- ☑ Service provider
- ☐ Professional

What does the company sell?
- ☐ Goods
- ☑ Services

Describe your goods or services:

What type of range does the company have?
- ○ Local
- ○ Regional
- ○ National
- ○ International

Figure 2-1:
Web Site
Planning
Form
(download
at www.
dummies.
com/
go/web
market
ing).

© 2006 Watermelon Mountain Web Marketing www.watermelonweb.com

What type of range will the Web site have?
- ○ Local
- ○ Regional
- ○ National
- ○ International

Web Site Goals

Rank the applicable purposes of your site, with 1 being the most important.

_____ Information
_____ Branding
_____ Lead generation/qualifying prospects
_____ Sales revenue
_____ Ad revenue
_____ Internal needs
_____ Transformation

Financial Profile

Break-even point: $ _____   Within: _____
Return on investment: _____ %   Within: _____

Web Site Budget for First Year

Outside development: $ _____
Special elements (such as video): $ _____
Marketing: $ _____
Inhouse Labor: $ _____
Other materials: $ _____

Total: $ _____

Sample Objectives

Repeat for each goal within timeframe specified (for instance, 1 year).

Traffic objective (# viewers per month): _____   Within: _____
Conversion objective: _____ %   Within: _____
Sales objectives (# sales per month): $ _____   Within: _____
Average $ per sale: $ _____   Within: _____
$ revenue per month: $ _____   Within: _____
Other objectives specific to your site: _____   Within: _____
_____   Within: _____
_____   Within: _____

© 2006 Watermelon Mountain Web Marketing www.watermelonweb.com

Marketing Profile

Describe your target markets. Give specific demographic or segment information. For B2B, segment by industry or job title.

_____

_____

_____

_____

_____

_____

_____

What is your marketing tag?

_____

Value proposition: Why should someone buy from your company rather than another?

_____

_____

Name at least six competitors and their Web sites.

_____   _____

_____   _____

_____   _____

_____   _____

_____   _____

_____   _____

© 2006 Watermelon Mountain Web Marketing www.watermelonweb.com

Setting Goals for Your Web Site

After you've outlined your business goals, you need to decide what your Web site must accomplish from a marketing perspective. The goals you set for your site plus the definition of your target market should drive both your Web design and marketing campaigns.

Business Web sites generally have one of the seven goals in the following sections as a primary goal, although large, sophisticated sites now address several categories. Rank the functions that apply to your site on the Web Site Goals section of the Web Site Planning Form (refer to Figure 2-1), with 1 being the primary purpose of your site.

Unless you have a large enough budget and staff to handle the demands of marketing to multiple audiences, select only one or two of these goals. You can add others later after benefits from your site start flowing to your bottom line.

Providing customer service through information

Brochureware or business card sites are an inexpensive solution. These sites, which contain no more than the minimal information included in a small tri-fold brochure, might provide a small business with an adequate Web presence. For example, the two-page interior design site at www.lmkinteriorsltd.com (shown in Figure 2-2) briefly describes services, linking to a second page with contact information and a project inquiry form. Other, information-based sites are much more extensive. Medical, technical support, or news sites may contain hundreds or thousands of pages in a searchable, linkable, static format. Businesses save money by hiring fewer staff to provide the information live while taking advantage of the Internet to offer support online 24/7 to accommodate customers worldwide.

Figure 2-2: LMK Interiors' brochureware site informs customers of available services and lets them submit an inquiry.

Courtesy Cheryl K. Perkins & Assoc. (Website Designer)

Branding your company or product

Sites like Coke.com primarily serve a branding function. Branding sites may include games, coupons, entertainment, feedback sections, interactive functions, and corporate information, but they generally don't sell the product online. They generate leads or sales only indirectly. For instance, consumers can buy a key chain or other branded paraphernalia on the Coca-Cola site (www.coke.com) but cannot buy a bottle of Diet Coke.

Branding can be tricky, even on a sales site, when the name of a site is not the same as the existing business. Plaza Bakery, located on the central plaza in Santa Fe, New Mexico, solved this problem by modifying its former logo, incorporating the name of its Web site (SweetSantaFe.com), and moving its business name below the image. (See Figure 2-3.)

Figure 2-3:
SweetSanta-
Fe.com
resolved a
branding
problem on
its new
Web site
by revising
its logo in
the upper
left corner.

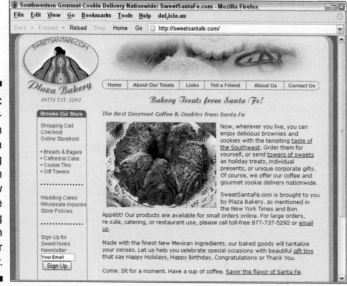

Courtesy Plaza Bakery

Generating leads or qualifying prospects

Some sites, especially those for services and expensive products such as cars and homes, allow potential customers to research offerings, but customers must call, e-mail, or visit the brick-and-mortar establishment to close a sale. Interactive techniques, such as the Live Chat feature used by staffing agency Aerotek (www.aerotek.com/default.aspx), build relationships that turn prospects into customers. (Chapters 4 and 6 describe many interactive techniques you can use on your site for this purpose.)

If you're clever, you can qualify your leads online. For instance, SantaFe Wedding.com, a destination wedding site, asks for the groom's name on its form inquiry page (http://santafewedding.com/request.html). That question alone reduces the number of false leads by more than 60 percent.

Generating revenue through sales

Transaction sites, which are, perhaps, the most familiar type of site, are used to sell goods or services online. Travel reservations, magazine subscriptions, organizational memberships, B2B (business to business) sales, and even donations fall into this category, as do retail sites from Amazon.com to the smallest, home-based micro-store. Good transaction sites take advantage of the Web to gather information about customer demographics, needs, and preferences and to test response to special offers.

Generating revenue through advertising

A business model that calls for generating revenue by selling ads operates in a fundamentally different marketing mode. When you sell advertising, the primary product is the audience you deliver — either the number of eyeballs that view an ad or the number of click-throughs to an advertiser's site.

Achieving internal needs

Sites in this category attract investors, identify strategic business partners, locate suppliers, recruit dealers, or solicit franchisees. The audience for these sites is quite different from the audience for a site targeted at customers or clients. This distinction is critical because elements of your marketing plan are derived from the definition of your target market.

Transforming your business through process innovation or creative techniques

Transformation applies to more than giant corporations whose Web sites integrate just-in-time inventory, smooth supply chains, online sales, and accounting systems. Many innovative small businesses create online processes that fundamentally change the way they do business.

Surprisingly, innovation doesn't have to cost much. Pablo's Mechanical (www.pablosmechanical.com), a plumbing and heating contractor, captured the second-home market in the rural tourist area near Angel Fire, New Mexico. Pablo's Mechanical realized that second-home owners are usually well off, are frequent Internet users, and often live out of state, perhaps in a different time zone. His simple, inexpensive site directs his customers to click onto large plumbing manufacturers' sites to select fixtures and then send him an e-mail with what they want installed.

Specifying Objectives for Your Web Site

What can convince you that your site is successful? After you establish goals, you need to specify the criteria that satisfy them. That means establishing measurable objectives. First, enter your calculations from Chapter 1 for break-even point, return on investment (ROI), and budget onto the Financial Profile section of the Web Planning Form in Figure 2-1. Your budget and ROI expectations might constrain how much you can spend on marketing and, therefore, on how much traffic your site will receive. Take this into consideration as you specify numerical targets for your objectives and the dates you expect to accomplish them. There's no point in setting unrealistic objectives that doom your site to failure before you start.

Table 2-1 suggests some possible measurements for different Web site goals, but you have to determine the actual quantities and time frames for achievement. Define other objectives as appropriate. Enter the numbers and time frames for the criteria you'll use on the Sample Objectives section of the Web Site Planning Form. These numbers are specific to each business.

Table 2-1	Site Goals and Objectives
Site Goal	*Possible Objectives to Measure*
Managing customer service	Number of phone calls and e-mails, amount of traffic to various pages, hours of site use, cost savings, time savings
Branding	Onsite traffic, time onsite, activities performed, coupons downloaded, gross revenues
Generating qualified leads	Number of phone calls and e-mails, conversion rate of visits to leads, conversion rate of leads to sales as compared to other lead sources, traffic to various pages, number of e-mail addresses acquired, cost of customer acquisition

Site Goal	Possible Objectives to Measure
Generating online sales	Conversion rate of buyers to visitors, sales revenue, average dollar value of sale, number of repeat buyers, profit from online sales, cost of customer acquisition, promo code use, sales closed offline that are generated from Web, if possible (that is, enter phone orders into the system)
Generating ad revenue	Ad revenue, click-through rate, page views per ad, traffic to various pages, visitor demographics
Measuring internal goals	Conversion rates for various actions, site traffic, other measurements (depending on specific goals)
Transforming the business	Site revenues, costs, profit, time savings, costs savings, other measurements (depending on specific goals)

If you don't have objectives, you won't know when you've reached or exceeded them. Setting objectives ahead of time also ensures that you establish a method for measurement.

For instance, you can obtain site traffic numbers from your Web statistics, as I discuss in Chapter 14, but you can't count leads that come in over the phone that way. Your receptionist must ask how a caller heard about you and tally results. Or you can display a separate number, e-mail address, person, or extension for Web visitors to use, just as you would establish a separate department number for a direct mail campaign.

Try to track data for a 13-month period so you can compare same-date results. Almost all businesses experience some cyclical variation tied to the calendar.

Defining Your Target Market

In the Marketing Profile section of the Web Site Planning Form (refer to Figure 2-1), you need to define your target market(s). For each goal you select on your Planning Form, decide who your audience is. Phrases such as "everyone who eats chocolate" or "all airplane passengers" are way too broad. Unless you are Toyota or General Mills, you won't have the funds to reach everyone, so you need to segment and prioritize your markets.

Note: I discuss how to fill out the rest of the Marketing Profile section in "Writing Your Online Marketing Plan," later in this chapter.

Understanding market segmentation

Market segmentation (dividing your market into smaller sets of prospects who share certain characteristics) takes many different forms. You need to select the one that's the best fit for your business. For your online marketing plan, you need to locate the various sites on the Web where your target audiences hang out, so you need to know who they are. Think about it for a moment. The sites that appeal to opera lovers might not appeal to teenagers, and vice versa.

One caveat: Your online target audience might differ slightly from your offline audience. It might be more geographically diverse, wealthier, older, younger, more educated, more motivated by price than features, or vice versa. You discover these variations only from experience.

Here are a few forms of market segmentation:

- ✔ **Demographic segmentation:** Sorts by age, gender, socioeconomic status, or education for B2C companies

- ✔ **Lifecycle segmentation:** Acknowledges that consumers need different products at different stages of life (teens, young singles, married couples, families with kids, empty nesters, active retirees, frail elderly)

- ✔ **Geographic segmentation:** Targets areas as small as a neighborhood or zip code or as broad as a country or continent

- ✔ **Vertical industry segmentation:** Targets all elements within a defined industry as a B2B strategy

- ✔ **Job segmentation:** Identifies different decision makers (such as engineers, purchasing agents, and managers) at specific points of the B2B sales cycle

- ✔ **Specialty segmentation:** Targets a narrowly defined market (such as 45- to 65-year olds, female caregivers of people with Alzheimer's, or 16- to 35-year-old male owners of classic Mustangs)

Follow classic guerrilla marketing principles: Focus on one market segment at a time, gain market share and profits, and then invest in the next market segment. Otherwise, your limited marketing time and advertising funds are spread too thinly to have a significant impact. For more information on market segmentation, try www.businessplans.org/segment.html or http://money.howstuffworks.com/marketing-plan12.htm.

Researching your market online

If you aren't sure how to define your market segments, check some of the online market research sites in Table 2-2. These sites offer a wealth of statistical data about the demographics of online users, what types of products sell well, and the growth of Internet use by demographic segments.

Table 2-2	Online Market Research Sites	
Name	**URL**	**Content**
ClickZ	www.clickz.com	Marketing stats, resources, articles, and more
Internet Systems Consortium	www.isc.org/index. pl?/ops/ds	Internet domain survey host count
internet.com	www.internet.com	Online marketing newsletters and resource-providers lists
MarketingSherpa	www.marketingsherpa. com	Free articles and case studies, fee-based online marketing library
Web Marketing Today	www.wilsonweb.com	Resource links with online and e-commerce marketing information

If your target audience isn't online, the Web should not be part of your marketing mix for end user sales! It can still fulfill other functions, of course. Check the Harris Interactive report at http://harrisinteractive.com/harris_poll/index.asp?PID=668 for details about who's online. As of May 2006, Harris found that 77 percent of U.S. adults — 172 million — were online at work, school, or home and that Internet access now looks a lot more like the nation as a whole than it did several years ago. More seniors, minorities, and low-income users now have Internet access, shrinking the digital divide.

Writing Your Online Marketing Plan

Your business might have a formal marketing plan, or perhaps you have been in business so long that your marketing basics are second nature. For the sake of completeness and easy communication with others, fill out the additional questions of the Marketing Profile section of Figure 2-1:

✔ **Marketing tag:** Enter your *marketing tag,* which is the five- to seven-word phrase that describes what your business offers or who you are. This phrase probably appears (or should) on almost all your stationery, business cards, advertising, and packaging. Like your logo, your marketing tag helps define your public image. Your marketing tag should appear on your Web site as well! Many companies include it in their header graphic to reinforce branding. You can see examples in Figure 2-2 and the figure in the "Planning for success at a museum Web site" sidebar near the end of the chapter.

✔ **Value proposition:** Why should someone buy from your company rather than from a competitor?

✔ **Competitors:** Enter the names of at least six competitors and their Web addresses.

After you go online, your universe of competitors expands phenomenally. If you've been selling locally but plan to expand your market size, you'll find lots of other competitors online. You'll find competitors for your type of business in search engines, online Yellow Pages, or online business directories. This effort can be a bit sobering, but it's better to be prepared than surprised.

Before writing an online marketing plan, consider how three other traditional marketing concepts apply in cyberspace: the classic four Ps of marketing, Maslow's Triangle (which I discuss in further detail in the "Understanding why people buy: Maslow's Triangle" section later in this chapter), and the obvious but often-forgotten need to fish where the fish are. Use these tools as part of your planning process to resolve problems before they impede your online success.

Examining the four Ps of marketing

Marketers name product, price, placement (distribution), and promotion as the traditional elements of marketing. These terms apply to the Web as well.

If you plan to update an existing site, it's particularly important to review the four Ps. For instance, you might think you need a site update because you receive too little traffic from search engines, but after a review of the four Ps, you find out that the real issue is pricing. Chapter 14 explains how to diagnose problems with the four Ps by using your Web statistics.

Product

Your *product* is whatever good or service you sell, regardless of whether the transaction takes place online. Review your competition to see what features, benefits, or services they offer. (To find your competitors, look up your product in Google or another search engine.) Product also includes such elements as performance, warranties, support, variety, and size. If you have an online store, look at your entire product mix and merchandising, not just individual products. Ask yourself the following questions:

- ✔ Do you have enough products in your online catalog to compete successfully?

- ✔ Are you selling what people want to buy?

- ✔ Are you updating your product catalog regularly, quickly removing items that are out of stock and promoting new items?

Price

The expanding presence of discount stores online puts significant *price* pressure on small businesses. Price comparison sites like Shopping.com, which cost-conscious shoppers check frequently, also compel lower prices. Use those sites to assess your prices against your online competition. Are you significantly higher, lower, or price competitive? What about your shipping prices?

I talk more about shipping in Chapter 5, but for now, remember that high shipping costs account for 75 percent of abandoned shopping carts. If necessary, bury some of the handling and shipping costs in the basic product price and reduce the visible price for shipping.

It's very hard for your small business to compete in the market for standard goods like baby clothes or DVDs unless you have really good wholesale deals from manufacturers or distributors. But you can compete pricewise on customized goods or services or by offering unique benefits for buying from your company. If you must charge higher prices than your online competitors, review your value proposition so that people perceive an extra benefit. That could be a $5 promotional code for a discount on another purchase, a no-questions-asked return policy, exclusivity, or your reputation for quality service.

You don't need to compete with offline prices because people value the convenience of, and time saved by, shopping online. It's perfectly okay to price online products higher than identical items in your brick-and-mortar store.

In a drive to compete, many dot com businesses drive themselves into the ground by charging less for products than they cost. The more products they sell, the more money they lose. What a business model! While every business sometimes offers loss leaders, you have to cover the loss with profits from other products.

Placement

Placement refers to your distribution channels. Where and how are your products and services available? Inherently, the Web gives you an advantage, with 24/7 hours of operation for research, support, and sales online. However, you might face distribution challenges, particularly if you're constrained by agreement to a particular territory or are a distributor or manufacturer who plans to sell online directly to consumers.

Avoid *channel cannibalization* (the use of multiple distribution channels that pull sales from each other). Don't compete on price with your retailers. Otherwise, your direct sales might cost you sales from other outlets, in a destructive cycle of eating your own. Before competing with retailers, review the increased level of staffing and expenses that are required to meet expectations of consumer support. Are you really able to take this on? If so, you might want to open a completely separate retail site at a different URL from the one that your dealers and distributors see.

Promotion

Your Web marketing plan is one of the four Ps. All the different ways you communicate with customers and prospects are part of *promotion*. Include marketing your Web site as much as you market your company and products. Careful integration of online and offline advertising is critical. Are your methods reaching your target audience? Are you sending the right message to encourage customers to buy? In the next section, you can see how to use Maslow's Triangle to craft a message that appeals to customers' motivations.

Understanding why people buy: Maslow's Triangle

By now, you realize that online marketing requires more than getting listed in search engines and waiting for the money to roll in. Maslow's Triangle is another way to gain an edge. Advertisers have long understood the power of messages that address people's emotional needs, taking advantage of a theory developed by humanistic psychologist Abraham Maslow in the late 1960s. You can do this, too!

According to Maslow's hierarchy of needs (displayed as a triangle in Figure 2-4), everyone has to satisfy certain needs before they can achieve their maximum potential. In marketing terms, people buy certain products or seek certain types of information to satisfy one of more of those needs. Of the five levels in Maslow's Triangle, the bottom two (Physiological and Safety) are basic needs. The top three (Social, Esteem, and Self-actualization) are growth needs. At this point, people can find Web sites to satisfy every need in the triangle. Here's a list of those categories along with a description of each:

- ✔ **Physiological needs:** This category covers air, food, water, sleep, sex, health, and shelter. To satisfy these needs, people might research homes online, look for apartments to rent on Craigslist.org, purchase apparel from Patagonia.com, arrange a grocery delivery from Peapod.com, search for a dentist's name, look for nutrition advice, or locate an oxygen bar like the OxygenExperience.com.

- ✔ **Safety needs:** These types of needs include security items and information for times of emergency, social disorganization, or personal trauma. At this level, people might seek hotline numbers, fire or flood evacuation information, earthquake kits from SurvivalKitsOnline.com, fire extinguishers from AmericanFireEquipment.net, car alarms from SlickCar.com, or GPS systems from MagellanGPS.com.

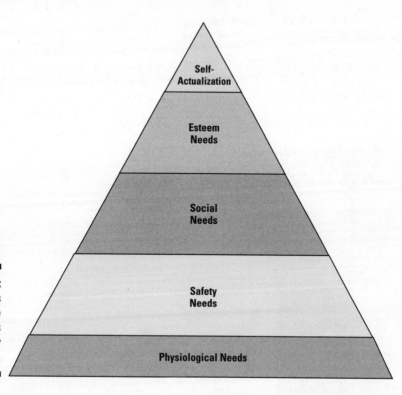

Figure 2-4: Maslow's Triangle shows his hierarchy of needs.

Self-Actualization

Esteem Needs

Social Needs

Safety Needs

Physiological Needs

Planning for success at a museum Web site

The Museum of New Mexico Foundation Shops (MNMF Shops) operate retail stores at four, state-owned museums in Santa Fe, New Mexico: Palace of the Governors, Museum of Fine Arts, Museum of International Folk Art, and Museum of Indian Arts and Culture. MNMF Shops had already managed a successful, retail Web site at www.shopmuseum.com for three years when it received an economic development grant to promote New Mexico artists and artisans with marketing exposure beyond Santa Fe, itself the third-largest art market in the U.S.

In March 2006, John Stafford, Director of Retail Operations, wrote a ten-page business plan revamping the existing site and adding two new sites, www.newmexicocreates.org and www.worldfolkart.org, for the Foundation's board of directors. The business plan included sections named Executive Summary, Mission Statement, Target Market, Business Model, Value Proposition, and Business Objectives, as well as sections on Merchandising Strategy, Operations Plans, Marketing Plans, and Financial Plans. It concluded with a Timing and Action Calendar.

Stafford added sections important for the board: Critical Success Factors highlighted areas that needed direct attention; Risk Assessment and Contingency Plans addressed issues that might affect the achievement of financial objectives. Thanks to the detailed plans, NewMexico Creates.org launched in July 2006 with nearly 1,000 pieces of art from 400 artists. WorldFolk Art.org launched at the end of October 2006. Both sites are on target to meet their objectives.

The MNMF Shops contribute all net income from online and offline sales back to the Foundation for distribution to the four museums for education and acquisitions.

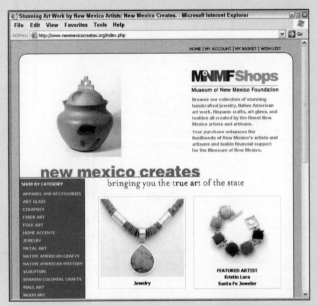

Courtesy Museum of New Mexico Foundation Shops

✔ **Social needs:** This category indicates our human cravings for caring and belonging, including products and services that make us more attractive to others. This need drives the appeal of popular social networking sites as diverse as MySpace.com and PunkyMoms.com, as well as cosmetics from ElizabethArden.com, spa memberships, self-help books from Amazon.com, hobbies, clubs, civic activities, churches, and other groups.

✔ **Esteem:** This refers to an individual's need for self-respect and respect from others. This need motivates the purchase of items like jewelry from Tiffany.com, fine wines from WineWeb.com, a monogrammed leather wallet from FineLeatherGifts.com, or a search for a Hummer dealer at Humvee.net, all of which carry a sense of status, prestige, and power.

✔ **Self-actualization:** A sense of creative self-fulfillment may come from artistic, musical, educational, spiritual, or religious pursuits. Individuals with self-actualization needs might visit sites related to creative or spiritual pursuits, such as Buddhanet.net, AcademyArt.edu, or ClevelandOrch.com, and they might buy books, music, classes, concert tickets, or art.

To increase your *conversion rate* (the percent of site visitors who buy), match your message to the needs your products fulfill. If you identify the specific benefits that people are looking for, you're more likely to close the sale. For instance, an esteem message would talk about the exclusivity of owning jewelry from Tiffany's, not about saving money.

Fishing where the fish are

When you advertise offline, you put your ads where the target market is likely to see them. Ads for muscle cars run in the sports section of the paper or on billboards near gyms. The same thing applies online. You need to place your lures where your fish hang out.

Figure 2-5 lists the marketing methods discussed in this book. As you read different chapters, check off methods you think are possibilities for your site. I also recommend that you compile a marketing notebook with ideas, articles, and Web sites, and create marketing folders on your hard drive to store online research.

Over time, you'll gather enough information to fill out a Web Marketing Spreadsheet like the one shown in Figure 2-6. On this form, you finalize the marketing methods from your checklist and specify marketing method, audience, *impressions* (number of times an ad is seen), costs per month, venues, and delivery schedule for each one. (In Chapter 12, I explain more about cost per thousand impressions, or CPM. You have to research costs for each technique.) You can incorporate offline marketing in this spreadsheet or duplicate this arrangement for offline expenses and then add the two together.

The combination of marketing methods you decide to implement is called your *marketing mix*. When completed, this spreadsheet encapsulates your marketing plan, showing how your marketing mix will achieve the objectives you've already established. The example in Figure 2-6 includes some objectives for a mock B2C site.

If you lose direction, you'll end up wasting money. After several months, discard the methods that don't work and put more money into the ones that are successful — or add another method or two. Over time, you'll develop an optimized, online marketing program that you can monitor and tweak as needed.

Marketing online is part of overall marketing

Exclusive online promotion of a Web site is rare. Your Web address should appear on your stationery, packaging, and brochures, at the very least. As you build an online marketing plan, you might decide to redirect some of your existing advertising dollars, but don't abandon successful offline advertising. Will you still need a listing in the Yellow Pages? Will you still hand out promotional items or exhibit at trade shows?

Put your *domain name* (that's just a techie word for *Internet address*) everywhere that you put your phone number and more. Put it on your shopping bags. Put it on your outdoor signs. Put it on your business truck! Heck, you can even hire someone now to put it on his shaved head.

What you already know about your business is right — the Web is a new medium, not a new universe. Don't let technology fool you into abandoning hard-won knowledge of your business, your target markets, or how to appeal to them. When in doubt, follow your instincts and let your bottom line guide your decisions.

Figure 2-5:
Web
Marketing
Methods
Checklist
(download
from www.
dummies.
com/go/
web
market
ing).

Web Marketing Methods Checklist

Offline Promotion
- ☑ Community events
- ☐ Direct mail
- ☑ Marketing collateral (brochures, spec sheets)
- ☑ Offline advertising
- ☑ Offline public relations and press releases
- ☐ Packaging
- ☐ Product placement
- ☐ Promotional items (specify)
- ☑ Site launch activities
- ☐ Stationery

Free E-Mail Techniques

☐ Autoresponders
☐ FAQs and packaged blurbs
☑ Group or bulk e-mail
☐ Signature blocks

Onsite Promotion

☐ Affiliate program
☑ Automatic updates (specify type of content, such as date, quote)
☐ Awards posting — ~~contest of the week~~?
☑ Blog
☐ Bookmark reminders
☐ Calls to action
☐ Chat room
☑ Content updates
☑ Contests, drawings, and games
☑ Coupons and discounts
☐ Downloads (postcards, sound effects, animation)
☐ Endorsement logos (BBBOnLine, TRUSTe, VeriSign)
☐ Favicons
☑ Free offers (giveaways)
☐ Guest books
☑ Make This Your Home Page tool
☑ Internal banners
☐ Live events onsite
☑ Logo
☐ Loyalty program
☑ Message board
☐ Nonprofit donation marketing
☐ Onsite auction
☑ Onsite newsletter registration
☐ Onsite search
☐ Other interactive or rich media
☐ Product reviews (onsite)
☐ RSS (Real Simple Syndication) feeds
☐ Samples
☐ Social networks (onsite)
☐ Surveys and polls
☐ Tell a friend (send a link)
☐ Testimonials
☑ Viral marketing
☐ Vlog (video blog)
☐ What's New page
☐ Wiki

maybe a new joke of the day relating to college, alcohol, one night stands.

Online Promotion (Buzz Campaigns)
- ❑ Award site submissions
- ❑ Blogging
- ❑ Hot sites submissions
- ❑ Inbound link campaign
- ☑ Online link campaign
- ❑ Online press releases
- ❑ Podcasting
- ❑ Posting to chat rooms, message boards, and social network sites
- ❑ Posting to review and opinion sites
- ❑ Reciprocal links
- ❑ Text messaging
- ❑ Viral techniques
- ☑ Webinars or Webcasting
- ❑ What's New announcements
- ❑ Wireless marketing and cell phones

Opt-In E-Mail Newsletters
Specify audience, frequency, and method.
- ❑ Own e-mail lists
Audience:_____ Frequency: _____ Method: _____
- ❑ Paid (subscription) newsletters or e-zines
Audience:_____ Frequency: _____ Method: _____
- ❑ Public mailing lists
Audience:_____ Frequency: _____ Method: _____
- ❑ Rental e-mail lists
Audience:_____ Frequency: _____ Method: _____
- ❑ Viral e-mail
Audience:_____ Frequency: _____ Method: _____

Search Engine Submissions
- ❑ Basic 4
- ❑ Directory submissions
- ❑ Industry engine submissions
- ❑ International search engines
- ❑ Local and map submissions
- ❑ Shopping search engines (free)
- ❑ Specialty search engines (for blogs, videos, images, and so on)
- ❑ Paid submission service
- ❑ Search engine optimization onsite
- ❑ XML feeds

Paid Online Advertising
- ☑ Banner advertising
- ❑ Banner exchange
- ❑ Classifieds online
- ❑ Google AdWords PPC and other options
- ❑ Newsletter sponsorships
- ❑ Nonprofit sponsorships
- ❑ Other PPC engines and directories
- ❑ Overture PPC
- ❑ Shopping PPC
- ❑ Site sponsorships
- ❑ Yahoo! Search Marketing PPC and other options

© 2006 Watermelon Mountain Web Marketing www.watermelonweb.com

Target Market	Marketing Method	Venue (Site Name or Source)	Estimated Impressions per Year	Cost per 1000 Impressions	Jan.	Feb.	Annual Cost	Est. Visits @ 5% Imp.	Estimated Conversions @ 2% Visits	Mktg Cost per Conversion	Mktg Cost as % Revenue @ $x per Sale
All Cyclists	Banner Ad			$		$	$			$	%
All Cyclists	Onsite Message Board				$	$	$			$	%
Bike Clubs	Affiliate			$	$	$	$			$	%
Bike & Fitness Press & Trade	Press Release			$	$	$	$			$	%
Budget Cycle Shoppers	Shopping Search Engine			$	$	$	$			$	%
Competitive Cyclists	Third-Party Blog			$	$	$	$			$	%
Existing Buyers & Opt-Ins	Inhouse Newsletter			$	$	$	$			$	%
Fitness	Google Ads			$	$	$	$			$	%
Fitness	Newsletter Sponsor			$	$	$	$			$	%
Gym Members	Rented E-Mail			$	$	$	$			$	%
Spinning Enthusiasts	Banner Ad			$	$		$			$	%
Women's Health > 45	Banner Ad			$	$	$	$			$	%
Monthly Totals											

Examples of Sales Objectives (take from your planning form)

By End of Year 1 (Post Launch): Reach $25K per month gross revenue.
Reach $300K per year extended.
Reach 500 sales per month.

By End of Year 2 (Post Launch): Reach $50K per month gross revenue.
Reach $500K per year extended.
Reach 1000 sales per month.

Estimated Average Sale:	$40
Monthly Target Amount:	$25,000
# Sales Needed per Month:	625
# Visitors Needed at 2% Conversion per Month:	31,250
# Impressions Needed at 5% CTR per Month:	625,000
# Visitors Needed at 4% Conversion per Month:	15,625
# Impressions Needed at 5% CTR per Month:	312,500

© 2006 Watermelon Mountain Web Marketing www.watermelonweb.com

Figure 2-6: Web Marketing Spreadsheet for a mock site selling cycling gear (download from www.dummies.com/go/webmarketing)

Chapter 3

Taking the First Steps to Your Online Presence

After you've done your homework on marketing goals (see Chapter 2), you're ready to create — or redesign — your Web site for success. Many business owners err by viewing their Web site as a separate project, independent of marketing and sales, even when they have an online store. In reality, site design is intricately intertwined with every marketing decision you make.

In this chapter, I explain the critical importance of selecting the right providers to bring your business vision to cyberspace. I show you how writing a *site index* (a table of contents for your site) and *request for proposal* (RFP) allows you to communicate your marketing and technical needs effectively to potential developers as well as evaluate their responses. If your budget is tight, I recommend using template-based hosting companies rather than a do-it-yourself approach.

You also find out how to select a good domain name and become familiar with the three characteristics of successful Web design: a site that attracts new visitors, keeps them with stickiness, and brings them back for more.

Deciding Who Will Design Your Site

The Oracle at Delphi was famous for the saying, "Know thyself." Web design reinforces the importance of self-knowledge. Be honest about your skills. Are you a programming geek? A gifted photographer? A colorful writer? Do you dream in Web-safe colors, JavaScript, or Flash animation? No? Then designing your own Web site is probably not your forte. Don't be hard on yourself. With the possible exception of Leonardo da Vinci, should he be reincarnated in the 21st century, everyone needs help of some sort with Web site development.

As the owner of a business with a passion for excellence, or the person delegated to oversee the company Web site, your job is that of *producer,* not creative director or technical manager. There's wisdom, not weakness, in playing to your strengths as a business owner and leaving the implementation to someone else. As producer, you select the team and coordinate their efforts, cheer them on when the inevitable problems arise, answer their marketing questions, resolve conflicts based on your business acumen, and arrange the celebration when the site goes live.

Understanding why it's not practical to do it all yourself

Besides overseeing the content, managing the money, and handling the marketing, are you going to educate yourself in HTML, PHP, JavaScript, database programming, Dreamweaver, FrontPage, marketing communications, copy writing, photography, and graphic design in the next six weeks? Are you also fantasizing about winning the Tour de France, or are you just a victim of some misbegotten belief that this will save you money? Forget about it!

Unless you're already a professional Web designer, don't do it all yourself; this is the biggest mistake you can make. Playing with your personal Web site is one thing, but creating a successful business Web site is a job for the pros. Would you let someone without experience design your ads, dress your store window, serve customers, buy goods from vendors, or negotiate contracts? Then why trust your Web site to a novice?

Novices might include your friends, neighbors, children, or siblings, unless they have experience creating business sites for a living. Even then, treat people you know as you would any professional — write up an agreement so that expectations are clear. Believe me, an agreement won't only save you aggravation and disappointment, it might save your relationship.

Time is money! A nonprofessional who does Web sites on the side and takes three or four times as long as a pro will end up costing you marketing opportunity and sales as well as money.

Deciding who will design your site is a strategic marketing decision. How will your site measure up if it's obviously homemade, with links that don't work, but your competitors' sites look professional and run smoothly? If your competition's sites are equivalent, this is not as much of a factor, but you're wasting an obvious opportunity to get an edge.

Using a professionally designed template to create your site

Do you remember when desktop publishing software first came out? Unskilled users distributed newsletters that looked like font catalogs, using every imaginable typeface and style. The resulting newsletters were almost unreadable. You can avoid the Web site equivalent of desperado design by using a professionally designed template.

Templates are not as flexible as a custom site, but they can save you significant money while maintaining graphic integrity. You can launch a template site very quickly and be confident that navigation will work. With a template to take care of design and programming, you can focus on content.

Think of templates as the equivalent of buying business stationery from an office supply store. You can hire a graphic designer for custom work or order letterhead and business cards from a store catalog, customizing ink colors and paper stock. In terms of the Web, you select a template with navigation and customize it with your color selection, logo, text, and photographs. (I discuss selecting templates for online stores in Chapter 5.)

If you can't afford a custom design when you start, use a template as a strategic placeholder. Put your money into marketing until you build a Web presence and set aside the revenues. Later, you can redesign the site with your profits.

Choices, choices! You can choose templates at three different levels: cost, customizability, and skills required:

- ✔ Select a package solution that includes your choice of template design, hosting, and a variety of other options, based on your needs. This is the simplest and usually the least expensive option. On the downside, package solutions are usually the least flexible. If you want, you can hire a designer to advise you on color choice or to tweak the template a bit. Figure 3-1 shows a template-based site created with WebSiteTonight, available through GoDaddy.com as the host. BossTin (www.bosstin.com) had a designer customize the template and create additional page layouts.

- ✔ Buy a template design that is specific to your industry and upload it to a host that you've selected separately. This requires more knowledge and skill.

- ✔ Hire a company that specializes in a particular industry, with a selection of templates that they customize for you. This is more expensive than the other two solutions but still less costly and less time consuming than a fully custom design.

Courtesy Boss Tin, LLC

Figure 3-1:
BossTin customized a template to create its site.

Table 3-1 lists just a few of the many, many template offerings available from sites that supply multiple industries and from sites addressing a sample of vertical sectors. Do an Internet search for *Web templates for [your industry]* (such as restaurants, authors) to find more alternatives.

Table 3-1	**Some Template Sites**	
Type of Sites (Y/N)	*URL*	*Hosting Provided*
Artists	www.foliolink.com	Y
B&B/Hotels	www.alaskainnkeeper.com/ website-templates.htm	Y
B&B/Hotels	www.lynda-design.com/htm/ 2208.htm	N
Construction	www.visionwebservices.com/ solutions/construction/ webservices.php	Y
Dentists	www.dentalwebsitemarketing.com	Y
Lawyers	http://legalwebdesigner.com	Y

Type of Sites (Y/N)	URL	Hosting Provided
Musicians	www.groovindesign.com	N
Musicians	www.musicaladvantage.com/webtemplates.htm	Y
Pet & Vet	www.templateshunt.com/template.php?id=8066	Y
Real Estate	http://corporate.homes.com/agentsWebsite.cfm	Y
Real Estate	www.realestatelaunch.biz	Y
Restaurants	www.restaurantwebdesign.net	Y
Multiple	www.bizland.com/bizland/index.bml	Y
Multiple	www.creatingonline.com	Y
Multiple	http://gowebsite.com/WebsiteTonight.html	Y
Multiple	www.perfectory.com/search.htm	Y
Multiple	www.templatemonster.com	N
Multiple	www.websitesource.com	Y

Opting for professional Web design services

If you've decided to invest in professional Web design services, you need to find the right designer for your objectives.

Deciding what expertise you need

For most business sites, it helps to select designers who come from a marketing communications background, not a pure programming or art background. Your developer must have the ability to design with an eye towards your target market, be knowledgeable about achieving business objectives, and be skilled enough to do the programming tasks required. Not every designer is right for every type of business or has staff with the experience to meet the specific requirements described in your request for proposal (RFP), described later in the chapter.

The designer is only one of several professionals you might need, as you can see from the following list:

- ✔ Web developer/designer
- ✔ Graphic designer
- ✔ Illustrator
- ✔ Photographer
- ✔ Copy writer
- ✔ Merchandising expert
- ✔ Videographer
- ✔ Audio engineer
- ✔ Animator (Flash, virtual reality)
- ✔ Ad agency
- ✔ Online marketing specialist

Developers with enough staff might be able to help with all tasks in the preceding list, or they might subcontract these services out, saving you the trouble of finding providers yourself. At the very least, they probably have a list of people they recommend.

Most small businesses can't afford all these professionals. Decide which aspect of the site is most important to its marketing success. For instance, online stores and tourist sites depend on high-quality photography. A content-rich site inherently demands good writing, while a multimedia site might need an animator, videographer, or audio engineer. Prioritize by outsourcing the most critical element. Do the best you can with the rest.

Finding good providers in your area

Locating qualified professionals is like finding any good service provider. A recommendation can't be beat. Take the time to review designers' and other providers' portfolios online to ensure that you like their style and to assess their talents. Match their description of skills and experience against your RFP. (I go into more detail on the RFP in the upcoming "Writing a Request for Proposal (RFP)" section.)

Always check references — not only those that providers give you, but also several others randomly selected from their portfolio. Try one of these techniques or sort through one of the typical directories of providers listed in Table 3-2. Professionals generally self-submit or pay to be in these directories, so a listing might not say anything about their quality or suitability for your needs.

Table 3-2	Sample Web Provider Directories	
Name	**URL**	**Types of Providers Listed**
Freelance Designers	www. freelance designers.com	Advertising designers, Flash designers, graphic designers, photographers, search experts, videographers, Web designers, Web developers, writers
Marketing Tool	www.marketingtool. com	Copy writers, Flash designers, illustrators, photographers, PR firms, search experts, videographers, Web designers, Web hosts
Web Design Directory	www.designdir.net	Advertising designers, graphic designers, Internet marketers, PR firms, Web designers, Web hosts
WebDesigners-Directory	www.webdesigners-directory.com	Graphic designers, logo designers, Web designers
Web Wiz Guide	www.webwizguide. info/developers/ directory/default. asp	Flash designers, graphic designers, Internet marketers, photographers, Web developers by specialty

Here are a few ways to find good Web professionals:

✔ If you have bookmarked a list of sites you love since Chapter 1, start by approaching those designers.

✔ See who designed your competitors' sites.

✔ Ask others in your local trade association for names of providers they use.

✔ Look at Web sites for regional or statewide associations of Web professionals.

Generally, you get what you pay for! You can pay a lot for someone who isn't capable, but you can't pay a little for someone who's really good at what they do.

Creating a Site Index

A preliminary site index helps you gather your ideas in one place. Outlining — the way you learned in junior high — is one easy way to organize and track site content. As you can see on the site index for the fictional SillySox.com in Figure 3-2, the top-level navigation, which appears on your main menu, shows up as Roman numerals in the outline. Secondary pages under that topic appear as capital letters, and third-level pages appear as Arabic numerals.

Organize your site index strategically, with the most important information for each level at the top of its section. Then review the site index against your site objectives that you wrote in Chapter 2. (If you skipped ahead to this chapter, no worries! Just go back to Chapter 2 and come back to this when you've established your objectives.) Keep rearranging the index until it reflects the marketing goals you want to accomplish. Be sure to include any special functions the user might need to access, such as a Contact Us page, newsletter signup, or audio/video players. The site index might change after discussion with your developer and during the development process.

The order in which navigation items appear on the screen is crucial. The viewer's eye goes first to the upper-right corner. Place there the most important action you want your audience to take. The top of the left navigation is the second most important spot. The less-important activities go in the middle of the list of activities on the left side or in the middle of horizontal navigation across the top. You can see how the index in Figure 3-2 reflects placement on the screen shown in Figure 3-3. Chapter 4 offers additional detail about placement for marketing effectiveness; Chapter 5 talks about placement for sales efficacy.

Your site index becomes an important planning tool for scheduling and budgeting. As part of your RFP (described in the next section), it will have a direct impact on the bids you receive. You can later convert the site index into tables to track which pages need to be written, which pages need photographs, and which pages are complete.

You can find out more about organizing your Web site in *Web Design For Dummies,* 2nd Edition, by Lisa Lopuck (Wiley Publishing).

Sample Site Index for SillySox.com (fictional)

Top Navigation

(from left to right, with the element at the top right being most important)

I. Home

II. About Us

    A. Links

    B. Advertise With Us

        1. Traffic & Demographics

        2. Media Kit

III. Sock It To Me

    A. Kid's Game 1 (Sock Design Coloring Contest)

    B. Kid's Game 2 (Follow the Footprints)

    C. Kid's Game 3 (Land of the Lost Socks)

IV. Sign Up for Sox Savings News

Left Navigation

(from top to bottom, with the element at the top right being most important)

V. Onsite Search

VI. Shop Our Catalog

    A. Women's Socks

        1. Knee Socks

        2. Short Socks

        3. Patterned Tights

    B. Children's Socks

        1. Knee Socks

        2. Short Socks

        3. Baby Socks

    C. Shoelaces

    D. Accessories

        1. Hair Ornaments

        2. Scarves

VII. Customer Care

    A. Shipping & Wrapping

    B. Return Policy

    C. Payment Methods

    D. Privacy & Kids Policies

VIII. Contact Us

Figure 3-2: Sample site index for SillySox.com (fictional).

© 2006 Watermelon Mountain Web Marketing www.watermelonweb.com

Figure 3-3: Because acquiring e-mail addresses is considered the most important marketing activity for SillySox.com, that function appears in the upper-right area of the navigation.

Second most important action

Most important action

© 2006 Watermelon Mountain Web Marketing www.watermelonweb.com

Writing a Request for Proposal (RFP)

You can't buy a custom Web site the way you buy running shoes or a massage. People use a written request for proposal (RFP) document as a convenient way to get bids from service providers on the same set of tasks. An RFP saves you time explaining your project to multiple bidders and enables you to compare prices and services more easily.

The process of writing an RFP can be as formal or informal as you'd like. The more complex and expensive the site, the more likely you will want a formal process, perhaps with an evaluation by a team and including an interview. You'll find forms with questions to ask Web developers and their references on the book's companion Web site (www.dummies.com/go/webmarketing).

The RFP, with negotiated modifications, can be incorporated in the contract. An introductory page for a fictional RFP appears in the sidebar titled "A sample RFP for SillySox.com (fictional)."

Elements of a good RFP

A good RFP conveys your marketing intentions and site needs in a concise form. It often includes

✔ A cover letter including a method and due date for a response

✔ A summary of the goals, objectives, and target market for the site

✔ A list of desired features, site size, and other details

✔ A draft site index

✔ A list of special services needed

✔ A timeline for development

✔ Information on how and when proposals will be evaluated

Establishing a development timeline

Be sure to include a development timeline in your RFP. A fixed date for a trade show, presentation, or holiday sales cycle might drive your schedule for *going live* (making your site available to the public) or *launching your site* (driving traffic through promotional activities).

Without a target date, a site will never be finished. A realistic timeline allocates half the elapsed time to planning and content development, a quarter of the time to actual programming and stocking the site with content, and another quarter to testing and revisions.

While you can launch small template sites quickly, three months is a realistic minimum for most custom sites. The determining factor in the timeline is not likely to be your developer but the amount of time it takes to prepare good content for a larger site. Expect a fair amount of back-and-forth interaction during the design/approval process.

Everything will take twice as many labor hours as your most optimistic projections and cost at least twice as much!

Knowing what to expect from the developer

After asking you a series of questions, including what sites you like and hate, most Web developers give you several rough design comps (compositions) that show the look and feel of the prospective site. They then create detailed designs for several pages with the look and feel you select. Only after you approve the design does the developer start programming. It's usually easier (and cheaper) to make changes during the design phase than during programming. While the developer is programming, you should work on content.

A sample RFP for SillySox.com (fictional)

SuperSillyStuff, Inc., which manufactures and sells a variety of novelty clothing lines, invites you to bid on Web site development and hosting for a new e-commerce site at www.sillysox.com. The new site will sell primarily a line of novelty socks for women and children, with additional matching accessories and shoelaces.

The primary target audience for the site is women ages 18–35 with children and a moderate socioeconomic status. The secondary audience is women ages 18–65 buying gifts. The objective for the site is $1,000 in gross revenues per month after 6 months and $3,000 per month after 12 months. Socks will sell in packages of 2–4 pairs for $10, depending on the size and design. Holiday socks and scarves will sell for $8 each, with shoelaces and hair ornaments running $2–$5. There will be a minimum required sale of $10. Your bid should include

- Eight pages of HTML text with a content management system for easy client updating.

- A method of newsletter registration.

- Internal banners to announce new products, specials, free gift wrapping, and other news.

- A catalog of about 100 different items with text, photos, prices, and inventory that can be updated without tech support. Size and color alternatives should be available as drop-down selections.

- A secure server for transactions. Include screening out children too young to purchase.

- A complete set of traffic and sales statistics, annual hosting, and one hour of maintenance per month.

The online store should use a prepackaged store builder, including catalog, shopping cart, and check stand with real-time credit card processing. Our graphic designer will provide graphic design elements, subject to modification, for the Web. We will supply all digital photos, text and meta tags. Another contractor will handle all Web promotion, including search engine submission. SuperSillyStuff, Inc. will own the copyright and other intellectual property rights to the site and to any code produced as a work for hire. The complete RFP includes a detailed scope of work, a site index, a background questionnaire, the criteria for selection, and a list of competing sites. Please let us know by 4/24 whether you intend to bid.

Bids due electronically	05/03	[to sales@sillysox.com]
Interviews	05/10	
Developer selection	05/17	
Initial developer meeting	05/24	
Comps due	06/15	
Final design	06/30	
Site ready for testing	08/15	
Site launch	09/07	

Finding the Right Domain Name for Your Site

Selecting or changing a domain name (sometimes called a *URL* for *uniform resource locator*) is a critical marketing decision. The problem is more than just a simple search for availability on NetworkSolutions.com, GoDaddy.com, BuyDomains.com, or another registration site. The following sections give you the lowdown on how to choose the right name for your site.

Understanding what makes a good domain name

A good domain name is

- **Easy to say in person.** It's unwieldy to say "digit" before a number in a URL, or the word "dash" or "hyphen"; besides, people have a hard time finding the dash character on a keyboard.

- **Easy to understand over the radio or on the phone.** Words that include the *ess* and *eff* sounds are often confused when listening, as are certain consonant pairs like *b/p, c/z, or d/t.* If you're selling in other countries, confusion between English consonants is different, such as *b/v* in Spanish or *r/l* in Japanese.

- **Easy to spell.** Using homonyms might be a clever way to get around a competitor who already owns a name you'd like to have; however, you're just as apt to drive traffic to your competitor as to gain some for yourself. Also, try to avoid foreign words, words that are deliberately misspelled just because they are available (for example, *valu* rather than *value*), or words that are frequently misspelled.

- **Easy to type.** The longer the URL, the more likely a typo. Your domain name can be as long as 59 characters, but unskilled typists average an error every 7 keystrokes!

- **Easy to read in print and online ads.** You can insert capital letters or use a different color for compound domain names to make them easier to read. Be sure your domain name can also be read easily in black and white, and in a logotype if you design one.

- **Easy to read in the address toolbar.** You can't use colors or capitalization to distinguish parts of a compound name or acronym in address or search engine boxes. Depending on the browser fonts set by the user, the letters *m, n,* or *r* next to each other (mrnrnm) are very hard to read, as are the characters l/i (lilllil), or the similar digit/letter combination of 1/l.

✔ **Easy to remember.** Words or phrases are easier to remember than a stream of letters in an acronym, unless your target audience already knows the acronym from extensive branding (for example, AARP). Your domain name may be, but doesn't need to be, your business name, unless you enjoy a preexisting brand identity.

One of the more complicated URLs I've heard is "1uffakind.com." The interactive design company that owns the name wants to distinguish itself from OneofaKind.com, which is owned by a competing company. The name is memorable enough, but radio ads must spell out the homonym as "the digit one followed by *you-eff-eff-a* kind dot com." That expensive airtime could be spent on a message rather than on spelling!

Stick with original, top-level domains (the primary categories into which Internet addresses are divided): .com for businesses, .org for nonprofits, .net for network providers. Avoid top-level domains like .info, .biz, or odd countries just to get the name you want. People won't remember them and won't find your site.

Don't bother taking the same name with multiple, top-level domains unless you think your audience might be confused. You probably won't want to spend money branding your URL with both extensions; generally one site redirects to the other. The one exception is international selling. You might want to register the same domain in different countries with a large target market, such as members of the European community or Japan, so you can get into search engines restricted by national registration.

With more than 71 million domain names registered, finding a name might seem impossible. Take comfort in knowing that nearly as many domain names are now expiring as new ones are registered.

If your first choice of domain name isn't available, try the suggestion tool available on many registration sites. Use those suggestions to brainstorm more names. Get reactions from friends, customers, clients, and strangers about your options. If you're really desperate to get a particular name, go to the WhoIs database at www.networksolutions.com/whois/index.jsp or other registrar sites to see who owns the domain name and bid to buy it. You can also reserve a name in case the current owner decides not to renew.

Renaming your site: Pros and cons

It's always a challenge to handle renaming a site that doesn't have a great URL. The upside, new traffic from word of mouth and advertising, must offset the downside to be worth it. You face the following risks:

✔ Losing repeat visitors

✔ Losing search engine ranking

✔ Losing inbound links

✔ Losing brand recognition

✔ Incurring added costs for reprinting, packaging, or signage

Change your domain name only if you have little to lose. A site with poor search engine rankings, little traffic, and few inbound links is a pretty safe bet for a change. However, if you have significant offline brand-name recognition and your brand appears in your URL, stick with what you have.

Sometimes, you can segment several domains by marketing purpose. Apply the new, user-friendly domain to B2C sales or lead generation while repurposing the old domain name for corporate identity or B2B use. You can link frequently between the two sites, if you need to. You now have to maintain and host two sites, which has its own time and cost implications, but those consequences might be small compared to the loss you'd face from abandoning the old domain name entirely.

If you decide to abandon your primary domain name, ask your developer to redirect your old domain name to your new one for at least four to six months. (See the next section.) That gives other inbound links, internal links, image links, and search engines a chance to catch up. Don't forget to submit your new name to search engines and to request inbound links again. Essentially, every domain name requires its own online promotion campaign.

Playing Games with Page Names

This section might make your eyes glaze over; if so, show the upcoming Technical Stuff paragraph to your developer. Whether you change your domain name, redesign your site, delete a page, or simply move one to a different folder, you can easily frustrate visitors who have entered the URL for a specific page that no longer exists.

Generally, they receive the totally useless message 404 Page Not Found and are left adrift on the cybersea. More than 99 percent of them will say, "forget this" and go to another site, costing you a visit, a prospect, perhaps even a customer. Not a good marketing decision! So what's a Web site owner to do?

Try a custom 404 redirect like Apple's at www.apple.com/anypage. Rather than see a meaningless Page Not Found message, users see standard navigation and a directory of links to help them get where they want to go. You can change the message in a custom 404 redirect to whatever you want. You can set this HTML meta redirect (also doable in JavaScript) to allow a delay for viewers to read a message, or you can make it instantaneous. A custom error message without a redirect or links is not very helpful. Although not the friendliest solution for search engines, this is still one of the most commonly used techniques for rescuing lost viewers.

A 301 redirect is a better solution if the site is hosted on a server running Apache. It is efficient, user friendly, and search engine compatible. Interpreted as moved permanently, the 301 redirect sends visitors to an appropriate page you designate. Or you can default any unfound page to the home page. Ask your host the best way to implement a 301 redirect in your environment. Or try one of the following references:

- ✔ www.pandia.com/sew/163-301-redirect.html
- ✔ www.lefthanddesigns.com.au/47896.php
- ✔ http://websitehelpers.com/seo/redirecting.html

Don't make a habit of duplicating content on two pages with two different URLs. Search engines might think you're trying to scam them and penalize you.

One other type of redirect has some marketing functionality. Many domain name companies like MyDomain.com (http://mydomain.com/domains_urlfwd.php) will redirect a newly purchased domain name to a Web page with a different name hosted at any location. It's a cheap way to redirect traffic to a free, one- to two-page site that you got from your ISP or to a certain portion of your own site as part of a particular promotion. You can use the new name in your offline marketing without any problems.

Some search engines (including Google), some pay per click (PPC) advertising sites, and some banner ad sites don't recognize a domain name that redirects this way. Do this for tactical reasons, such as tracking from a particular print ad, promotion, or trade show, and only for a short time. I discuss other ways to track traffic from ads in Chapters 12 and 14.

Understanding What Your Site Must Accomplish

A business site has to succeed on multiple levels to pull a prospect or visitor into your marketing orbit. Without initial curb appeal, your site doesn't have a chance to establish itself in visitors' minds. Without strong content, visitors don't have a reason to stay on your site long enough to find out what you have to offer and how wonderful you are. And without a reason to return, visitors might never establish enough confidence to purchase your goods or services. Chapter 4 covers design in greater detail, but the following quick introduction helps.

Catching the visitor's attention

You have only four seconds — that's right — four seconds to make a first impression. That's not enough time for a visitor to read your content. It's time enough only for our emotion-based lizard brains to react to color, layout, design, navigation (maybe), and perhaps, a headline. If you haven't caught people in your cybernet by then, they're gone, probably never to return. Gila Wilderness Ventures (`www.gilawildernessventures.com`) in Figure 3-4, for example, catches viewers' attention and imagination with its Western concept. Its 3-D perspective pulls the eye into the site and intrigues the viewer with the potential for discovery.

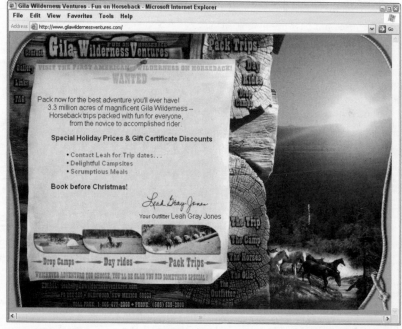

Figure 3-4: The conceptual theme of the Gila Wilderness Ventures site quickly captures the visitor's attention.

Courtesy Gila Wilderness Ventures

Fonts, images, activities, everything on the site must appeal to the target audience you're trying to reach. You wouldn't put bright colors on a site selling urns for pet ashes, or pastels on a site aimed at teenagers. A high-tech site in silver and black has a very different look and feel than one selling country decor with gingham and duckies. A site selling high-priced goods needs lots of white (empty) space to look rich; a discount site does well with crowded images. That's why I recommend finding a designer who knows about marketing communications.

Getting visitors to stick around

Stickiness is the technical (!) term for keeping people on a Web site. If your average viewers visit fewer than two pages of your site (see site statistics in

Neopets.com: Stickiness supreme

Only five years after its founding in 1999, Neopets.com found itself named the fourth stickiest site in the world by Nielsen/NetRatings, with enviable statistics: average interaction time of more than four hours per user per month, 1,000 or more page views per user per month, 70 million global members (of whom about half are active), and 4.2 billion page views per month from kids, teens, and young adults. Alexa.com currently ranks it as the 139th most-visited site on the Web.

Users of Neopets create virtual pets, playing 160 or so fantasy games in the mythical land of Neopia. They play games individually or interactively and earn Neopoints to buy food or toys for

their virtual Neopet. The free site also offers auctions, greetings, messaging, news, and more.

The site is supported by what Neopets call *immersive advertising,* which is similar to product placement in the real world. Advertisers must incorporate their ads into a branded game, shop, or other offering, such as a Neopet screen saver. Neopets has become a worldwide phenomenon, translated into Japanese, Chinese, Korean, Spanish, French, German, and Italian. With constantly changing content, Neopets generates recurring visits and brings in new visitors by word of mouth and, I suspect, by kids copying what their older siblings do.

Chapter 14) or stay less than 30 seconds, most of them see only your home page and flee! You need more cyber-glue. Ideally, you want the average visitor to stick with the site for a minimum of three pages and at least a few minutes. Otherwise they haven't spent enough time to figure out what you have to offer.

Lay down a sticky trail with content, calls to action, things to do, media to download, and interaction with site elements. Every action users take, every click they make, binds them kinesthetically to your site. For example, Neopets.com (described in the nearby sidebar) is famous for its stickiness, which makes it especially appealing to advertisers.

Bringing 'em back for more

Finally, research shows that many people don't buy on the first visit to a site. Some use the Web simply for research before making a purchase in a brick-and-mortar store. Others research multiple sites for comparison shopping but return only if they have a reason. Lawrence.com in Figure 3-5 offers viewers many reasons to come back, from quirky movie reviews to an excellent calendar of activities in this university community. Those with late-night munchies can visit the site to see which restaurants are open, even at 2 a.m.

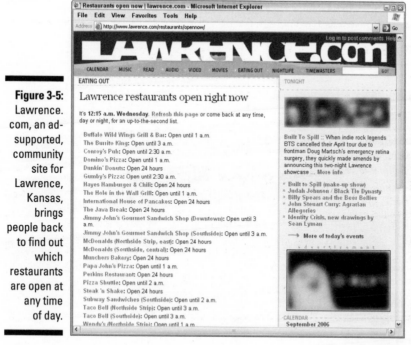

Figure 3-5: Lawrence.com, an ad-supported, community site for Lawrence, Kansas, brings people back to find out which restaurants are open at any time of day.

Courtesy Lawrence.com

Gearing the Site to Your Visitors' Interests

Sorry to be the bearer of bad tidings, but customers and clients don't really care about *you*. They care about themselves! In terms of gaining business, a Web site has to make clear what you can do for the visitor, not why you got into business in the first place or your favorite products, places to visit, or movies (save that for your blog!).

Throughout this book, you can find techniques to ensure that your Web site answers the question "What's on this site for me?" immediately and repetitively. As long as visitors are having a good time, finding useful information, or locating products and services that appeal to them, they will stay on your site. As soon as you lose their interest, you lose their business.

You sell benefits to visitors through graphics, content, and interactive opportunities — and providing reasons for repeat visits. In Figure 3-6, the State of Alaska tourist site at www.travelalaska.com uses the second person (you) in the first paragraph and calls to action (imperative verbs) in the third paragraph to focus on benefits for its visitors, not on itself.

What's in it for me? Answer that question at every step, and your Web site will work magic for you.

Second person (you)

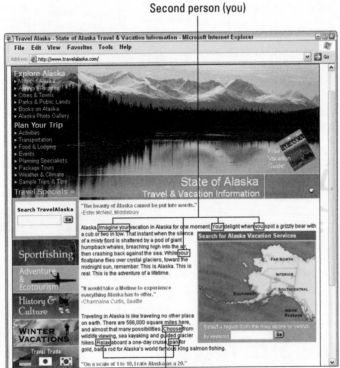

Courtesy Alaska Travel Industry Assn.

Figure 3-6:
The content
on the State
of Alaska
travel site
makes clear
what's in it
for me.

Imperative verbs

Part II
Building a Marketing-Effective Web Site

The 5th Wave   By Rich Tennant

"So far, our Web presence has been pretty good. We've gotten some orders, a few inquiries, and nine guys who want to date our logo."

In this part . . .

Marketing is only part of your Web site, but all of your Web site is marketing. Successful business Web sites don't happen by accident. This section addresses marketing that occurs right on your site. If you drive site design and features by target audience and business goals, you'll jump over half the Web marketing hurdles.

From the look and feel of your site to navigation, content, and features, Chapter 4 looks at how marketing affects the various components of Web design.

Chapter 5 does the same, specifically for companies that sell online. Opening an online store is like opening a brick-and-mortar store in a new location. It takes just as much planning, time, money, maintenance, and care. Forget those commercials about money rolling in while you sit back and count it!

Chapter 6 talks about specific techniques you can use on your site to attract new visitors, keep them on your site, and bring them back for repeat visits. Onsite marketing is fairly inexpensive, requiring more labor and creativity than cash.

Chapter 4

Producing a Successful Business Web Site

Successful business Web sites don't happen by accident. Companies with a sophisticated Web marketing staff deliberately place every item in a specific place on a page, think through each headline, and consider every graphic element and photograph for impact. They don't spend hundreds of thousands of dollars on the mere chance that a site will achieve its marketing and sales objectives.

If those companies can be organized, so can you. This kind of detailed care may take more time, but it doesn't have to cost you any more money.

Your defined business goals and target audience drive site design. Those factors determine how a site looks on the screen and how visitors navigate through it, which is often called the *look and feel* of a site. This chapter focuses on the marketing elements for any site. The next chapter considers, specifically, the marketing aspects for a successful online store.

Incorporate your business goals and objectives, your list of competitors, and your target audience in your request for proposal (RFP). (See Chapter 3 for more on RFPs.) If you've already selected a developer, take your planning pages to your first meeting, along with a list of sites you like and sites you hate. A good developer should ask for all this information, regardless of whether you come prepared.

Thinking About the Structure of Your Web Site

The most important criterion for a successful business Web site is whether it accomplishes its objective. Your site doesn't have to be beautiful or cutting edge as long as it ultimately has a positive impact on your bottom line. The second most important criterion is how well the site works from the users' perspectives. The easier you make it for users to achieve what they want — whether buying a product, obtaining information, or connecting with others — the more likely your site is to succeed.

Using AIDA to guide visitors toward specific actions

Direct marketing techniques are highly useful for coaxing users into taking actions you want them to take. The four standard steps of direct marketing (known as AIDA) apply to the structure of Web sites:

- ✔ **Attention:** Get viewers' attention by using graphics, a headline that grabs, and a benefits-based lead. You have four seconds to convince them they'll find something of value on the site.

- ✔ **Interest:** Build interest with site design and navigation. Include intriguing options that pull people to additional pages on your Web site, giving you time and space to expose visitors to your products, services, and benefits.

- ✔ **Desire:** Create desire and a sense of urgency as visitors move themselves toward taking an action. If you think visitors are almost ready to buy, post a reminder to Buy Now for Free Shipping. If you think they're doing research, remind them to Bookmark This Page or Tell a Friend. It's tricky, but you can prod users to do what you want them to do. Use whatever content tools that will build desire in your audience, from marketing copy, photography, and special offers, to online activities or onsite entertainment.

✔ **Action:** Right from the beginning, make it obvious what you want visitors to do, whether it's to buy online, make a call, send an e-mail, or sign up for a newsletter. Then ensure visitors that it's extremely easy for them to take those actions.

You can't count on a linear experience. Web sites aren't like most books, read from front to back. Visitors might not arrive on your home page, and they might skip all around your site. Not every visitor wants the same thing, so you must juggle appeals to multiple subsegments of your target audience.

Assessing your Web site or others

Most business owners say, "I don't know anything about Web design, but I know what I like." Are you in that category? If so, a few simple terms can help organize your visceral reaction when it's time to evaluate other Web sites, plan your own, or communicate effectively with your Web designer and staff. While many people use different wording, these five elements cover the ground of site design:

✔ **Concept:** The underlying design metaphor for your site intimately connected to your brand and target audience

✔ **Content:** All the words, products, pictures, audio, interactive features, and any other material you put on your site

✔ **Navigation:** The way users move through a site by using menus, links, and sitemaps

✔ **Decoration:** All the supporting design elements, such as buttons, fonts, and graphics that your designer creates

✔ **Marketing efficacy:** Methods such as calls to action or signup forms that get users to do what you want them to do

The form in Figure 4-1 provides a detailed breakdown for assessing sites. Try it on your existing site if you have one, or on any of the sites that appear in this book. See what happens when other people evaluate the same sites by using this form. You might be surprised! The higher the score, the better, but you may find that others rate a site quite differently from the way you do. If several people consistently score a site below 50, it is probably in real trouble. (If a question doesn't apply, just ignore it and reduce the possible total by 5 points.) You can download this form on the book's companion Web site at www.dummies.com/go/webmarketing.

Most of this chapter deals with the elements in the preceding list in more detail.

Web Site Assessment Form

Concept or Presence

	Lowest				Best
How well is a coherent, visual metaphor carried through the site?	1	2	3	4	5
How well is that metaphor carried through on each screen?	1	2	3	4	5
How well does the metaphor fit the company image?	1	2	3	4	5
How well does the metaphor suit the purpose of the site?	1	2	3	4	5
How well does the metaphor suit the target audience?	1	2	3	4	5

Concept Subtotal: _____

Content

	Lowest				Best
How appropriate is the text-intensiveness of the site?	1	2	3	4	5
How well does the site answer any questions you might have?	1	2	3	4	5
If you have unanswered questions, how easy is it to ask questions via e-mail and/or phone? How prompt is the response?	1	2	3	4	5
How well does the content suit the purpose of the site?	1	2	3	4	5
How well does the content suit the target audience?	1	2	3	4	5

Content Subtotal: _____

Navigation

	Lowest				Best
How consistent is the navigation?	1	2	3	4	5
How obvious, simple, or intuitive is the navigation?	1	2	3	4	5
How easy is the access to the menu, site index, and home page from each screen?	1	2	3	4	5
How accessible are navigation tools (screen visibility/position)?	1	2	3	4	5
How effectively are internal links used to move through the site?	1	2	3	4	5
How well arranged is the content (number of clicks needed)?	1	2	3	4	5

Navigation Subtotal: _____

Decoration

	Lowest				Best
How attractive is the decoration?	1	2	3	4	5
How well does the decoration support the concept?	1	2	3	4	5
How well does the decoration support the content?	1	2	3	4	5
How well does the decoration support the navigation?	1	2	3	4	5
How well does the decoration suit the purpose of the site?	1	2	3	4	5
How well does the decoration suit the target audience?	1	2	3	4	5

Decoration Subtotal: _____

Marketing Efficacy

	Lowest				Best
How well does the site convey its central value message?	1	2	3	4	5
How well does it meet the buying needs of the target market?	1	2	3	4	5
How effectively does it use calls to action?	1	2	3	4	5
How well does the site promote itself within its own pages?	1	2	3	4	5

Marketing Efficacy Subtotal: _____

Site Total: _____

Figure 4-1: You can use this form to assess your own site or others.

© 2006 Watermelon Mountain Web Marketing www.watermelonweb.com

Creating a Concept

Concept is the design metaphor that holds your site together. For example, look at NYCabbie.com in Figure 4-2. The site uses a taxicab-yellow background with a checkered rule as the metaphor for this site, which sells photographs of life in New York City from a cab driver's perspective. The content extends the concept with sections called Dear Cabby, Taxi Stories, and Taxi Tips. After photographer/cab driver Michael Krygier handed a card with his Web address to a passenger — who just happened to work for the British Broadcasting Corporation — the site became so successful that Krygier got what he most wanted, recognition as an artist.

A good designer integrates marketing communication principles, branding considerations, and your target audience into the concept for your Web site.

Figure 4-2:
NYCabbie
uses an
immediately
recognizable
visual
metaphor
with a
checkered
design
element and
yellow
background.

Courtesy NYCabbie

Applying marketing communications principles to your design

Marketing communications integrates marketing and sales principles with graphic design to achieve business objectives. It acknowledges that the presentation of information affects emotional response and thus influences buying decisions. Designers ask about your target audiences to be sure to select or create appropriate design elements.

While essential for any type of sales collateral or packaging, marketing communications is particularly critical because of the short window for grabbing attention on the Web. Experienced Web designers intuitively adjust the font style, graphic style, colors, images, and white space to have a positive impact on your marketing process while reinforcing your brand.

For example, the red, white, and blue design for automotive site Checker Auto Parts (www.checkerauto.com) is quite different from the golden aura of Fairytale Weddings (www.santafewedding.com) in Figure 4-3. Checker Auto uses strong graphics, photos of vehicles, and thick, italic fonts that suggest speed and power. Fairytale Weddings uses romantic photos with delicate flourishes of script. Red conveys strength, power, and excitement; gold conveys warmth, richness, and excellence.

The upper-right corner of the screen below the header graphic is valuable real estate because the user's eye starts there. Because that's an excellent location for an important call to action or special offer, Checker Auto uses that space to solicit e-mail addresses. On its entry page, Fairytale Weddings recognizes that the last item in a list gets more attention than those in the middle, letting prospects know immediately that they can "Make a Request."

How quickly can you identify the different demographics of the audiences for these sites? Gender is obvious. What about economic status? Can you identify any similarities between these sites?

Color meaning is culturally dependent. If you sell internationally, research the meaning of colors in your target country. For instance, in many Asian countries, white, not black, signifies death; red, not green, symbolizes prosperity.

Branding with logos and favicons

Put your company logo on your Web site, just as you would on any other advertising or packaging; it's an essential part of your brand. If you don't have a logo, this is a good time to get one. Ask your graphic artist to design one for you, make one at sites like LogoMaker.com, or search for *free logos* to find the names of companies that sell logo software or inexpensive, pre-made logos.

The upper-left corner of a page is the standard location for a logo, or *logotype* (a logo that is done completely with lettering), as shown in Figure 4-4. That may vary depending on the overall design. Usually, clicking the logo takes the user to the home page.

Figure 4-3:
Compare the design concepts for Checker Auto and Fairytale Weddings. The two sites appeal to different audiences, but both immediately tell you what they're about.

Checker Auto site courtesy CSK Auto, Inc.
Fairytale Weddings site courtesy Fairytale Weddings with photographs © 2006 Insightfoto.com

Figure 4-4:
The
favicons
on the
navigation
bar add to
the branding
impact
of the
respective
logos in the
upper-left
corner of
these sites.

CHEETAHMAIL® and the CheetahMail logo are registered trademarks of CheetahMail, Inc., an Experian company. The CheetahMail website is © 2006. CheetahMail, Inc. an Experian company. All rights reserved. Trend Watching images courtesy Trend Watching.

Favicons, a contraction of the words *favorites icons,* are relatively recent tools for secondary branding. They appear to the left of the URL in the browser address bar, as shown in Figure 4-4, as well as in the drop-down menu of favorites, in the history bar, and on the links toolbar. Favicons are visible in most browsers, including Internet Explorer (version 5 or later), Firefox, Opera (version 7 or later), and Netscape (version 7 or later). However, a favicon doesn't show up in Internet Explorer the first time a user visits the site — it shows up only when the user has bookmarked it.

Go to www.make-a-favicon.com or www.webdevelopersjournal.com/articles/favicon.html for directions on how to create one of these tiny (16-x-16 pixel) icons.

Developing Content

Content refers to everything you provide for the Web site, from written copy to photographs, from product information for a database to a calendar of events. As I discuss in Chapter 3, you might decide to outsource content production to a copy writer, designate one or more of your employees as *content expert(s),* or combine the two solutions. In any case, you or an employee should allow time to provide a rough draft or raw materials, establish directions, and review content for accuracy and quality. No outsider knows your business the way you do.

Writing and photography for the Web face different constraints than they do with print or film. However, they remain just as critical online as offline when it comes to moving your prospects along the AIDA (attention, interest, desire, and action) pathway. You still need headlines that grab attention, images that pique interest, copy that builds desire, and calls to action that move Web visitors to buy.

Writing effective marketing copy

People don't read online; they scan to save time. That makes sense because it takes 25 percent longer to read the same material onscreen than it does to read it on paper. Because of the limitations of time and screen space, you need to adapt your writing style for the Web. Try to follow these precepts:

- ✔ **Use the inverted pyramid.** Use the journalistic convention of the inverted pyramid, with the most important information at the beginning of each page. Readers might never reach the end of the first paragraph, let alone the end of the page.

- ✔ **Grab readers with headlines.** Good headlines grab readers by the lapels. Subheads help break up the text on a page, making it easier to read. If you use a different font size, style, or color for your headings and if your headlines or subheads include a search term, you might receive extra points in search engine rankings.

- ✔ **Write strong leads.** The first sentence on the page is called the *lead*. Hook readers with benefits, telling them what they'll find on your site, store, or page. It improves search engine ranking to include three to four search terms in the first paragraph.

- ✔ **Stay above the fold.** Keep the most important information *above the fold* — that is, keep it above the part of the page that users have to scroll to see. Depending on the audience, perhaps fewer than 50 percent of your visitors will scroll below the fold.

- ✔ **Avoid long, scrolling pages.** Many short pages of 150 to 200 words are preferable to a few long pages. If long text is unavoidable, consider creating HTML files that users can download and print out easily. Alternatively, use the Frequently Asked Question (FAQ) format. At the top of a page, create a list of links to *anchor paragraphs* (text, often below the fold, that viewers access from links at the top of the same page, without scrolling).

- ✔ **Limit use of PDF files.** While designers like PDF files because PDFs preserve designs, this file format isn't great for users. Generally, restrict PDF files to distributing long documents intended for print, not for reading online.

- ✔ **Use active voice.** Shun passive voice in favor of active voice. That is, the subject performs the action rather than receives it. The active sentence, "Search engines skip Flash pages" is preferable to the passive version, "Flash pages aren't read by search engines." Hints that you are using passive voice: forms of the verb *to be,* including the constructions *there is, there are,* or *it is.*

- **Emphasize second person.** Use *your* or *you* explicitly as the subject, or implicitly with imperative verbs, such as *buy, review, call,* or *sign up*. Second person forces you to talk about benefits, not features, thus telling visitors what they'll get from your site. Even the New York Times notes the growing use of *you, yours, my,* and *ours* as Madison Avenue follows the trend toward customization and personalization. Think MySpace.com. Possessives imply ownership, empowering consumers. Your marketing copy must establish a relationship that breaks through the boundary of the screen.

- **Use first and third person judiciously.** You can slide in some first person (*our* or *we,* especially in sentences like "We offer a money-back guarantee"). Just don't spend a lot of time talking about yourself and your business. Your readers don't care. On most sites, third-person descriptions of product (*it* or *they*) are fine, but don't put off your visitors with pages written in third person. Those pages often become impersonal and distant.

- **Stay informal.** With a few exceptions, an informal, conversational tone works better than dissertation-style, proper English. That's no excuse, however, for obvious grammatical errors such as subject/verb agreement.

- **Keep it short.** People are busy and don't have time to read everything. Use short words, short sentences, short paragraphs, and short pages, always placing the most important words and information near the beginning.

- **Use bullet lists.** Sentence fragments are fine, especially in bulleted lists. Think PowerPoint style, not essay.

- **Include text links.** Link liberally to other parts of your site within the text. These contextual, internal links help users find in-depth information quickly and move people to multiple pages of your site. If the linked text happens to be one of your search terms, you might earn extra points toward improved ranking in search engine results, too.

Of course, the basic principles of good writing still apply. Especially, keep these points in mind:

- **Write vividly.** Use specific nouns and verbs rather than strings of gratuitous adjectives and adverbs.

- **Skip the jargon.** Use your readers' ordinary language.

- **Be yourself.** In spite of all these directions, let your personality shine through. When appropriate, include an emotional jolt of humor or wit as a payoff to the reader.

- **Check spelling and grammar.** If you don't have a content management system (see the "Choosing a way to update your content" section, later in the chapter) that checks spelling and grammar, write the text first in a word processing application. Save your checked and corrected content as a `.txt` file, or in Notepad to remove formatting.

✔ **Have others read what you write.** It's easy to get too close to your writing. Have someone else read it for clarity, accuracy, and omissions.

✔ **Proofread your text.** Read your text out loud. It's the fastest, easiest way to find mistakes. A site full of errors gives visitors the impression that you're sloppy. If you don't care about your own site, how do visitors know you'll care about them as customers?

Gardener's Supply Company writes appealing prose for product descriptions on its Web site (www.gardeners.com). In Figure 4-5, note the use of the second person "you," the vivid description of the planter, the benefit statement "self-watering convenience," a link to a related product, and the call to action, "Place Your Order Here."

Table 4-1 lists three good resource sites for Web writing.

2nd person active voice

Figure 4-5: Good marketing copy is more than half the battle. In this case, Gardener's Supply Company has already won.

Call to action

Courtesy Gardener's Supply & Dutch Gardens

Table 4-1	Resources for Web Writing
Name	*URL*
W3C Style Guide for Online Hypertext	`www.w3.org/Provider/Style`
Web Style Guide, 2nd edition	`www.webstyleguide.com/index.html?/index.html`
Writing for the Web (Jakob Nielsen)	`www.useit.com/papers/webwriting`

Choosing fonts

The easier you make it for people to read your content, the more of it they absorb. The low resolution of computer screens causes eyestrain. While they might not know why, visitors will reward your efforts to make the screen easier to read. Ask your designer about these suggestions:

- When using HTML, select fonts that were designed for the Web: Verdana and Trebuchet for sans serif type and Georgia for serif. (This doesn't apply to text that appears within graphics.)

- Keep the length of a text line to less than half the width of the screen, even though that means only 8 to 12 words per line.

- Surround text with white space. Allow margins to rest the eye rather than push text to the left or right edge of the page.

- Avoid italics in HTML.

- By convention, use underlined text only to represent links.

- Limit use of reversed-out text (light colors on a dark background). It is too hard to read and might complicate printing.

- If you use different colors to distinguish visited from unvisited links or navigation, be sure that there is enough contrast to set apart the two states.

- If you target an audience of people older than 40, default to a larger size font than you might otherwise. It's easier to read.

Telling stories with pictures

Photography is a powerful method of reaching your audience with immediacy and impact. While it's absolutely critical to show pictures — including close-ups — of any products that you sell, that's not the only reason to use photography. Well-selected and appropriately positioned images can tell a story about your business, your processes, your tourist destination, and most important, your people. Good photos are good sales tools!

Sometimes, the Web seems to exist in a strangely depopulated part of the universe. Many sites omit photographs, perhaps because of a legacy of concern about download time. Others have photographs only of buildings, machines, products, landscapes, nature, or artwork.

That's fine, but the most powerful images in the world have faces; our human brains are designed to react to them. When viewers see a picture with people, they can imagine themselves visiting that place, doing that activity, or using that product. They move themselves one step further along the buying process.

While faster access has made it easier to use photos, a page that takes more than eight seconds to download will lose much of its audience.

To reduce download time, be sure to save photos in the correct format for the Web: JPGs with a file size of 100K or less. Use smaller images of 10–20K, called *thumbnails,* that people click to view an enlargement in a pop-up window. This process is especially common on pages with multiple images, such as catalog pages for an online store. Here are a few other tips for using photos on your Web site:

- ✔ Photos that work in print don't always work online, especially as thumbnails. Long shots or images with multiple points of interest might look fine when expanded, but not as small images.

- ✔ Crop photos to remove extraneous background information that detracts from the message you're trying to send.

- ✔ It's worth the cost of digital doctoring if the picture helps tell your story. Some photos might need additional processing in Photoshop to improve their color, contrast, brightness, or hue, or to erase something that you don't want seen. Of course, ethical and professional constraints limit manipulation of images for reasons other than quality.

- ✔ Start with a high-resolution photo resized and saved for the Web as a JPG. You cannot make a low-resolution photo better, but you can easily make a high-resolution photo smaller while maintaining image quality.

- ✔ If you expect users to print pages with photos, make sure the photos are "readable" in black and white.

If photographs are an integral part to the story you're telling or the appeal you're making, they need to be good ones! Look at the role of photos on ExperienceWashington.com in Figure 4-6 for instance. Hire a pro or buy stock photos from a source like www.istockphoto.com. A photo that is too small, out of focus, too busy, or poorly framed makes your company and your products look as bad as the photo.

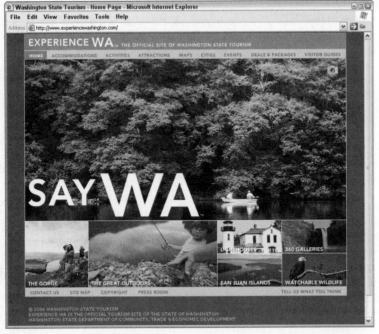

Figure 4-6: The home page of Experience Washington. com, the tourism site for the state of Washington, uses photos effectively to tell a story and involve the viewer.

Courtesy Washington State Department of Community, Trade, and Economic Development

Using rich media

Multimedia, sometimes called *rich media,* has increased in popularity as broadband use has exploded. Audio clips, music, video, virtual reality, and Flash animation all fall into this category. If rich media appeals to you, here are a few reasons why it might be worthwhile for your site:

✔ **The media adds marketing value.** It might extend your brand, help sell a product — as a virtual reality tour of real estate or a complex product might — or explain a process or service, as a video could. It might also demonstrate your capabilities, such as music clips for a composer selling songs online or animation for a Web designer.

✔ **It makes the site easier to use or otherwise enhances the user's experience.** For instance, a live Web cam at a daycare center offers clients security and reassurance — assuming access is password-protected so only parents can view it.

✔ **The goal for your Web site demands it.** A site that earns its keep by advertising might use rich media techniques to keep visitors on a site longer, encourage more page views, or attract repeat visits.

✔ **Your target audience wants or expects it.** Younger audiences are much more attracted to rich media than older ones; a consumer audience with time for entertainment is more susceptible to rich media than a busy, B2B audience of engineers — unless there's a reason for the rich media, such as a product demo.

✔ **You need rich media to stay even with, or ahead of, your competitors.**

If you're now convinced that rich media is right for your site, here are a few other important considerations before you take the final plunge:

✔ Will your target audience have the plug-ins, know-how, and access speed to take advantage of rich media?

✔ Can you afford the cost of doing it right? Good multimedia is rarely cheap. If you can't afford to do it right, don't do it at all. Visitors won't know what they're missing, but they will know if something doesn't work properly or looks terrible.

✔ Can you locate professionals to create the rich media, whether a good audio recording studio, a videographer, or an animator? Very few Web designers can do everything, but they might know subcontractors who can help. As always, review portfolios, get several bids, and check references.

✔ Can you launch your Web site without rich media and add it later, or is it intrinsic to the purpose and design of your site? Adding features later lets you test site operation and assess the value of your baseline site first. Later, you can announce new features in e-mail, newsletters, press releases, and on the site itself. Implementing rich media can delay the launch of your site, as it might be the most complex and time-consuming element of your site.

✔ Can you display your Flash, video, or other rich media on a page other than a splash page? (A *splash page* is an introductory Web page used as a lead-in to the home page. Splash pages are usually graphically intensive or use rich media, but lack navigation other than a link to enter the site. A splash page with navigation is called an entry page.) Search engines can't read Flash pages.

✔ Can you give your visitors a choice of viewing a Flash versus nonFlash version of your site?

✔ How much use would justify the expense? Will your statistics (see Chapter 14) display the number of visits or downloads for your rich media? Can you track an association from rich media access to business outcome?

Do not use rich media just because you can. Establish a reason, an objective measure of value, and a way to measure impact on something other than your ego.

Figure 4-7 shows one page from the all-Flash site for the Tijuana Flats restaurant chain (www.tijuanaflats.com). Everything is in motion on this site, which figuratively clears the table, complete with sound effects, as you shift between sections of the site. The static navigation, which appears on the napkin in the upper left, has animated highlights when you hover over an option. Violating the rules of consistent navigation, secondary navigation specific to a section shows up in different places on the screen.

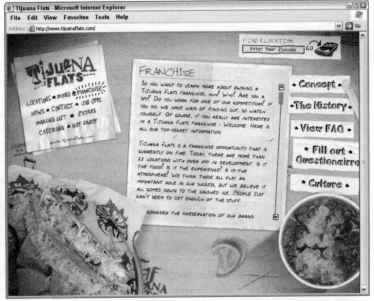

Courtesy PUSH/Mindflood

Figure 4-7:
The Tijuana
Flats
restaurant
site uses
Flash
throughout
the site.

In this case, breaking the rules establishes the carefree, slightly over-the-top experience that patrons can expect, as well as the attitude the chain wants to see in its employees and franchisees. One quibble: Users can't tell that the Hot Sauce option on the menu takes them to an online store to purchase sauces and branded gear. Tijuana Flats won a 2006 Webby Award in the restaurant category.

If you're uncertain about rich media, apply the KISS principle. (Keep it simple, stupid.) Be sure that sophisticated rich media will be worth the investment of money, time, and effort that it will take. It's nice to have bragging rights but even nicer to have a profit.

Choosing a way to update your content

Chapter 6 discusses the importance of updating content regularly and the type of information that should be updated. To make changes cost-effectively, you need a method of changing content that doesn't require knowing HTML or paying your Web designer every time you need a small change.

Updates are critical to your customers' perceptions of your company, as well as to search engine ranking. Decide how you will update your site before you start developing it. You have several choices, none of which require technical knowledge beyond word processing:

✔ **Have your developer handle the updates.** On a small, HTML-only site, updates are fairly easy. Ask your developer to quote a price for development and/or hosting that includes an hour of support per month.

✔ **Do the updates yourself.** Template-based sites allow you to update content at any time, without any special knowledge.

✔ **Use Macromedia Contribute.** Macromedia Contribute software (www.adobe.com/products/contribute) allows you and/or other content experts to update an HTML site without knowing any HTML. Let your developer know in advance if you plan to use this software, which starts at $149 for a single site license.

✔ **Use your developer's CMS.** Many developers have written their own password-protected, inhouse, content management systems (CMSs). They might call this capability their *admin pages* or *backroom*. Some customize CMS software that they purchase to offer all their clients. The complexity and flexibility of a proprietary CMS depends totally on the developer, but it rarely requires technical knowledge. However, a proprietary CMS is generally tied to a particular developer or host. If the company goes out of business or you switch to another provider or host, you might lose this access.

✔ **Use an open source CMS.** *Open source* (software whose source code is available to developers to use, modify, and redistribute without charge) CMSs are free, with many customizable options. They're generally designed for fairly large sites with many pages, a product database, or a structured approval process. Of the dozens of alternatives, your developer will select one based on the type of Web site you have, the language it's written in, the features you need, the skills of your staff, and what they themselves are familiar with. Most online store packages (see Chapter 5) already incorporate the ability for ordinary staff members to manage the product catalog and store; you need a separate CMS for nonstore pages.

✔ **Buy a commercial CMS.** Paid CMSs exist at all prices and levels of sophistication. They're often built in to high-end, enterprise-level, Web development systems. In large, corporate environments, many content experts need different levels of access to specific pages. Some such Web development packages are designed for certain environments, such as colleges or publications.

Figure 4-8 shows an editing page from the content management system for SweetSantaFe.com. The first page of this CMS lists all pages of the site with options to create new pages, or edit, preview, or delete existing pages. This particular CMS lets users add or remove pages that appear in the navigation.

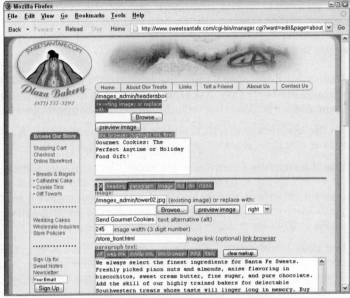

© Courtesy Plaza Bakery. CMS developed by Web site designer, Desert Heart Multimedia, DesertHeart.com ©2006

Figure 4-8:
The password-protected CMS for SweetSanta-Fe.com offers a WYSIWYG (what you see is what you get) editor.

Check out the sources in Table 4-2 for CMS resources.

Table 4-2	Resources for Content Management Systems
Type of Resource	**URL**
Lists CMS options	`www.cio.com/summaries/web/content`
Lists CMS options	`www.la-grange.net/cms`
Lists CMS options	`www.oscom.org/matrix/index.html`
Reviews of CMS	`www.openadvantage.org/articles/oadocument.2005-04-19.0329097790`
Reviews of CMS	`http://techupdate.zdnet.com/techupdate/stories/main/0,14179,2897730,00.html`
Open source CMS	`www.mamboserver.com`
Open source CMS	`http://joomla.org`
Open source CMS	`http://drupal.org`

Ensuring Easy Navigation: A Human-Friendly Site

You have marketing goals and objectives for your site, but if visitors can't find the information they want or can't execute an action, you don't have a chance of meeting those objectives. Most good marketing Web sites follow a few, essential principles of navigation:

- The main menu of options appears consistently on every page in the same place.

- The footer of each page includes links to the main pages so users don't have to scroll back to the top of a page to navigate elsewhere. (This is also helpful for search engine optimization.)

- Secondary menus cue users with a glimpse of what they will find within a section.

- A linkable sitemap or index offers the overall layout of a site at a glance. (This, too, is helpful for search engine ranking.)

- The appearance of contextual and navigation links changes to let users know where they are and where they've been.

- An onsite search engine is available for large, information- and product-loaded sites so visitors can quickly find what they're looking for. Onsite search has a high marketing value. Be sure your developer makes results of failed searches available to you. This immediate consumer feedback tells you what your site is missing.

- The navigation has words, not nameless icons that visitors have to remember. It's even better if those words are also search terms. Search engines can't read icons.

- All contextual and navigation links are verified to be sure they work, open correctly, and go to the right content page.

The Collectors Guide site in Figure 4-9 (www.collectorsguide.com) uses many elements of navigation to help users find their way around. Note the consistent, horizontal navigation at the top of the screen. Hovering over menu items brings up both secondary and third-level navigation choices. Color changes and check boxes indicate where users are on the site. Note the onsite search box in the upper-right corner and the directions for scrolling to read current news stories in the box on the lower left. Items are grouped by concept, with the most important calls to action (Buy Art/Subscribe) in the upper-right corner. A sitemap is available under the About Us drop-down menu and in a limited set of linkable footers on other pages.

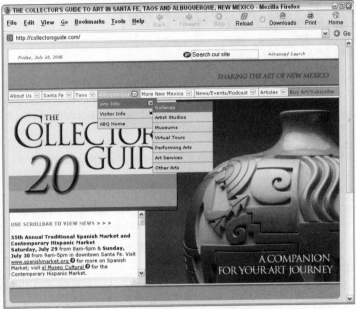

©2006 Wingspread Guides of New Mexico, Inc.

Figure 4-9:
The navigation on Collectors Guide is obvious, consistent, and user friendly.

Mastering usability issues

Navigation is just one of several usability factors that might dramatically affect the success of your Web site. A site that is obvious and easy to use gives viewers a positive impression of your company. A site that doesn't run on their browser does just the opposite!

Generally, you don't know how any specific users have set their browser options — whether they block all pop-up windows, which plug-ins they've installed, how accurately their monitors display colors, what screen resolution they use, or how fast their Internet connections might be. Some high-end application developers purchase software like BrowserHawk (`www.cyscape.com/products/bhawk`) to detect users' browser settings.

The rest of us need a feel for the numbers. For instance, more than half of all U.S. users have broadband access and more than half have a monitor set for 1024 x 768 resolution or higher. While almost all members of a B2B, high-tech, target audience have fairly recent, if not the latest and greatest, in technology and access, an audience of older, retail consumers shopping from home might struggle with older browsers and lower-speed connections.

You can garner some browser-use statistics for your site over time (see Chapter 14) and by all means, research configuration across a more narrowly defined group of users in your target market. Because that still doesn't tell you what will happen with a specific user, you might need to provide directions for setting up a browser, like BestConnectionJewelry.com (www.bestconnectionjewelry.com) does in Figure 4-10. Consider offering users a choice of dialup versus broadband versions or Flash versus nonFlash.

Better yet, make sure that your site operates on all popular, current browsers and versions (Internet Explorer, Mozilla Firefox, Opera, and Safari) by testing them for compatibility and download speed. Sites like www.netmechanic.com/products/browser-index.shtml and www.browsercam.com sell software for developers to use for multiple clients or offer less expensive versions for one-time, limited use, often for $20 or less.

Figure 4-10:
Best
Connection
Jewelry
helps its
users
configure
their
browsers
for an
optimal site
experience.

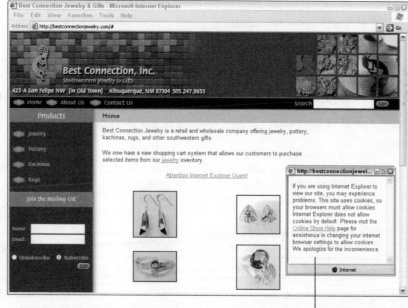

Browser setup instructions

Courtesy Best Connection Jewelry & Gifts

Taking human factors into consideration

Every Web site places a significant cognitive load on users, who basically learn to use a new piece of application software for each site they visit. The more your site conforms to Web conventions and to the reality of the human mind, the easier it is to use. Visitors reward your efforts by staying on the site.

Some human factors to consider as you design your site include:

- ✔ **The brain is built for recognition, not recall.** Don't make your users try to remember what icons mean or how to find information.

- ✔ **The brain likes the number seven.** Seven seconds is the limit for short-term memory. It is also the number of things that most people can remember at once (so don't overwhelm them with choices) and the number of times they need to see a name or ad to remember it.

- ✔ **Contrast helps the mind organize information.** Contrast in design might occur in type, color, empty space, or size.

- ✔ **Brains like patterns.** Group objects by function or appearance and use consistent page design and site operation to give your viewers a boost.

- ✔ **Users need reassurance.** Provide feedback within a reasonable time, such as thanking a visitor for submitting a form.

- ✔ **The kinesthetic experience of click actions reinforces a message.** Ask visitors to click to request something, download an item, or submit information. The act of checking a box on an order form puts shoppers in the mindset to buy.

- ✔ **Provide easily accessible help to use the site.**

Table 4-3 provides more sources on human factors design, including UseIt.com, the Web site created by Jakob Nielsen, one of the grandfathers of research on the computer/human interface. The table also lists sites with examples of bad design you can learn from.

Table 4-3	Resources for Web Usability and Design	
Name	*URL*	*What You'll Find*
Jakob Nielsen's UseIt.com	www.useit.com/papers/ heuristic/heuristic _list.html	Principles of Web usability and design
Jakob Nielsen's Top 10 Mistakes in Web Design	www.useit.com/ alertbox/9605.html	Laugh and learn from the mistakes of others
Microsoft Usability Guidelines	http://msdn.microsoft. com/library/default. asp?url=/library/en- us/dnsiteplan/html/ improvingsiteusa.asp	Principles of Web usability and design
Worst of the Web	www.worstoftheweb.com	Laugh and learn from the mistakes of others

Name	URL	What You'll Find
Web Pages That Suck	www.webpagesthatsuck.com	Laugh and learn from the mistakes of others
Yahoo! Directory	http://dir.yahoo.com/ Arts/design_arts/ graphic_design/web_ page_design_and_layout	Directory of articles on Web design and usability

Making your site accessible

You must design your site with specific, human factors in mind when your target audience includes children, seniors, or people with disabilities. Accessibility is particularly important for information-intensive sites, social service organizations, political sites, newspapers, and other public communications.

Concerns range from readability levels to the use of <alt> tags that enable speech synthesizers to read images, as well as text, out loud. At the very least, try to make your site accessible to Level 1 of the W3C Web Accessibility Initiative (www.w3.org/WAI).

Planning for accessibility broadens your audience by welcoming older users, visitors with low literacy or who are not fluent in English, people with slow access or old equipment, and new and infrequent Web users. Google, which is beta testing a version of its search engine for blind and visually impaired users, estimates some 11 million such users in the U.S. alone.

Federal law (www.usdoj.gov/crt/508/508home.html) requires that government and public education sites be accessible to people with sensory or motor deficits. Go to http://cast.org or www.anybrowser.org/ campaign/abdesign.html for more information, and go to http:// webxact.watchfire.com to test a page of your site for accessibility. A fully featured testing product for accessibility is available at www.watchfire. com/products/webxm/bobby.aspx.

Decorating Your Site

When people think about Web sites, more often than not they think about surface decoration. *Decoration* encompasses colors, buttons, backgrounds, textures, rules, fonts, graphics, illustrations, photos, sounds, and any other elements that support the overall concept.

Ask your designer to establish a stylebook specifying colors, fonts, and other elements that should be followed as the site expands. Otherwise, the site can lose its visual coherence over time as staff leave and memories fade. A stylebook might specify:

- ✔ Icons
- ✔ Typography
- ✔ Photography
- ✔ Windows
- ✔ Sounds
- ✔ File formats

The site for NatureMaker (shown in Figure 4-11) is an excellent example of using decoration to support a concept. Table 4-4 lists just a few of the many online resources providing decorative elements to use on your site.

Figure 4-11: The bark background on the splash page for Nature-Maker echoes on all other pages of the site in a subtle, screened-back form.

Courtesy NatureMaker, Inc.

Table 4-4	Some Web Design Resource Sites	
Description	*URL*	*Free (Y/N)*
Bullets, arrows, icons	`www.stylegala.com/features/bullet madness/`	Yes
Cascading style sheets	`www.csszengarden.com`	Yes
Clip art, Web sets	`http://resources.bravenet.com/clipart`	Yes
Clip art, Web sets, graphics, cartoons	`www.desktoppublishing.com/free.html`	Yes
Clip art, Web sets, photos	`http://build.tripod.lycos.com/imagebrowser/index.html`	Yes
Fonts	`www.1001freefonts.com`	Yes
Fonts	`www.urbanfonts.com`	Yes
Photos	`www.istockphoto.com/index.php`	No, but inexpensive
Search engine	`www.freefind.com`	Yes with ads; no without ads
Sound effects	`www.partnersinrhyme.com/pir/PIRsfx.shtml`	Yes
Sound effects	`www.thefreesite.com/Free_Sounds/Free_WAVs/`	Yes

Improving Marketing Efficacy

Marketing efficacy refers to other onsite techniques that encourage users to do what you want them to do. Chapter 6 covers many onsite features that pull visitors to the site, keep them there long enough to establish a positive memory, and bring them back for repeat visits. One technique deserves special attention here: the call to action. Calls to action are usually, but not always, imperative verbs (such as *buy, view, register,* and *get*). They move visitors from one page of the site to another, building interest and desire until visitors take the desired action.

On average, sites lose about half their visitors with every additional click. If visitors wander around your site without finding what they want, they're likely to be goners.

The conversion funnel

Conversion rate is one of the most important statistics you track for your site. It is the number of people who take a desired action divided by the number of people who visit. Across the board, the average conversion rate is only 2–4 percent, as shown in Figure 4-12. That's a sobering number. While conversion rate varies widely — from 0.1 percent to 30 percent — from site to site, the 2 percent to 4 percent number is a useful yardstick for predicting and assessing success.

Figure 4-12:
The conversion funnel illustrates why it's so important to move your visitors through your site until they take a desired action.

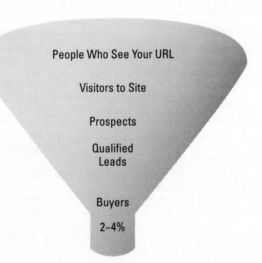

People Who See Your URL

Visitors to Site

Prospects

Qualified Leads

Buyers

2–4%

To achieve the standard conversion rate, you must bring 25–50 times as many visitors to your site as the number of conversions you're looking for. In turn, that number dictates elements of your strategic marketing plan. Again, on average, only 5 percent of people who see your URL somewhere end up visiting your site. Therefore, you must generate somewhere from 500–1,000 URL impressions for every conversion you want to make.

Calls to action

A few, simple rules for calls to action can help improve the conversion rate of your site.

✔ **Set up 2 clicks to action.** Enable users to take the action or action(s) you most want in two clicks or less. Keep your primary calls to action, such as Buy Now or Sign Up to Save, on the main navigation or catalog pages at all times. A second click submits the request. Your site is off and running!

✔ **Generate leads.** In the world of Web marketing, e-mail addresses are gold. If you don't have a newsletter, create another reason to collect addresses, such as, `We'll e-mail a copy of our free white paper to your inbox. Submit your e-mail address now.` Offer a benefit when asking visitors to sign up or register. Of course, let people know they're giving you permission to contact them by e-mail in the future.

✔ **Use links as internal motivators.** A link is an implicit call to action, with `click here` understood at this point by most Web users. With the right phrasing, a link call to action pulls the user to another page with an appeal to self-interest. For instance, a link might read `Live longer` or `Warm Nights, Cool Drinks, Hot Dates`.

Cherry Moon Farms (`www.cherrymoon.com`), the fruit brand line of ProFlowers, uses six different calls to action on the purchasing page shown in Figure 4-13. The text reads, `Send a special delivery of Cherry Moon Farms' freshest and juiciest premium fruit. . . .`

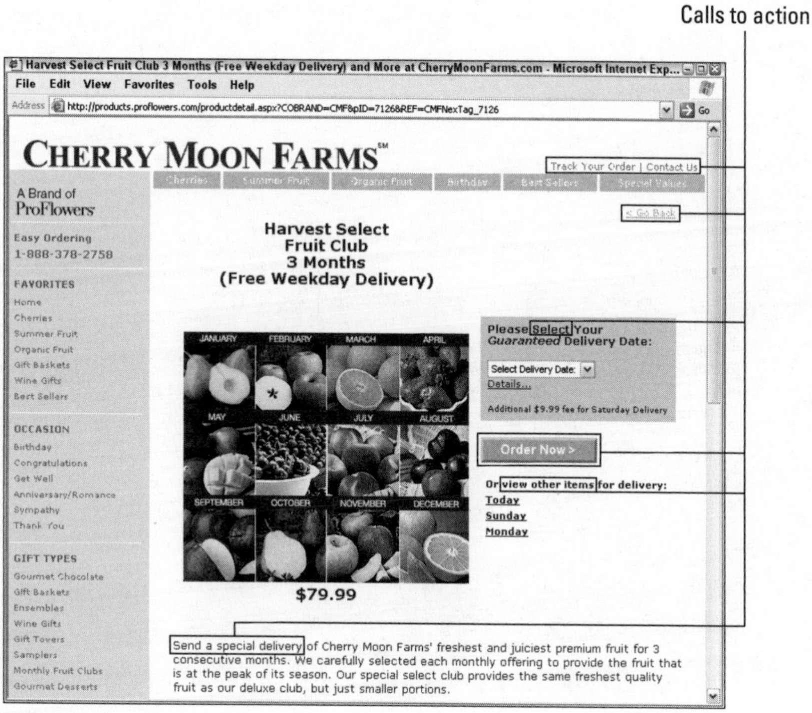

Calls to action

Figure 4-13: Six calls to action on the Cherry Moon site make it clear to users what actions they can take.

Courtesy Cherry Moon Farms

The four-letter word that starts with F

Free is marketing's magic word. Especially on the Internet, with its legacy of free information, visitors expect to get something for nothing. It might be free shipping, a free gift with order, a free newsletter, a free, five-year warranty, free gift wrapping, free maintenance tips, free color chart, or free tech support. Offer anything, as long as it's free. *Free* works even when targeting wealthy retail customers or B2B prospects.

Free is one call to action that doesn't need a verb. By itself, the word *free* generates an impulse to act. Without a doubt, *free* is one of the most potent tools in your online marketing workshop.

The Zen of Web sites: intention and attention. Build your site with deliberate marketing intent and pay attention consistently to make sure that your site is working hard for you.

Chapter 5

Creating a Marketing-Effective Storefront

*O*nline stores come in two forms: *pure-play* stores that exist only online and *bricks-&-clicks* stores that supplement a real-world storefront with a cyberstore. Both require the careful decision making that businesses routinely devote to opening a new location on Main Street. Online stores achieve maximum value when they're customer-centric, anticipating users' needs and filling them.

Don't get snookered by TV commercials that show money rolling in from online sales. Success requires a realistic estimate of how much time and money you need to invest. It also requires that you apply what you already know about retail marketing to your cyberstore.

This chapter emphasizes the marketing characteristics of a successful online store, rather than the technical details of implementing a storefront solution. It covers merchandising, simplifying the online sales process, enhancing revenue, and offering customer support.

If you're interested in finding out more about setting up an online store, check out *Starting an Online Business For Dummies,* 4th Edition, by Greg Holden (Wiley Publishing).

Examining the Key Components of an Online Store

When the tough go online, the tough go shopping. If you're not already an online shopper, that's your first assignment. Look at other storefronts, particularly your competitors'. Buy products. Assess not only your competitors' products and prices, but also the ease of using their sites, customer support, return policies, product quality, order fulfillment, and shipping processes.

Study some of the online stores consistently ranked among the best to get ideas of how a good store operates: Amazon.com, BarnesandNoble.com, eBags.com, or LLBean.com.

Only then are you ready to start building your store. It will share a few standard components with others, such as:

- ✔ **Product catalog:** The catalog component organizes your inventory and presents products consistently. Unless you have only a few products, you generally enter your product list into a database or spreadsheet that includes at least the product name, category, description, price, and photo filename.

- ✔ **Shopping cart:** Users place their tentative purchases into a cart, which tracks the contents, allows shoppers to delete items or change quantities, and provides a subtotal of the amount due. If you have a small store with only a few items, you can use an online order form rather than a cart. Be sure your developer programs the form to handle arithmetic automatically. Too many people can't multiply a price by two or add a column of numbers.

- ✔ **Check stand:** This portion of your online store computes shipping and taxes, totals the bill, and accepts shipping and billing information (including credit card numbers) in a secure manner. The check stand or other element of the storefront should issue an onscreen `Thank You` to confirm order submission, and e-mail an order confirmation as well.

- ✔ **Reporting and order tracking:** Unless your store is very small, it helps to have easy-to-understand reports on sales, customers, and product popularity. The larger your store, the more store analytics you'll want. Order tracking allows you, and your customer, to know the status of an order in terms of fulfillment and shipping.

- ✔ **Other add-ons:** Large, sophisticated stores might interface with inventory, point of sale, and accounting systems. They might also integrate with live sales interaction capability, customer relationship management (CRM) systems that track a customer's experience with your business, or other enterprise-level solutions.

Online shoppers buy convenience and time, not just products.

The same four Ps of marketing I discuss in Chapter 2 in the context of your overall business also apply to your online store.

- ✔ **Product:** The products that sell well online are not necessarily the same as the ones that sell offline.

- ✔ **Price:** You don't have to price products the same in online and offline environments unless your online audience is likely to come into the store to purchase. Your competition, overhead, cost of sales, and cost of shipping might differ between online and offline stores, just as they might between stores in different physical locations. If you decide to keep prices the same, you might need to adjust the price in both channels to maintain profit margin.

- ✔ **Placement:** The placement of items on a page determines how much attention they receive and, therefore, how well they sell. Think of your site as containing multiple, internal distribution channels.

- ✔ **Promotion:** You can use onsite promotion, such as internal banners, discounts, upsales, and other techniques to move products and increase sales.

For more detailed information about each of these Ps, page ahead to "Merchandising Your Online Store."

Selling B2B (Business to Business) with an Online Store

You might be surprised to find that nearly 90 percent of online transactions in North America are from B2B sales, not B2C (business to consumer). If businesses are your primary customers, you can establish your online store very much like a retail one. Customer friendliness and ease of use remain primary. Other than a different online promotional strategy, your main changes will be pricing, merchandising (how you stock your store), and packaging — most businesses buy larger quantities than individuals.

If you're looking for resellers or franchisees, include a secure application form with spaces for a state resale number and credit references. At the very least, ask them to call or e-mail! You might also have an online form for them to apply for a trade account and pay by purchase order (PO). At `https://cart2.barnesandnoble.com/poaccounts/application/page1.asp?z=y` in Figure 5-1, you can see how Barnes & Noble handles PO account applications. It might take a bit of work to accept POs online and to integrate them with accounting software for proper billing.

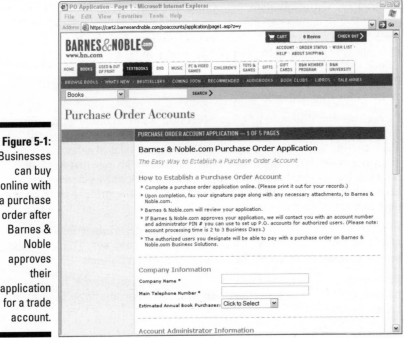

Courtesy Barnes & Noble

Figure 5-1: Businesses can buy online with a purchase order after Barnes & Noble approves their application for a trade account.

If you're a wholesaler or manufacturer, consider implementing a password login so only approved dealers can view your wholesale prices and place orders.

Don't undercut your retailers by competing with them directly on price. As I mention in Chapter 2, you can lose more revenue from channel cannibalization than you make from selling directly. Instead, link customers to your dealers' Web sites to buy, and have dealers link back to your site for product details or tech support. Consider offering co-op support for dealers' online advertising — it'll pay off in additional business for your company.

If you must sell online B2C, perhaps because you're opening up a new territory or your business plan calls for a second income stream, sell your products at manufacturer's suggested retail price (MSRP) and let your dealers offer discounts.

Merchandising Your Online Store

Merchandising refers to the selection and display of products in your store. If you have a bricks-&-clicks operation, you're under no compulsion to sell *any* of the same products both online and offline, let alone *all* of them. For example, Jelly Belly discovered that the 1-pound packages of jelly beans so popular in their stores were a dud online, but high-margin, accessorized gift packages performed better on the site. While customers can still buy jelly beans online, JellyBelly.com is merchandised quite differently from Jelly Belly shops in malls.

Selecting and pricing products

Your product selection and pricing levels are key elements to your online success. Some products sell better online than others, just as different products sell in different locations of the country. At the same time, price competition online is intense. You need to make astute business decisions about what you'll sell and at what price. Don't be afraid to run financial projections, or to ask your accountant for help.

Deciding what types of products to sell

First, decide what you'll sell, whether a subset of your inventory or all of it. If you're just starting a business, check out the criteria for picking products suitable for online sales at `http://onlinebusiness.about.com/od/startingup/a/product.htm`. Items that sell well on the Internet change over time. The current list, in descending order of online sales dollars in 2005, is shown in Figure 5-2.

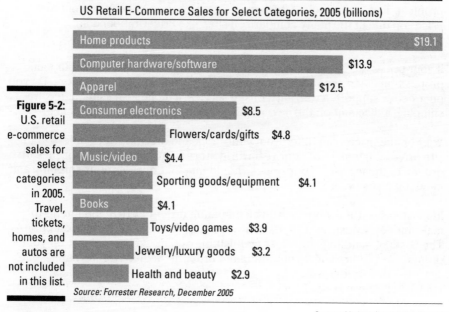

US Retail E-Commerce Sales for Select Categories, 2005 (billions)

Home products	$19.1
Computer hardware/software	$13.9
Apparel	$12.5
Consumer electronics	$8.5
Flowers/cards/gifts	$4.8
Music/video	$4.4
Sporting goods/equipment	$4.1
Books	$4.1
Toys/video games	$3.9
Jewelry/luxury goods	$3.2
Health and beauty	$2.9

Source: Forrester Research, December 2005

Figure 5-2: U.S. retail e-commerce sales for select categories in 2005. Travel, tickets, homes, and autos are not included in this list.

Source: eMarketer (www.emarketer.com)

Choosing specific items to include in your catalog

Your second decision is how many items will be in your catalog — to start with and eventually. Catalog size is one of the main factors to consider when selecting a storefront solution. Given intense competition online and shoppers' desires for good selections, you need a critical mass of products and choices — unless you have a very narrow niche with high demand.

If you have only one or two products to sell, review your business plan to determine whether an online store will be profitable. Also, consider whether you might do better selling through another outlet, such as one of these:

- eBay or another auction site
- Amazon.com Marketplace (www.amazon.com/exec/obidos/subst/misc/sell-your-stuff.html)
- zShops (www.amazon.com/gp/help/customer/display.html/002-5030947-8079226?nodeId=1161404)
- Google Base (http://base.google.com/base/help/checkout.html)
- A distributor at another online store
- A classified ad on a site like Craigslist.org

Pricing your products

Finally, decide on pricing. Your planning guides from Chapter 2 come in handy as you set price points. (If you skipped ahead and didn't read Chapter 2, no problem. Just take a look at it when you get a chance.) Check competitors' prices on one of the many comparison sites like PriceGrabber.com, Shopzilla.com, MySimon.com, or BizRate.com.

If your prices are going to be substantially higher, be sure to state your value proposition clearly so that shoppers perceive a benefit for paying more. Do you offer better support, a warranty, onsite service, a money-back guarantee, free shipping, a discount on the next purchase, free add-ons, or gift wrapping?

Your online prices can differ from your brick-and-mortar prices unless your site drives customers to your real-world store to make purchases or pick up orders. In those cases, your prices should match. Consider your shipping and handling costs before finalizing prices.

In most cases, think about setting a minimum order of $10 if you intend to make money. (Music and similar downloads at $1–$2 each are an exception.) The costs of handling, customer acquisition, and marketing can eat up your profits. Let visitors know your minimum order immediately. Alternately, package low-price products together, such as three pairs of socks for $9.99.

Displaying products

Most online stores are arranged hierarchically. At the top level, a storefront page displays thumbnails representing each category (equivalent to a department). Depending on the nature and size of the inventory, categories are sometimes broken down with navigation into subcategories that make sense to shoppers. You might subdivide the category Shoes into Men's, Women's, and Children's, for instance. Clicking a category or subcategory takes the user to a thumbnail display of products within that category. Clicking a product thumbnail brings the user to a product detail page.

Here are some key decisions you need to make for each product category:

- **Choosing which products to feature:** You might want to feature products within a category because they are bestsellers, have high profit margins, or are ready to be dumped. Place featured items at the top of a category display, and certainly *above the fold* (high enough on the page that users don't need to scroll to see them). Put the others in descending order of importance. That way, new customers can quickly find the products they're most likely looking for. Online always plays to strength!

- **Sorting products:** Don't give into the temptation to sort strictly by alphabet or price, even if you have a very large store. Sometimes inserting an extra space before a product name forces that item to the top of the display, much like putting "A" before your company name so it appears at the beginning of the Yellow Pages.

- **Positioning special items on the page:** Think grocery store. The upper-right corner of your home or catalog pages acts like an endcap in a supermarket — that's where your specials go. You can use that space for sales, gifts, events, seasonal items, or an internal banner. Link from there directly to a specific product detail page where users can make a purchase.

The rows of products above the fold are like shelves at eye level, holding items that are heavily promoted, like high-margin granola or fancy soups. The rows below the fold display items that people will search for, no matter how inconvenient, like corn flakes or chicken soup, on the bottom shelf at the grocery. By implication, it's better to have a category layout with three to four items in each row than to arrange category contents in a long, scrolling column only one-product wide.

Informing users of product options

Product detail pages should offer shoppers choices of color, size, or other attributes, as does the product detail page from ExOfficio (www.exofficio.com) in Figure 5-3. Actual attributes vary according to what you're selling.

If your storefront doesn't allow attributes, each available combination requires a separate entry and stock keeping unit (SKU) number. Most storefront software won't let you assign the same SKU to two separate entries.

You or your staff enters all this information into a product database, generally with a minimum of technical training. Try to select staff familiar with your stock to enter the data. Make sure that you designate all the possible categories in which a product should appear.

Spell check your product names and descriptions before you open the store. Also proof prices, SKUs, category assignments, product attributes, and photos. Data entry errors are very common.

If a product is out of stock, either remove it immediately from your catalog or notify customers onscreen at the category or page level. Offer a substitute online, and/or let people know how long they must wait for a back order. If you wait until checkout to inform a shopper that a product is unavailable, you will probably lose that customer forever.

Product details

Figure 5-3: ExOfficio. com lets shoppers select combinations of color and size on its product detail pages.

Courtesy ExOfficio

Enhancing revenue with upsales, impulse buys, and more

Depending on the storefront software you use, you can implement revenue-enhancing features to increase the dollar value of an average purchase or to improve the likelihood that customers make repeat visits. You'll find almost all these concepts on highly ranked selling sites, like Amazon.com, which displays ten revenue-enhancing options in Figure 5-4. A date reminder service appears after clicking Gift Idea List in the drop-down menu. An 11th option, the treasure chest icon, leads to time-limited discounts, personalized for individual interests.

Revenue-enhancing options

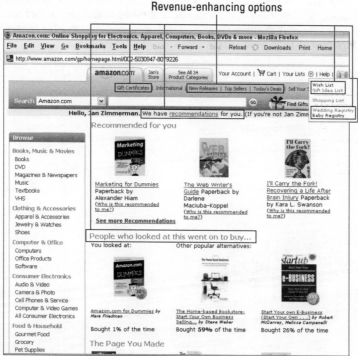

Figure 5-4:
Amazon.com is an excellent site to study for revenue-enhancing options.

© 2006 Amazon.com, Inc. or its affiliates. All Rights Reserved.

Given your products and target markets, mark the features in the following list that you think would be most valuable to implement:

- ✔ **Cross-sales** usually appear on a product detail page, with a sentence like `People who buy this, also buy....` The recommendations, which are derived from a long record of what has appeared in shopping carts, list products related by interest, such as birdfeeders for people who buy birdbaths.

- ✔ **Upsales** usually appear on a product detail page, with a sentence like `If you are interested in this, you might also like....` or the term `Suggestions`, as shown on Eastern Leaf's site (`www.easternleaf.com`) in Figure 5-5. Upsales, which you code into the product database, are directly related to the product on view. They might be a more expensive, larger, or more powerful version of the same item, or they might be add-ons that make the product more useful or attractive.

- ✔ **Personal recommendations** might appear when an existing customer logs in. These are derived from the individual's own history of purchases, rather than from other customers' histories.

- ✔ **Bestsellers** often appear as a category within your storefront. Usually, the software calculates this list automatically across the entire store based on sales made over a specified period. Larger stores might let you specify bestsellers within a specific category. A bestseller list is actually a subtle testimonial. Which brand and model of digital camera do other people buy? Could they all be wrong?

Figure 5-5:
Eastern Leaf offers two upsale items: a display stand and bonsai fertilizer.

Upsale items

© 2006 Eastern Leaf, Inc.

✔ **What's New** appears as a category within your storefront. Coding items from across your inventory as `new` in the product database makes it easy for repeat and frequent customers to see these items quickly. A great feature for sites with collectibles or one-of-a-kind items.

✔ **Special or Hot Deal** items appear as a category within your storefront. This category — like Filene's Basement — pulls bargain hunters with a wide range of interests. Because you code these in the product database, you can change them at any time.

✔ **Gift recommendations** might be presented as a category or subcategory and coded in the product database. In essence, these prepackaged search results make it easy for gift buyers who "don't have a clue what to get." These recommendations are especially helpful to shoppers in a hurry. In Figure 5-6, Yardiac (`www2.yardiac.com`) displays Gifts for Her. The site also prompts for Gifts for Him, Children's Gifts, Top 10 Gifts, and Gift Certificates.

✔ **Impulse buys** are the last-minute purchases you see on or near the counter as a sales associate rings up your purchase. Many store solutions allow you to place one or more impulse buys on shopping cart or check stand pages. With this feature, you can offer something (a vase for flowers, a scarf to go with a dress) at the crucial moment when customers figuratively have pulled out their wallets.

✔ **Gift registries** are a navigational feature equivalent to the shower, wedding, baby, or housewarming registries available at almost any department or big-box store. Honorees designate the items in the store that they're interested in receiving. The registry tracks which items have been purchased and makes it easy to ship items directly to the gift recipient. Recipients drive their friends to your site to buy.

✔ **Wish lists** are a variant of a gift registry. Users can mark items to purchase for themselves in the future, which might be after depositing their next paycheck or doing further research. Gift givers can view the lists to see what others want for their birthdays or holidays. Wish lists bring customers back for another sale in the future or drive new people to your site.

✔ **Date reminder services** e-mail shoppers a week or two before an event to remind the user to send a gift. The electronic equivalent of a birthday book for the forgetful, this feature is actually a simple variation of calendar or scheduling software. The e-mail reminder includes a link to buy a gift from your site. The option usually appears somewhere on the navigation.

✔ **Sending gifts or gift certificates** must be planned in advance. Be sure there is a place at checkout not only for a separate recipient address, but also for a gift message and wrapping option. If there's a fee for wrapping, you need to include it in check stand calculations. Not all storefront solutions allow you to issue gift certificates and track their use, though there are third-party alternatives.

✔ **Promotion codes**, too, need some forethought. Most storefronts can calculate and apply only certain types of promotions, including one for marketing's favorite option, Free. Because users enter these discount codes during checkout, the check stand must calculate them on the fly. You specify sometimes intricate rules for which products they apply to, when they expire, and when they can be compounded. It's a best practice to put promo codes not only in your newsletter or other ads, but also onscreen to encourage buying.

Figure 5-6:
Yardiac
suggests
"Gifts for
Her" and
other
presorted
suggestions.

Courtesy Yardiac.com

Including product detail

In the real world, shoppers might use all five senses to evaluate a product and make a decision. Online shopping constrains the user to sight and sound at best. There's no way yet for users to sample your new chipotle dip, to enjoy the fragrance of freshly baked chocolate chip cookies or the scent of perfume, to run their fingers over soft-as-silk leather or plush velvet. No way to hold a sparkling ring up to the light or to tell whether the black-on-black labels on the DVD player will be readable.

To the greatest extent possible, you must overcome those constraints with text, photography, 3-D, or virtual reality accessed on product detail pages. Product photography is absolutely critical to a sales site. Close-ups are essential, sometimes from multiple angles. Complex equipment or items, such as sculpture, that visitors need to see from more than one side benefit from 3-D, virtual reality, or video. If you can't hire a professional, at the very least:

✔ Check out tips for tabletop photography at www.tabletopstudio. com/documents/HowTo_page.htm or www.shortcourses.com/ studio/tabletop/studio.htm.

✔ Buy a decent digital camera.

✔ Set up a simple, tabletop studio with two lights at a 45 degree angle from above the product and a simple, solid-color background. Better yet, buy a studio light tent, like EZ Cube.

✔ Use a tripod.

✔ Crop and maximize the appearance of your photos by using Photoshop or similar software.

✔ If you're selling gift items, display how the wrapped package will look when received, complete with bow.

✔ Photograph packaged sets of goods priced as one basket or kit.

✔ When possible, picture people using or modeling your products. The added interest factor increases sales. SkyStone Trading (www. skystonetrading.com) incorporates people as jewelry models on its site, as shown in Figure 5-7.

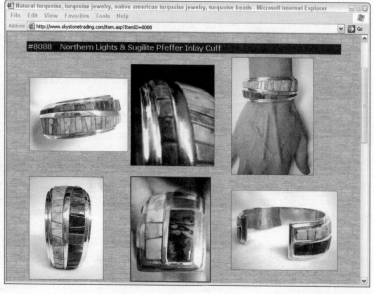

Figure 5-7: SkyStone Trading offers multiple close-ups of each piece of jewelry, including display on a live model.

©1998–2006 All rights reserved.

You enter the filenames for photos in your product database, along with product descriptions. Write sparkling copy, as I describe in Chapter 4, offering benefits and distinguishing which products are best for which applications. In other words, anticipate answers to questions that customers might ask.

Include text information about warranties, service, technical support, and other specifications according to the product. If your products offer color choices, display color swatches on the detail page. This is not trivial. Different manufacturers have different color palettes — it's not easy being green!

Making It Easy for Your Customers to Buy

From a marketing perspective, you need to convert shoppers to buyers. Make it easy. Studies show that many online shoppers give up early in the process, long before they open a shopping cart. Many shoppers' complaints are the same as those for any Web site: poor navigation, long download times, and inability to find what they want. The following sections detail some ways that you can enhance the shopping experience for your customers.

Providing a product search engine

The larger and more complex your store, the more you need an onsite product search engine. Besides the obvious category and subcategory choices, users might want to search by the following criteria, alone or in combination:

- ✔ Product name
- ✔ Product type
- ✔ Price
- ✔ Product attributes, such as size, color, or material
- ✔ Brand

Depending on your storefront solution and the nature of your site, you might want two search engines: one that searches the product database and another that searches content-rich HTML pages.

As always, the trade-off is between flexibility and complexity. Don't make the search function more complicated than most of your users can handle.

Search engines can locate items only if the entered keyword appears somewhere in the product record. Ask which fields of a record are searched. High-quality search engines can respond by algorithm (rule) to misspellings and synonyms. Otherwise, you might want to include misspellings and synonyms in a nonprinting field of each record.

Try to use drop-down searches wherever there might be confusion about the data, such as whether to include dollar signs in a price or how to spell a brand name. Drop-down lists that work with the search engine allow visitors to choose from a list of search options rather than type in a keyword. (Or, you might want to presort products into some of these categories and put them in the storefront as navigational choices instead.)

Product search is a great source of market intelligence! Confirm that you can get reports on both successful and unsuccessful searches. Unsuccessful results tell you what your customers are looking for but can't find. Now that's market intelligence!

Some storefront solutions come with a built-in search engine, which ranges from fully customizable to completely inflexible. Your developer can install a third-party alternative on some storefront solutions; others won't allow it.

Google's powerful search algorithm is available free at `www.google.com/searchcode.html`, but only in exchange for displaying Google ads on results pages and offering Google Web search. Because these options might lead to a competitor, you might want to license one of Google's advertising-free solutions (Google Mini — more information is available at `www.google.com/enterprise/mini/index.html#utm_source=bizsols&utm_campaign=miniC`) after calculating cost versus benefits. You can search for other free or advertising-supported, third-party search engines.

Implementing 2 clicks to buy

The same principle of 2 clicks to action I discuss in Chapter 4 applies to your online store. To move clients toward purchase as quickly as possible, put a Buy Now (good) or Add to Cart (better because it doesn't remind shoppers that they are spending money) button at the level of category thumbnails, as well as on product detail pages. Don't force users to click any more than necessary if they're hot to trot.

The standard, View Cart button usually opens a full-page window with shopping cart contents. Open that, instead, in a small window or pop-up that shows users a summary of their cart contents, or show the cart contents on each page of the Web site. (Web developers call that a *minicart*. This saves users two clicks: one to view their cart and the other to return to shopping. Mama's Minerals (`www.mamasminerals.com`), whose before-and-after screens are shown in Figure 5-8, implemented the last approach when it relaunched its online store. Details about its redesign appear in the nearby sidebar "Prospecting for online treasure."

Figure 5-8:
Before (top)
and after
(bottom)
screens for
Mama's
Minerals
show
how the
company
incorporated
many user-
friendly
shopping
features on
its new site,
including a
minicart
display with
shipping.

Minicart

©1998–2007 Mama's Minerals, Inc.(r) 1100 San Mateo Blvd. NE #15, Albuquerque, NM 87110.
RockZ NewZ(tm) is Mama's Minerals quarterly ezine. Used with permission.

Offering multiple payment options

Making it easy for customers includes making it easy to pay. Even though online ordering has become more secure and commonplace, some customers still worry about providing credit card information online. It's a best practice to offer options for calling in an order, printing out and faxing the shopping cart and payment information, or mailing an order with a check. Besides, multiple payment options increase your conversion rate.

Any significant online store really needs to accept credit cards. Ask your developer or hosting company about options.

If you already have a merchant account, you can process credit card transactions offline as long as you have a secure server (HTTPS) for this portion of your site. After you reach about ten sales per day, you might want to shift to *real-time card processing* (cards are verified online before the transaction enters your system, rather than offline like phone orders). At that point, the savings in labor costs offset the increased cost of real-time processing.

Real-time gateways (the software that manages real-time processing) also validate credit cards for billing address, card verification number, and spending limits, all of which reduce your risk as a merchant. Ask your developer or template host for pricing. Unless they're included in your storefront package, both the secure server and real-time gateway usually incur start-up and annual fees.

Other payment options, including the following, are available for special situations:

- **PayPal:** Like similar services, allows you to take credit card payments without having a merchant card account. Find out more at `www.paypal.com`. Many e-commerce hosts aggregate their stores through similar services.

- **Google Checkout:** Provides a new, one-stop checkout for stores with compatible check stands. A buyer enrolls to use a saved profile on Google that completes billing forms on other sites with one click. Google advertisers receive credit toward the transaction fees that Google charges (2 percent, plus 20 cents per transaction.) See `http://checkout.google.com/sell?promo=sha` for more information.

- **Prepaid deposits:** Debits for small purchases, such as downloading articles, music, or photos. This approach reduces the per-transaction cost that might otherwise make credit cards too expensive to accept for small purchases (unless you have the volume of iTunes). It also establishes a minimum order amount.

REAL WORLD

Prospecting for online treasure

Mama's Minerals, a bricks-&-clicks retailer of gems, minerals, and related products, is something of an Internet pioneer. As shown in Figure 5-8, the old store had confusing navigation and long, scrolling pages with Buy buttons hidden well below the fold. Dozens of products appeared on separate, static HTML pages, whose dark background led to slow loading times for every one of them. While it brought in sales every month, the site needed constant maintenance from an HTML programmer. State-of-the-art when launched in 1998, Mama's Web site was sadly outdated five years later.

Already rich with information, resplendent photographs, and a database of thousands of e-mail addresses, Mama's was a prime candidate for an extreme makeover. Within a year, Mama's

redesigned site, shown in Figure 5-8, rocketed its online sales to new highs. The new, database-driven storefront is built on the Miva Merchant shopping cart base, with front-end navigation and graphics designed by Desert Heart Multimedia. E-commerce manager Art Ofner, who's not a programmer, now presides over an online inventory of more than 1,200 items in the product database and sales six times what they were before.

Mama's added multiple sales enhancements, including a minicart with shipping estimates in the lower-left corner. Ofner promotes the store through monthly What's New newsletters, quarterly RockZ NewZ e-zines, search engine optimization, PPC (pay per click) ads, onsite promotions, and direct mail.

✔ **Electronic bill presentation and payment (EBPP):** Works well for billing and payment on a monthly basis, or for B2B stores using purchase orders. Basically, EBPP allows you to invoice electronically and then receive payment by electronic funds transfer from the customer's bank account to yours. This service is available from multiple providers, such as Anypay www.anypay.com/site/ml/eng/htm/business/eft.htm, Electronic Banking Systems EFT, www.ebseft.com/dpage.php?idp=9&idt=1, and Inovium Electronic Funds http://electronicfunds.com.

Supporting customers

Keeping customers satisfied throughout the sales cycle might start online, but it finishes offline when customers are happy with the products they receive.

REMEMBER

Always respond to e-mail and phone inquiries within one business day. Sadly, companies often violate this most basic rule offline as well as online. If problems occur with order fulfillment or shipping, let your customers know as soon as you recognize the problem, and offer a substitution. An honest effort retains customers; delay or denial loses them for eternity.

To offer customer support through the buying process, try the following:

✔ **Enable customers to communicate with a real person.** If you sell online, get a toll-free number. Publish the hours when the phone is answered in an obvious place on the site. If your customer base and geographic area become large enough, you might need to create or outsource a call center for sales and technical support. Alternately, offer live chat or live calls online.

✔ **Build trust.** Publish your business hours and a street address, not a post office box, to establish basic, business credibility. Post the logos of all organizations that validate your standing, preferably in the footer so they appear on every page. At the very least, post them on the About Us page. Include the logo of

- The company that supplies your secure certificate, such as VeriSign (`www.verisign.com`)

- Safe shopping services, like the electronic Better Business Bureau, (`www.bbbonline.org`), ePublicEye (`www.epubliceye.com`), or TRUSTe (`www.truste.org`)

- Business rating services, such as the free Shopzilla Customer Certified Rating program (`http://merchant.shopzilla.com/oa/registration`)

- Memberships in the local chamber of commerce or trade associations

✔ **Spell out warranty, refund, and return policies.** Look at your competitors' sites to understand what's standard in your industry. If you offer something special, such as `Satisfaction Guaranteed` or `Free Shipping on Returns`, be sure to promote it on your site. Anything that reduces customers' perceived risks encourages purchase. It's equally important to be clear about constraints; for example, `DVDs can be returned only if unopened`, `Exchanges Only`, or `No Refunds after 30 Days`. Some sites use Warranties and Return Policies as separate navigational items. Others group them together with Privacy and Security statements under a Customer Support or Customer Care tab.

✔ **Ensure privacy and security.** Reassure your customers that their personal information, including e-mail addresses, won't be used elsewhere, rented, or sold. Tell them about encrypting data — not just during transmission but when storing it on your computers. In these days of identity theft, never ask for anyone's Social Security number. Chapter 15 has more information about privacy policies.

✔ **Notify customers if you place cookies on their computer.** To reduce the amount of data entry on repeat purchases, many sites create a password-protected customer account on their server. Others place a *cookie* (a small data file with unique identification numbers) on the customer's hard drive that recognizes when a repeat customer visits the site.

> Cookies allow personalization, purchase history, keeping open shopping carts, and convenient reordering. However, some customers worry about them. If cookies are required, you might need to tell people how to modify cookie settings on their browsers; most don't know how.

Fulfilling orders

A customer doesn't separate your Web site from other aspects of your business. If he receives the wrong item or his package gets lost in shipping, he blames your business for a poor online shopping process, not for poor follow-up. You must ensure that the positive experience your customers have onsite carries through to completion.

In the best of all possible worlds, a customers receives an e-mail confirmation when she completes her order, as well as a reminder to print her order details. If your shipping process assigns a unique tracking number to the order, she can access a link directly to the carrier's site to keep an eye on the progress of her shipment, whether you use UPS, the U.S. Postal Service, FedEx, or other carriers.

Sophisticated, storefront packages offer additional automated features, including

- **Packing slips and shipping labels:** Well-integrated systems print out packing slips and shipping labels. This might require buying an additional module or third-party software.

- **Production tracking:** Some systems track an order through production, which is particularly useful if your products involve customization or have a long fulfillment cycle. A customer receives an e-mail when the products he ordered, such as checks or monogrammed towels, enters the production queue. Complex, B2B sites integrated with manufacturing systems might allow buyers to track progress on their orders.

- **Shipping confirmation:** You can set up your sophisticated storefront to send another e-mail to the customer when a package has shipped. This tells buyers when to expect their order and how reach you if there's a problem. It offers another opportunity to thank your customers for their order, remind them about your return policies, and link them back to your site. It's also a window for a customer feedback survey, but keep it short!

It's best practice to charge a customer's card only when a product has shipped. Check to see whether your software and/or manual transaction process can accommodate that.

Very large stores might arrange for third-party companies to handle their order fulfillment and shipping. Amazon.com, which has perfected this element of online selling, contracts its fulfillment service to many of its large merchant partners.

Remember that it's much less expensive to sell something else to a satisfied customer than it is to acquire a new customer.

Shipping Is a Marketing Issue

Probably nothing so infuriates online buyers as the price of shipping. In reality, shipping is expensive, especially as the price of gas rises. Research alternatives to decide which carrier and delivery choices you will offer. Not everything can go ground — baked goods and fresh flowers always need fast delivery!

The overall rate of shopping cart abandonment is 70 percent. That's right, 70 percent of all started shopping carts never result in a purchase. Of those, studies show customers abandon more than half due to high shipping charges.

Deciding what to charge for shipping

Decide whether the shipping charge is a flat fee per order or item, varies by price, or varies by weight. If you decide on weight, you need to enter the weight of each product in your product database. After you have an estimate of shipping volume, you might be able to schedule pickups and negotiate a discount rate with a carrier.

Handling isn't free either. You incur costs for packaging materials and wrapping, picking products out of inventory, packing cartons, and labeling.

If you're new to this business, test your packaging, shipping, and carrier selection, especially for fragile or perishable goods. Simply ship samples to yourself or friends.

Your store software should separately report revenues from product sales, taxes, and shipping charges. If you're careful with financial records, you can track shipping and handling costs against shipping revenues to be sure you aren't losing money on shipping. If you incorporate a portion of shipping and handling costs in the product price, adjust this calculation accordingly.

In many cases, it's better to bury some of the cost of shipping and handling in the online product price and reduce the published shipping price. This strategy reduces customer resistance to shipping charges perceived as high, relative to product price. People balk at paying $10 to ship a $20 item but don't blink at paying $10 for a $70 item.

Communicating your shipping policies

Create a separate page for shipping information that is quickly available on either main or secondary navigation. Let people know how long it takes for products to leave your facility or order fulfillment center — same day for orders received by 1 p.m.? next business day? a week for custom-made goods? Make sure your shipping page is covered by your onsite search function. Your policy should clearly inform buyers about shipping alternatives, from standard ground to overnight, and whether there are any limitations.

For instance, the U.S. Postal Service delivers to P.O. boxes, but FedEx and UPS don't. The Postal Service delivers on Saturday with no additional charge; FedEx charges extra; UPS doesn't deliver on Saturdays at all. Some companies or products ship only to certain countries. Some companies won't ship products like chocolate year-round unless the buyer pays for special, refrigerated handling and overnight delivery.

Don't surprise users at the check stand with shipping prices. Let people see in advance how much shipping is likely to be, as Mama's Minerals does in Figure 5-8. Clicking the Click for Shipping Estimate link in the lower left gives buyers a quick preview of costs by zip code and shipping choice.

Shipping decisions might affect many elements of your online business plan, from manufacturing to merchandising, from pricing to revenue projections.

Specifying Storefront Requirements

Plan your marketing and sales process before you develop your online store. Your input from a marketing perspective is essential to selecting the right storefront package. For instance, you may want promotion codes for special offers, statistics that tabulate sales by category and subcategory, and/or the ability to sequence the appearance of products on a catalog page.

The Storefront Checklist on this book's companion Web site (www.dummies.com/go/webmarketing) may help you think through this process. After you have made the strategic business decisions and decided on your budget, you can prioritize the needs that the storefront must meet. If you're sending out an RFP (request for proposal, which I discuss in Chapter 3), be sure to include this information. Because the ultimate selection might have technical consequences, let your selected developer determine the specific package to implement.

Assess prospective developers for their e-commerce experience and determine which solutions they're capable of implementing. Because of the complexity of some storefronts, developers often specialize in one product line. Your selections of software, hosting, and developer are interdependent.

Your choices for selling online start with the simplest — a listing on eBay — or an inexpensive template for starter stores with a small catalog. They range in complexity all the way to enterprise-level solutions for stores with thousands of products that integrate with inventory control, accounting, and retail point-of-sales (POS) software. As usual, the more flexible and complicated the store, the higher the price tag and the greater the technical skills required.

Selecting the right type of storefront

The easiest and least expensive storefront solutions offer the least flexibility and fewest features. If you're just starting your business, you can use one of these solutions to establish your store. Then invest in a more complex, fully featured, e-commerce solution as you grow. The following sections explain storefront options, sequenced roughly from simple to complex.

No-storefront selling solutions

By far, the least-expensive way to start selling online is to use the *no-storefront* selling solution. In other words, forego all the hassle of a Web site and storefront. Simply sell your products directly through Amazon Marketplace or zShops, eBay, other auction sites, CraigsList.org, or other classified sites. You won't have your own domain name, but you can link from a separate, small, HTML Web site to your listings on most of these.

One-stop storebuilders

As the e-commerce variant of the template sites I discuss in Chapter 4, *one-stop storebuilders* (think, Web Store in a Box) are generic, somewhat inflexible solutions, but they quickly solve most of your problems — except content. True, one-stop storebuilders help you buy a domain name, build template-based Web pages, stock a product catalog, supply the shopping cart and check stand components, provide a payment system through PayPal or a merchant gateway, and host your site. Very inexpensive and relatively easy to use, the entry-level versions work best for small stores. Many smaller hosting companies offer these packaged solutions, but they're also available through eBay Stores, Yahoo! Stores, and many registration companies like Network Solutions.

Specialty storebuilders

Sometimes called *malls,* specialty storebuilders have a mission. Usually, a hosting company decides to focus on a particular industry or geographical area and markets e-commerce templates specifically tailored to the needs of that audience. The host then creates a directory of all the shops as a virtual mall and promotes the mall as an online destination. Some high-end malls, like Shop.com, allow buyers to use a universal shopping cart across all their stores, saving the user time and making purchasing easier.

Watch out for malls that are really nothing more than a directory of links. Ask about traffic and promotion for the mall. Also, be cautious if a mall won't let you use your own domain name. When that happens, you can't promote the store in search engines; you need another Web site for promotion and branding.

Assembly storefronts

Many companies host a storefront solution on their third-party server that you link to from your site, wherever it might be hosted. These assembly storefronts have all the essential components for e-commerce, but you might need technical assistance to make the link interface smooth. In essence, you create and support two sites that share a similar look and feel. If you order a book at www.dummies.com, you'll see that the URL in the navigation bar changes to http://customer.wiley.com when you add something to the shopping cart. It changes again to https://customer.wiley.com (secure server) when you click Checkout Now.

Integrated storefronts

Developers integrate commercial, off-the-shelf, or open-source e-commerce components with your existing site to create a seamless online store solution. Depending on its size and other factors, your storefront might be hosted on a dedicated server, on your shared server, or on the developer's server. This approach is more complex, but also more customizable and flexible than others. Translation: It costs more money. Some developers license and resell the same storefront solution to all their e-commerce customers. This is fine, as long as the store does what you need. You have the advantage of working with someone who is expert in that particular package and security about the future as well. If something happens to your developer, you can find someone else who knows this package.

Custom e-commerce solutions

For maximum flexibility and control, some developers prefer to write their own e-commerce packages. The upside: A custom shopping site that's industry-tailored might be very cost-effective for your particular business. The downside: Depending on how many other stores use the software, it might not be fully debugged and might need a lot of testing. If you ever change developers, you're most likely to lose your storefront.

Enterprise e-commerce solutions

Usually expensive, integrated solutions for large, high-end stores interface with retail, point of sales (POS) systems, bookkeeping, inventory, manufacturing, customer relationship management (CRM), enterprise resource planning (ERP), and other systems. Choosing a solution at this level generally means you've made a significant investment and have a team of technical, merchandising, and content developers working with you. An enterprise solution from NetSuite was assembled to build the storefront for PartsforScooters.com in Figure 5-9.

Narrowing the options

Table 5-1 lists some storefront options in the categories described in the previous section, not as recommendations, but as examples for you to research. Unfortunately, there is no simple way to find the best solution for your business from literally hundreds of options. With so much competition, you can find an affordable solution that meets your needs. Base your individual business decision on the type of products you sell, the size of your catalog, your budget and development time frame, what your competition offers, and the expectations of your target market.

Figure 5-9: The site for Partsfor Scooters is an enterprise store solution from NetSuite.

Courtesy Parts for Scooters

Table 5-1	Some Storefront Options		
Name	**URL**	**Catalog Size**	**Minimum Monthly Cost**
MonsterCommerce (NetworkSolutions)	`www.monstercommerce. com/ecommerce_ shopping_cart_ pricing_small_ business.asp`	60,000	$99
Bigstep	`http://go.bigstep. com/products/ bigstep.htm`	100	$30
BizLand	`www.bizland.com/ bizland/index.bml`	Unlimited	$6
eBay	`http://pages.ebay. com/storefronts/ start.html`	15 pages	$16
HyperMart	`www.hypermart.com/ hypermart/hosting_ plans.bml`	Unlimited	$20
Microsoft Commerce Manager	`www.microsoft.com/ smallbusiness/online/ commerce-manager/ detail.mspx`	10,000	$25
ProStores Express (eBay)	`www.prostores.com/ express-store.shtml`	10 items, 2 pages	$7
ProStores (eBay)	`www.prostores.com`	Unlimited	$30
Yahoo! Small Business	`http://smallbusiness. yahoo.com/merchant/ ?p=PASSPORT`	Thousands	$40
ShopCapeCod (Mall)	`http://shopcapecod. com`	100	$29 with
1 of a Kind Jewelry Mall	`http://www.1ofakind jewelrymall.com/ vendor-faq.php`	Unlimited	$22
CafePress (graphics products w/mfg)	`www.cafepress.com/ cp/info/sell/shops/ shops_premium`	Not applicable	$7

Name	URL	Catalog Size	Minimum Monthly Cost
GlassArtWorld Mall	www.glassartworld.com/SignUp/MerchantOverview.asp	Unlimited	$20
Shop.com	http://www.shop.com/op/a-market-intro	Unlimited	Pay per order
Go Daddy	www.godaddy.com/gdshop/ecommerce/cart.asp	Unlimited	$10
Website Source	www.websitesource.com/ecommerce/overview.shtml	Thousands	$7 with osCommerce; $15 with Miva
StoreFront	http://www.storefront.net/solutions/new/default.asp	Unlimited	$600–$3400 (flat fee)
Miva Merchant	http://smallbusiness.miva.com/products/merchant	100	$600 flat fee
osCommerce	www.oscommerce.com/solutions/oscommerce	Unlimited	Free (open source)
CPOnline for Synchronics	http://www.synchronics.com/products/cpol.htm	10,000+	$125
NetSuite Small Business	http://www.netsuite.com/portal/products/nsb/webstore.shtml	Unlimited	By quote only
Retail Pro	www.uniteu.com/uniteu/deptasp?s%5Fid=0&dept%5Fid=2000&WT%2Esvl=deptnav1	Unlimited	By quote only

Start by reading reviews listed in Table 5-2. You might also ask the owners of several online stores what solutions they implemented (if the answer isn't visible on the site), or ask your business colleagues. The Storefront Checklist (available for download on the book's companion Web site at www.dummies.com/go/webmarketing) allows you to compare your wish list of capabilities with the capabilities found in different storefront solutions.

Table 5-2	Online Retailing Resources	
Name	*URL*	*What You'll Find*
About.com	`http://onlinebusiness.about.com`	Shopping cart, store front reviews, and more
ClickZ-Retailing	`http://clickz.com/showPage.html?page=stats/sectors/retailing`	Statistics about online retailing
c|Net Download	`www.download.com/E-commerce/3150-2649_4-0.html?tag=dir`	E-commerce software reviews
Direct Marketing Association	`www.the-dma.org/guidelines/shcharges.shtml`	Setting shipping and handling charges
eCommerce Times	`www.ecommercetimes.com`	News about e-commerce
Internet Retailer	`www.internetretailer.com`	Strategies and news for multichannel retailers
MarketingProfs.com	`www.marketingprofs.com/2/dixon1.asp`	What e-tailers can learn from retailers; free membership required
PC Magazine	`www.pcmag.com/category2/0,1874,4808,00.asp`	E-commerce software reviews
Practical eCommerce	`www.practicalecommerce.com/public/276/`	Shopping cart checklist; subscription e-zine and magazine for e-commerce
Shop.org	`http://shop.org`	Network for retailers online; part of the National Retail Federation
Shopping Cart Index	`www.shoppingcartindex.com`	Shopping cart software reviews
TopTenREVIEWS	`http://ecommerce-software-review.toptenreviews.com`	E-commerce software reviews
Top Ten Reviews	`http://shopping-cart-review.toptenreviews.com`	Shopping cart reviews

Watching Out for Storefront Do's and Don'ts

You might not have experience selling, but I can guarantee you have experience buying — at least offline. Use your common sense as you plan, stock, and build your store.

The golden rule of marketing: Don't do to your customers what you wouldn't want done to you.

What users hate about online shopping

According to a study by the Pew Internet & American Life Project (www.pewinternet.org/pdfs/PIP_Holiday_Report.pdf), holiday shoppers in 2005 continued to have concerns relating to "trust, reliability, price, and preferences." Shoppers who didn't buy online complained about

- ✔ Not being able to see gifts in person
- ✔ Sending credit card and personal information over the Internet
- ✔ Prices higher online than in stores or catalogs
- ✔ Late arrival of items (which was perceived as higher than actually occurred)
- ✔ Web sites that make online shopping confusing

What users love about online shopping

The same study showed that those who did buy online were pleased with the experience because it

- ✔ Was convenient.
- ✔ Saved money.
- ✔ Saved time.

The elements that the Pew study identified are consistent with findings for the past several years. In earlier studies, users commented on the ease of research, which is borne out by another Pew finding: Almost twice as many Internet users went to the Web to research gift ideas and compare prices than actually bought online.

While the digital divide is shrinking, the demographics of actual buyers still skews toward those from higher, socioeconomic categories (college educated, households earning more than $75,000) and those with more than three years experience online. Eventually, the later arrivals from lower socioeconomic categories will become buyers, too. Research shows that Internet users are more likely to become buyers the longer they have been online.

Projections indicate retail e-commerce sales in the U.S. will exceed $100 billion in 2006, a growth of more than 20 percent over 2005. However, that's still less than 3 percent of nearly $4 trillion in total retail sales in this country of shopaholics. Don't close your brick-and-mortar store yet! As you set up your online business, take this research into consideration as part of a realistic plan. Climbing to that pot of gold at the end of the cyber-rainbow might be a tad bit steeper than you hoped. But it will be fun.

Chapter 6

Pulling Repeat Visitors with Onsite Marketing Techniques

In This Chapter

▶ Enhancing marketing value with updated content

▶ Creating communities online

▶ Trumpeting your accomplishments

▶ Luring visitors with freebies and fun

▶ Letting others do the talking

▶ Marketing the viral way

*H*ave you heard the phrase "Marketing is only part of a business, but all of a business is marketing"? If you look at an organizational chart, you might point to little boxes labeled Sales and Advertising and say, "That's our marketing department." But what about the way a receptionist answers the phone? The appearance of the repair technician who visits a customer's office? The cleanliness of your store? The freshness of your products?

Everything your company does affects customers somehow. Everything contributes to the impression they have of your business and affects their expectation of the quality of service they'll receive. That, in a nutshell, is marketing.

The same thing is true of your Web site: Marketing is only part of your Web site, but all of your Web site is marketing. In Chapter 3, I identify the three goals your Web site needs to accomplish to be successful as a business tool:

✔ Attract new visitors.

✔ Keep them on your site.

✔ Bring them back as repeat visitors.

In this chapter, I describe some onsite marketing techniques to help you achieve these goals. Onsite marketing has a great advantage over other forms of advertising: It's fairly inexpensive, requiring more labor and creativity than cash. I recommend ideas that can increase traffic and win customers. No Web site needs all of them. The challenge is to select the best ones for your business.

Deciding Which Onsite Marketing Techniques to Use

Alas, I know of no rules that say, "do a blog or interactive media only if you have a young audience," or "women respond more to testimonials." You can implement many different combinations of the onsite, marketing features described in this chapter to create a site that grabs your audience and pulls them back for future visits.

Mark down the possibilities on your Web Marketing Methods Checklist from Chapter 2 as you go through this chapter. (You can download this handy planning form from the book companion's Web site at www.dummies.com/go/webmarketing.) By the time you complete your online marketing plan, you'll have a good feeling for several techniques to retain as the most appropriate for your site, staff, and budget. It's too expensive to do them all!

Always, always, do site updates to keep your content fresh. Next, incorporate the three, no-brainer options (internal banners, testimonials, and the Tell a Friend tool) because they're cost-effective to implement. Then select no more than one or two of the other techniques described in this chapter for your initial site launch or upgrade.

Follow the KISS maxim (Keep it simple, stupid.) whenever you do anything on the Web! You can always note options to implement downstream in Phase 2, 3, or 12 of your Web development plan. When it comes to choosing those initial, onsite, marketing techniques, consider these factors:

- What you're trying to accomplish with your site
- Your target market
- How much money you have budgeted for site development
- How your server is configured
- What your developer knows how to do
- How much time you have before site launch
- How much time you have to maintain the activity
- How much staff you have for maintenance
- How much interest you have in the technique
- Whether the potential payoff to the bottom line makes the effort worth it

Whichever techniques you select, be sure to include them in your Request for Proposal (RFP), explained in Chapter 3, or discuss them with your Web developer. This is essential for getting an accurate price estimate and for scheduling work on your site. Even if you don't implement special features all at once, it's important for your developer to know what you're considering in the future. In some cases, a developer can make provisions so that it's easy to add a feature downstream. Otherwise, you might face major programming costs to integrate a feature that wasn't planned for.

Freshening Your Content

Fresh content is the single must-do option in this chapter. If you visit a Web site marked `Last Updated March 14, 2001`, you're likely to immediately take off for another site. Why waste your valuable time looking at old, irrelevant content when there are dozens, if not hundreds, of other, more recent Web sites? Even if you're looking at a simple, information-only site whose URL you entered from a business card, you can't be sure that the hours of operation or location are still correct. Knowing that you still need to call the company for confirmation, you're more likely to visit another Web site instead.

Updated content impresses customers and prospects. It demonstrates your commitment to your Web site, and even more so, your respect for customers' time. As such, an updated site helps attract new customers in those first crucial seconds and brings them back for repeat visits. In addition, updated content is one of the factors that some search engines consider when ranking your site in search results. The more often a site is updated, the more relevant search engines consider it to be. As you discover in Chapter 10, you need every advantage in the competitive world of search engine ranking.

Establishing an update schedule

Your content update schedule depends on the nature of your site, as shown in the Sample Update Schedule in Table 6-1. At the very least, review all site content at least once a year, and budget a complete site overhaul every few years. During that time, viewers' expectations of a contemporary site change as technology improves and graphic styles evolve.

Table 6-1	Sample Update Schedule
Frequency	*Task*
Every 3–5 years	Site redesign, new content and features
Annually	Review and update all content and photos

(continued)

Table 6-1 *(continued)*

Frequency	Task
Monthly	Update at least one page of the site with news, seasonal content
Weekly	New products, special promotions
Daily	Automated date change
As needed	Product inventory, especially price changes, deletions, and back orders

Updating some content at least once a month is much better for search engines and very doable for most businesses. The more frequently you update your site with changing content, the more you need easy, inexpensive access through a content management system, a storefront administration package, or software like Macromedia's Contribute, as I discuss in Chapter 4.

Paying a developer for updates can get expensive, although some developers sell a hosting package that includes monthly update services. As a last resort, someone inhouse who is already familiar with HTML or various Web publishing software tools can make changes to your site and upload them via File Transfer Protocol (FTP).

Whatever the frequency of updates, decide who is responsible for doing them and who will confirm that they've been done. In other words, plan! I have yet to see a site that doesn't need updating.

Determining what content to update

There's a simple rule to decide what parts of your site to update: anything and everything! There's no need for a case of writer's block. Even small changes can keep your site current. For instance:

- ✔ Your home page might need changes, perhaps because you've introduced a new product or want to promote a special offer.
- ✔ Your About Us page might need to reflect changes in staffing. Perhaps you have updated summer hours, a new location, or new e-mail addresses for Contact Us.
- ✔ Your product pages might need to be amended with price changes, additions, or deletions.
- ✔ If you have a media page, you might want to add new press releases, newsletters, or mentions in other media.

Remember that your viewers are interested in what affects them, not what's important to you. While you might be very proud of your latest contract, that news probably doesn't belong on your home page unless your target audience consists of investors or business press.

Some people create a What's New page specifically to collect all the changes between site updates. What's New pages are helpful when you have a constant stream of changing news, but you will get more search engine mileage by changing multiple pages on your site. NMsitesearch.com, a regional economic development site, posts news constantly (www.nmsitesearch.com/whats_new/whats_new_home.htm). In Figure 6-1, the site calls out What's New in the left navigation, with five separate subcategories of news in secondary navigation. Old news stories drop off automatically six months after publication.

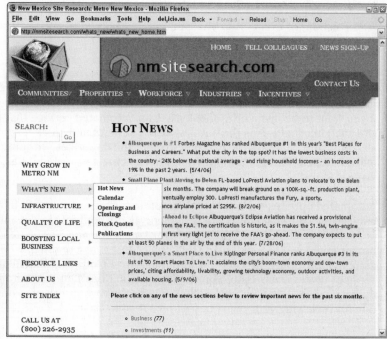

Figure 6-1: NMsite search.com is a news-heavy site that offers separate What's New categories, as well as ongoing content updates on other pages.

Courtesy Metro New Mexico Development Alliance

Your developer can also create a linkable, changing headline that is fast and easy for you to modify with your latest news or product promotion. Drawing a blank? Try some of these ideas:

✔ New products and services

✔ Seasonal specials or page appearance, especially for retail

✔ Sales and special offers

✔ Product modifications or deletions

✔ Price changes

✔ Trade shows you're exhibiting at, especially if you have passes for the show floor

✔ Planned speeches, signings, performances, or other public appearances where you can meet customers

✔ New distributors or retail outlets where customers can shop

✔ Schedule of classes or activities

✔ Changes in hours, phone numbers, addresses, location, maps

✔ Copies of press releases, newsletters, and mentions in other media

✔ Company news, such as new contracts or installations

✔ Calendar of events that you can update easily, with such software as CalendarScript (www.calendarscript.com)

Using content that updates automatically

If you want to be just a little sneaky, use an automated service that feeds your site such information as the date, weather, or news and stock tickers. You can also find sites that provide rotating word-of-the-day, jokes, or quotations to make it appear that content on your site has changed — and it has, as far as visitors know!

Automated updates are a reasonable option for businesses with information-only sites that remain fairly static, as long as the content is relevant to the purpose of your site and appropriate for your audience. For instance, a stockbroker might want to include a stock ticker, but a joke of the day could be quite inappropriate. Be cautious about using religious or political quotation services unless you're sure your audience won't be offended. Automated updates might help with your search engine ranking, but they're no substitute for reviewing your own content on a regular basis.

Some content services are free, some require that you link back to the source, and others charge a monthly rate for their service. Your developer can select the code that's right for your site. Your developer can place a date, stock ticker, or weather script directly into a server-side include (SSI) or footer so it appears on every page. Rather than use scripts, you can now use Real Simple Syndication (RSS) feeds to provide news, weather, or other information to your site, but these might not be seen as site updates. I discuss RSS in Chapter 13.

Table 6-2 lists a few of the many sources for scripts (code) that your developer can insert on your site. Sometimes, these are simple links to a third-party site; sometimes they require inserting a small piece of code. You can find many other such scripts simply by entering *scripts for ___* (fill in the blank with whatever you're looking for) in your favorite search engine.

The tables in this chapter give representative examples of the many options available in each software category; the listings don't imply endorsement of any of these products. Your developer needs to select the right software application or third-party link based on your budget, requested features, ease of implementation and maintenance, and the technical structure of your site.

Table 6-2	Sample Sources for Automated Content Updates
URL for Site	**Cost**
Business Quotations	
`http://en.thinkexist.com/DailyQuotation/customize.asp`	Free, links to source
`www.quotationspage.com/useourquotes.php`	Free, links to source
`www.sitescripts.com/Remotely_Hosted/Website_Content/Quote_of_the_day_Script.html`	Free
Date/Time	
`http://javascript.internet.com/time-date`	Free
`www.cgiscript.net/site_javascripts_date_time.htm`	Free
`www.scriptsearch.com/JavaScript/Scripts/Calendars`	Free
`www.webreference.com/js/scripts/basic_date`	Free
Stock Tickers	
`www.phpmaniacs.com/scripts/view/3256.php`	Free
`www.scripts.com/javascript-scripts/text-scrolling-scripts/stock-market-javascript-ticker`	Free

(continued)

Table 6-2 *(continued)*	
URL for Site	Cost
Weather	
www.weather.com/services/ oap.html?from=servicesindex	Free
www.weatherunderground.com/ about/faq/weathersticker.asp	Free

TIP

Don't use a visible, automated page counter on your Web site. While this may count as a content update for search engine purposes, a page counter can provide negative information unintentionally. If viewers stumble across a counter that reads 56 visits since 1999, they might wonder why they should bother reading the page. The page counter becomes a "reverse testimonial," in effect bad-mouthing your site. In Chapter 14 you find out about "invisible" page counters and other options for Web statistics to determine the number of visitors to your site.

Building an Online Community

As human beings, we not only need, but also want to communicate with one another. The Web offers a seemingly endless stream of techniques to do just that. Virtual online communities establish a give-and-take exchange with and among viewers who share a specific interest. Communities have sprung up on almost every subject, from movie star fan sites to do-it-yourself advice, from computer technical support to online investing. Healthcare information sites, among the most frequent targets of online searches, are also some of the most likely places to find online communities.

Supporting an online community on your Web site is one of the most reliable ways for you to ensure that visitors return to your site again and again. Online communities can also increase traffic, time on site, sales, and return on investment (ROI).

Keep in mind, however, that any online community requires a commitment of time, people, and attention to keep it from degrading. If you don't have time to oversee these communities, you're probably better off selecting other methods of onsite promotion. The size of the community, the number of participants, and the nature of the topic determine the amount of time required and the level of liability exposure you incur. On medical topics in particular, consult your attorney for disclaimer language to include on the site.

You might also find that you need to promote the site feature itself online and off to generate traffic and recruit members until you reach a self-sustaining, critical mass of participants.

Communication styles used in online communities

Online communities have two forms of communication styles: They use either a many-to-many communication style or a top-down, one-to-many communication style. Either style might occur *synchronously* (where everyone is online in real time) through chat rooms, or *asynchronously* (where messages are posted at different times) through message boards, blogs, or guestbooks. Here's a closer look at these two communication styles and how much time you'll need to commit for each type:

- ✔ **Many-to-many:** You don't have to do all the work with many-to-many communities. Community members help each other find desired products, exchange opinions, resolve problems, and give advice. On a regular basis, you still need to pay attention to what's transpiring. You can choose to stay in the background with a member-to-member community if you want.

- ✔ **One-to-many:** In one-to-many communities, an authority figure responds to queries and comments from multiple users, although others might chime in with their opinions. It's clear, however, that one individual is in charge. That expert might be you, an outside content expert contracted to answer questions, a tech support employee, or a guest "speaker" who appears at a specific time.

All online communities require a commitment of time and talent to manage them. It takes skill and judgment to monitor the messages, correct technical inaccuracies, remove offensive language before it posts, avoid liability, keep an eye out for online stalkers in a social network, write content for a blog, and recruit participants. Online communities are such a sponge for energy that some, like YouTube.com, ask members of the community to monitor each other and notify the administrator of objectionable postings. Reality check: Do you have the long-term interest to keep the community ball rolling? Does the content of the community fit well into the purpose of your site? Does the community feed into your business goals, either directly or indirectly?

Soapdom.com, shown in Figure 6-2, offers unmoderated chat rooms, message boards, and blogs for people interested in different soap operas. Moderated chats with soap celebrities are planned. If you visit the site, notice its privacy statement (www.soapdom.com/index.php?option=com_content&task=view&id=2237&Itemid=35) and Terms of Service for the message board, blog, and chat room (www.soapdom.com/index.php?option=com_content&task=view&id=2236&Itemid=35).

Courtesy Soapdom.com ©Soapdom, Inc.

Figure 6-2: Soapdom.com offers multiple online communities to meet the needs of its narrowly segmented audiences.

Message boards and chat rooms

Message boards — sometimes called *bulletin boards, discussion boards,* or *forums* — allow asynchronous communication on your site. Historically, bulletin boards were one of the earliest uses of the Internet, predating the development of the World Wide Web. The computer scientists working on the Internet originally created these boards to encourage open discussion of technical issues. Figure 6-3 shows a variety of moderated message boards from PeakOil.com.

You can use message board software to host one discussion topic or many, allow limited or unlimited participation, and select whether the boards are *moderated* (someone reviews the posts to filter them for propriety) or *unmoderated* (a posting free-for-all). Chat room software operates in a similar manner, except that everyone who participates is online at the same time. It can be more challenging to manage real-time chats, so, often, an expert handles the content response, while a separate moderator manages and edits the question flow. Table 6-3 lists some sources for message board and chat software that your developer might want to review, as well as several sites with evaluation criteria. She or he can also explore the alternative of linking to a third-party site that provides message board or chat service.

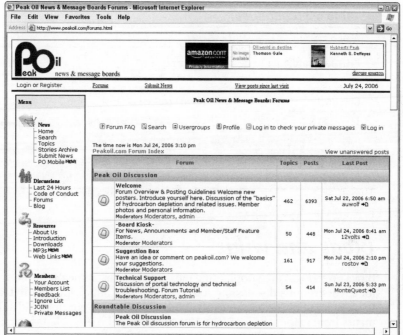

Courtesy PeakOil™

Figure 6-3:
Most of the message boards (forums) on PeakOil.com are moderated.

Table 6-3 Sample Sources for Message Board and Chat Software

Name	URL	Cost
Chat Room		
Bravenet	www.bravenet.com/webtools/chat	Free
2 Create a Website	www.2createawebsite.com/enhance/create-chat-room.html	Free
Chat Software Evaluation Site	http://wdvl.internet.com/Software/Applications/Chat/#resources	N/A
Message Board		
Simple Machines	www.simplemachines.org	Free

(continued)

Table 6-3 *(continued)*

Name	URL	Cost
PHP Junkyard.com	`www.phpjunkyard.com/phpmessage-board.php`	Free
CuteCast	`www.cutecast.org`	Free
Matt's Script Archive	`http://scriptarchive.com/wwwboard.html`	Free
Message Board Evaluation Site	`http://personalweb.about.com/od/addforumsandboards`	N/A

Blogs and wikis

Blogs (Web logs) are supplanting message boards as the preferred technique for asynchronous discussion. A *blog* is a form of online journal that allows you to wax eloquent (or tongue-tied) about a subject in your field and solicit comments from responsive readers. Unlike message boards, blogs look like Web pages, complete with links, graphics, sound, and video.

Once seen as a quick-and-easy alternative for individuals to publish online without needing a domain name or knowing HTML, blogs were quickly adopted for use as online diaries. Writers on media and political sites use blogs to comment without the limit of column inches of print media and to engage in dialog with their readers. Of course, on advertising-supported sites like those, a controversial blog that generates page views also generates ad revenues from additional eyeballs.

Many business sites now feature blogs to solicit user opinions and pinpoint trouble spots. Figure 6-4 shows an example of a business blog (from `www.allbusiness.com/blog/PhysicianBusiness/11417`). On business, financial, retail, and professional service sites, blogs are something of a chameleon. In addition to the community-building function of a message board, a blog might take on characteristics of an online e-zine or newsletter. You can use yours as an opportunity to educate your prospects on different aspects of your business or product while soliciting questions and comments. Table 6-4 offers some sources for blog and wiki software.

Courtesy AllBusiness.com

Figure 6-4:
A blog
aimed at
doctors
from
AllBusiness.
com.

Table 6-4	Sample Sources for Blog and Wiki Software	
Name	**URL**	**Cost**
bBlog	www.bBlog.com	Free
Movable Type	www.sixapart.com/movabletype	$200–$600
Greymatter	http://noahgrey.com/greysoft	Free
WordPress	http://wordpress.org	Free
MediaWiki	www.mediawiki.org	Free
MoinMoin Wiki	http://moinmoin.wikiwikiweb.de	Free
Serendipity	http://s9y.org	Free
Typepad	www.typepad.com	Starts at $5/month

(continued)

Table 6-4 (continued)

Name	URL	Cost
Blog Software Evaluation Site	`http://weblogs.about.com/ od/weblogsoftwareandhosts/ a/topfreeblogs.htm`	N/A
Wiki Software Evaluation Site	`http://en.wikipedia.org/wiki/ Comparison_of_wiki_software`	N/A

Business marketers have discovered that an onsite blog allows creative opportunities to

✔ Attract and retain traffic on a site

✔ Obtain positive and negative feedback from customers

✔ Generate links to other pages on the Web site

✔ Announce new products and test price points

✔ Build brand awareness

✔ Recruit beta testers

✔ Seed product promotions

✔ Identify opinion setters

Blogs can bite! While blogs might be a great way to position yourself as an expert, they have a way of producing challenging feedback. You might want to monitor how people respond to your postings, but don't get defensive if your customers, perhaps your competitors, make negative comments online. Like other forms of community building, blogs take lots of time. It helps if you like to write. You need to post at least twice a week to keep a blog lively and encourage feedback.

Depending on your marketing strategy, you might prefer to host your blog on another site, such as `www.blogger.com`, so the links to your site appear to be coming from another source. Google, in particular, ranks inbound links from blogs highly.

Wikis are related to blogs, but they're more of a democratic community. *Wiki software* allows multiple users to add, delete, and edit each other's Web content quickly without much technical knowledge, making wikis especially suited for collaborative writing. The Wikipedia.org free encyclopedia is a great example of group content that reflects many views.

Other community builders

Rather old-fashioned techniques from early Web sites have been recycled for community-building uses online. For instance, guestbook software — a variant of an unmoderated message board — was previously used to register visitors to a Web site and perhaps to gather e-mail addresses. With those functions now replaced by more advanced features, guestbooks are now used to share communal experiences, to solicit feedback from event participants, to collect congratulations on a wedding, or even to convey words of sympathy.

One client of mine set up a guestbook so vendors, friends, and customers nationwide could send condolences after five employees were killed in a tragic plane crash; the young son of one lost employee used the guestbook to write messages to his daddy in heaven.

Some of these applications have morphed into new, sophisticated, group-bonding sites that allow visitors to your site to connect to one another by using personal profiles. Successful, social network sites like MySpace.com, Facebook.com, Yub.com, Friendster.com, and Classmates.com testify to people's desire to form a community with others sharing a similar experience in the past or present.

You can install social network software on your Web site that allows your visitors to form their own groups of Harley riders, science fair participants, or whatever else makes sense for your target audience. For example, Figure 6-5 (from Catster.com) creates a social network of cat lovers with profiles of their animals — I don't think the cats are meeting online! Social networking is a great ice-breaker application to help people get to know each other quickly: first-year college students planning to attend the same orientation; people looking for roommates on a tour, conference, or retreat; or any other time people will be coming together for a brief, intense experience. You might password-protect this section of your site to assure privacy.

Ideas for community building are limited only by your imagination. People like to be asked their opinions and then return to see the results of a poll or survey. You can easily add script to conduct a simple poll (Who do you think will win the Oscars?) or a survey of attitudes toward any topic of interest to your audience.

Courtesy Dogster, Inc.

Figure 6-5: Catster.com is a site with a feline-friendly social network.

Table 6-5 lists some sources for building online communities on your Web site by using these methods. As always, the choice of software depends on your audience, how they will use the site, and your developer's technical assessment of the best software for your needs.

Table 6-5	Sources for Other Community-Building Software	
Software	*URL*	*Cost*
Bookmark		
Dynamic Drive	www.dynamicdrive.com/ dynamicindex9/addbook.htm	Free
Net Mechanic	www.netmechanic.com/news/ vol4/javascript_no1.htm	Free
Guestbook		
Chipmunk Scripts	www.chipmunk-scripts.com/ page.php?ID=13	Free
Big Nose Bird	http://bignosebird.com/ carchive/bnbbook.shtml	Free

Software	URL	Cost
CGI Extremes	www.cgiextremes.com/Scripts/Guestbooks	Free
Social Networks		
Build a Community	http://buildacommunity.com/bacfriends/index.html	Package 8 Community Builders $200
E-friends	www.alstrasoft.com/efriends.htm	Starts at $180
Survey/Poll		
SurveyMonkey.com	www.surveymonkey.com	$20/month or $200/year
Hosted Survey	www.hostedsurvey.com/home.html	First 250 responses free
Hot Scripts	www.hotscripts.com/Detailed/47579.html	Free

Tooting Your Own Horn

how about for site design have it shaped like glasses

Your Web site is no place to be shy! Because you have only one chance to make a first impression, you have to make it a good one. Consider using tried-and-true techniques on your site for shameless self-promotion: advertising (internal banners), testimonials, reviews, and awards. These tools can help you increase the time that people spend on your site.

Displaying internal banners

You know those ubiquitous banner ads that litter the Web? (I cover them in detail in Chapter 12.) You can take advantage of similar banners within your own site. Instead of paid advertising that links to someone else's site, however, link your internal banners to pages within your own site. Driving viewers to additional pages increases the time they spend on your site and the likelihood that they remember your business or buy your product.

While special features on your site should be easily accessible through navigation, the user's eye doesn't go to the navigation initially. Grab viewers' attention with an eye-catching banner that promotes a monthly special, takes them to the newsletter signup page, or accesses a community-building page. Internal banners are one of the no-brainers for onsite marketing, but plan them as part of the overall site layout and graphic design.

Collecting testimonials

Offline testimonials reassure prospects about the quality of the product or service you offer. Testimonials can come from an objective press rating, a celebrity, experts in the field, or other customers. Collect testimonials from satisfied customers and media mentions at all times, not just while you're working on site content. (The testimonial from your mother doesn't count. Sorry.) These recommendations are more no-brainers. There's some effort to collect them initially and to freshen them over time, but there is no cost.

If you have a business-to-business (B2B) site, get permission from your customers before using their names, titles, and company names. Some firms don't permit their names or their employees' names to be used in an endorsement; you don't want to risk losing their trade. Sometimes, you can get the same effect by using a job title and a description, such as `Director of Engineering, Fortune 500 Company`. The same principle applies if you have a recognizable celebrity or expert whose name carries cachet with prospective customers: Get permission first. The National Mail Order Association has a sample permission form at `www.nmoa.org/articles/dmnews/usingtestimonials.htm`, or you can simply Google *permissions testimonial*.

Although the situation is less sensitive with "ordinary" customers, you're still better off requesting permission. If you can't locate the source, you can use a first name and last initial, or vice versa, and their city or state: `J Zimmerman, Albuquerque, NM` or `Jan Z, Albuquerque, NM`. If your customer comes from a small town where he or she might be recognized or has an unusual name, use only the name or only the state or country: `P Tchaikovsky, Russia`. However, the less specific the attribution, the less potent the testimonial.

The location has value, especially if you want to communicate to prospects that your product has "reach," or that you've been able to satisfy customers from places like the one where they live.

There's no point in pasting a long list of testimonials on a single Web page — no one will read it! Instead, try these suggestions for getting the most out of this onsite marketing technique:

✔ Scatter the testimonials throughout the site.

✔ Judiciously select short phrases or single sentences that are relevant to the content of a particular page. In a case where Web media differs from print, an online testimonial carries more punch when it's short and to the point.

- ✔ You can break a long testimonial into several endorsements on different pages of the site.

- ✔ Consider rotating testimonials as part of your content update. You can do this manually or ask your developer to set up a quote database that posts a different testimonial every day, or every time your site is accessed. Testimonials can be effective on almost any site, as long as you don't overuse them.

Figure 6-6 shows how Hacienda Nicholas (www.haciendanicholas.com), a bed & breakfast in Santa Fe, uses testimonials specific to each room. Other pages carry more general testimonials from satisfied guests, such as "One of the best B&B's we've ever encountered" or "a special find — one of those places only insiders know about" from *Frommers*.

One other type of endorsement helps build trust in your site for online transactions. If you're a member of the Better Business Bureau (www.bbbonline.org), TRUSTe (www.truste.com) for privacy, or a well-established trade association that vouches for its members, display their seal(s) prominently on your site. These memberships generally require a fee and a site analysis, but they might give you a competitive edge in the online world.

Figure 6-6:
The site for Hacienda Nicholas makes effective use of testimonials.

Testimonial

Courtesy Hacienda Nicholas

Soliciting product reviews

Some people prefer the illusion that they make rational purchasing decisions rather than emotional ones. For these buyers, product reviews from a third party offer a perceived, objective rating. Sometimes you can get reviews by submitting your products or services to magazines, trade journals, or other press outlets. Or you can include your site for a fee on comparison shopping engines like Bizrate.com to solicit reviews. (Please see Chapter 12 for more information on shopping search engines.)

If you're confident in your products, open your site to ratings from customers with a link to `Review this product`. Sites like Hotscripts.com offer free rating scripts for your site. Go to `www.hotscripts.com/php/scripts_ and_programs/reviews_and_ratings/index.html` for more information. If you solicit ratings from customers, don't post only the good ones. If all reviews are uniformly excellent, viewers won't trust them. Many sites that offer product reviews are actually distributors, rather than creators, so they face no risk. For instance, users rate movies on Netflix.com, and they can rate or review absolutely anything on Amazon.com. These large sites compile the results or reviews, as well as what other people buy, to recommend new purchases based on what a viewer has already bought.

Submitting to award and hot sites

Some Web sites gain visitors and credibility by being ranked for their own quality. This is particularly true for graphic design and Web developer sites, industry-specific sites, professional service sites, and information-rich sites. There are general rating sites, including the well-known Webby Awards, and a range of others that are specific to certain businesses or that rate particular features, such as the quality of a database or flash animation. Search and apply for awards that apply to your business and site design. If you win, post the award on your site! Table 6-6 provides URLs for sites that list award opportunities as well as a few of the many awards that are out there.

Table 6-6	Sample Award Sites	
Award Name	*URL*	*Focus*
Web Marketing Association's WebAward	`www.webaward.org`	Multiple areas
Cool Netsites	`http://members.aol. com/skycheetah/ awardsites.html`	List of award sites

Award Name	URL	Focus
EduNET	www.edunetconnect.com/ awards/index.php	Educational sites
Kasina's awards for financial professionals	www.kasina.com/Page. asp?ID=493	Financial services companies
Interactive Media Awards	www.interactivemedia awards.com/default.aspq	Multiple business categories
Internet Advertising Competition	www.advertising competition.org/iac	Online advertising
IPPA	www.ippa.org	Web design
MuniNetGuide	www.muninetguide.com/ top_picks.php	Local government
Webby Awards	http://webbyawards.com	Multiple areas
Yahoo! Picks	http://picks.yahoo.com	Multiple areas

Incorporating Freebies and Fun

The onsite marketing techniques in this section are designed primarily to attract new traffic to your site and to increase your ROI. To use these techniques effectively, you need to publicize their existence on Web clearinghouses with master lists of links to coupons, free offers, games, and contests. Table 6-7 includes both source and publicity sites for items in this category.

Table 6-7	Sources and Listing Sites for Freebies and Fun	
Site Name	**URL**	**Function**
ContestAlley.com	www.contestalley.com	Contest submission site
ContestGuide.com	www.contestguide.com	Contest submission site
DynaPortal	www.dynaportal.com/ software/contests.cfm	Contest software, paid
FatWallet	www.fatwallet.com	Coupon submission site
Free Stuff Channel	www.freestuffchannel. com	Freebie offer submission site

(continued)

Site Name	URL	Function
Table 6-7 *(continued)*		
Miniclip	`www.miniclip.com/Downloads.htm`	Free, downloadable games
myClipper.com	`www.myclipper.com`	Coupon submission site
RefDesk	`www.refdesk.com/free.html`	Directory of sites for freebie submissions
Sweepstakes and More	`www.sweepstakesandmore.com/submitasweep`	Sweepstakes submission site
UbiDog Productions	`www.ubidog.com/cgi-bin/downloader/downloader.pl`	Free, downloadable contests

Coupons and discounts

Coupons and discounts work offline and they work online, particularly when your target audience has a bargain orientation. However, even high-end audiences like to believe that they are getting a deal. Even though most coupons are never actually used, they improve branding and name recognition. The online execution of a discount occurs as a promotion code that users enter during the checkout process on your Web site, while a coupon is printed out for use at your own or other brick-and-mortar stores. You need to figure how the cost of such discounts will affect your gross revenue and the average dollar value of a sale.

Not all shopping carts can accept all forms of discounts. It's important to ask your developer what your software can handle before you establish your discount plan. For instance, some sites can discount a total price by a flat dollar amount or percentage, but can't discount on a specific product. Some can't tie two purchases together to execute a complex instruction like `Buy one at full price and get the second at half off`. Some carts can't handle promotion codes at all.

Free offers

Free is marketing's four-letter word. (I talk about the power of *Free* in Chapter 4 as well.) You can tie a free offer to another purchase, such as a two-for-one deal, or a product that is paired with a purchase, such as `Free socks when` you buy shoes or `Buy one shirt and get a second free`. Or *free* can mean a separate promotional item shipped as a reward for taking an action, such as `Free bracelet when you sign up for our jewelry newsletter`. In either case, remember to include in your marketing budget the cost of promotional goods and their differential shipping expense. Be careful! Starbucks got burned in 2006 with an e-mail offer for a free iced coffee sent to a limited group of employees to share with family and friends. The e-mail spread so far and so wide that Starbucks had to cancel the promotion. You should also check with your shipping department to make sure that it can package and track shipping of promotional items.

Games and contests

Online games and contests often carry an age and/or gender appeal. The right game matched to the right audience can result in significant traffic to your site and many repeat visits. For this to pay off beyond traffic, you might want to sell advertising on your site or provide another business rationale for the game. It also helps to tie the award, if any, to the audience. Many games don't include prizes, while most contests do. Some contests are games of skill (for example, trivia or interactive contests); others, like sweepstakes or drawings, are simple matters of luck.

Whenever you include a contest or sweepstakes on your site, be sure to include a detailed page of rules and legal disclaimers. Consult your attorney if you have questions; some states have very strict rules.

Providing a Tell a Friend Option on Your Site

The best and cheapest form of advertising is word of mouth. There is no stronger recommendation for a product — or a Web site — than the approval of a friend. Fortunately, the Web offers an online equivalent to word of mouth. Tell a Friend scripts allow site visitors to e-mail others a link to your site. The message arrives from the sender's e-mail address, not yours, making recipients more likely to open it. Best of all, Tell a Friend is another no-brainer when it comes to onsite marketing. It's cost-effective and generally low maintenance unless you're offering a reward.

Many Web hosting and site template companies offer their customers a free Tell a Friend option, or you can use the same function from a newsletter provider like ConstantContact.com. Table 6-8 lists a few of the sites that offer free scripts for this feature. Be sure that the script includes a thank-you message following submission, and checks for such errors as leaving a field empty or incorrectly formatting the friend's e-mail address. Depending on your site, you might want to rename the feature according to your target audience: Tell a Colleague, Tell a Bride, or Tell a Hiker, for instance.

Table 6-8	Sources for Tell a Friend Scripts	
Site Name	*URL*	*Cost*
Bravenet	`www.bravenet.com/` `webtools/announce/` `index.php`	Free
SWS-Tech	`www.sws-tech.com/` `scripts/tellafriend.php`	Free
Tell-a-Friend Wizard	`www.tell-a-friend-` `wizard.com`	$6/month to $30/year

It's appropriate to include the Tell a Friend function on almost every Web site as a method of driving additional traffic with a recommendation from an extremely well-targeted audience of similar viewers. It is the simplest online equivalent of word of mouth. To improve the number of referrals, you might consider adding a minor incentive or chance to win a drawing for every friend someone notifies.

Keep it simple, though! Offering a reward might require programming, monitoring, and/or fulfillment. Giving someone a coupon for a free cup of coffee for Telling a Friend is a lot more effective (and easier) than requiring someone to tell four people, of whom one must subscribe, to get a chance to win a $50 dinner at a fancy restaurant!

Doing Viral Marketing without Catching a Cold

Viral marketing techniques use consumers to promote awareness of your product or site. Generally, but not always, viral marketing involves an e-mail message that is forwarded endlessly from one person to others. Tell a Friend scripts (which I discuss in the previous section) are a simple example, but any Web link, advertisement, graphic, video, or sound clip that is passed from user to user qualifies as Web-based viral marketing. Developing a good viral idea is difficult.

TIP

In the best of all worlds, a successful viral campaign offers consumers something of value, often a good laugh. The viral message has to be easy to send, containing nothing that will set off alarm bells, such as a huge graphic, or a subject line that looks like spam or porn. (See Chapter 8 for a discussion of e-mail subject lines.) Because a viral message might circulate for years, it doesn't work well for a limited-time or limited-supply offer. If you're lucky, you'll be able to track the number of forwards or visitors. Most newsletter services let you track forward-to-a-friend links if you send your original message out through them.

Often targeted at a techno-savvy group of 20- to 30-year-olds, viral marketing is a creative task at the cutting edge of advertising techniques. Take a look at some of the award winners and resource sites listed in Table 6-9 to get some ideas.

Table 6-9	Viral Marketing Resources	
Name	*URL*	*Description*
ClickZ Network	www.clickz.com/ experts/brand/brand/ article.php/3573036	Good article on viral marketing
Future Marketing Awards	www.futuremarketing awards.com	Viral marketing awards and archive
2CreateAWebsite	www.2createawebsite. com/traffic/viral- marketing.html	Directory of articles on viral marketing
Web Marketing Today	www.wilsonweb.com/ cat/cat.cfm?page= 1&subcat=mm_Viral	Directory of articles on viral marketing
Word of Mouth Marketing Association	www.womma.org/pages/ 2005/02/viral_award_ win.htm	Viral marketing awards

Viral marketing can take place through e-mail or on the Web by using a variety of techniques. Here a few with a history of success:

✔ **Send an e-mail-only message:** In 2000, Proctor & Gamble conducted a Send a Kiss promotion for Scope mouthwash. They provided a branded, animated e-mail of a kiss that users could send on Valentine's Day, Mother's Day, and other holidays. Hotmail spread its free e-mail service quickly because each e-mail that went out via Hotmail included a signature block with a link for recipients to get a free e-mail account, too.

✔ **Exploit chat rooms:** The low-budget horror pic, *The Blair Witch Project,* deliberately created a buzz in online chat rooms to drive traffic first to the film's Web site and from there to movie theaters to see the feature.

✔ **Create an interactive game:** Burger King scored big with its Subservient Chicken Web site (`www.subservientchicken.com`), shown in Figure 6-7, as part of the promotion for new chicken sandwiches in 2004. On the site, users can enter commands for the chicken to perform. Viewers quickly pass the link to their friends, generating millions of visits to the site. A more detailed description appears in the sidebar nearby.

✔ **Play to the creative ego:** Several sites, including Converse (`www.converse.com/index.asp?mode=mby&bhcp=1`), let people create and submit their own ads. MasterCard ran a famous contest (now over) to "Write your own Priceless Ad" (`http://www.priceless.com/film/film.html`), and needless to say, some of the ads push the limits of good taste and might even portray the company in a negative light. Still, the allure of creating their own ads draws visitors to the sites, encourages them to share their creations and the site with others, all the while burning the brands indelibly in the minds of the target audience these companies are trying to reach. It's a great exercise for anyone teaching an advertising class, by the way.

Figure 6-7:
Burger King's Subservient Chicken viral campaign.

™ and © 2006 Burger King Brands, Inc.

The story behind Subservient Chicken

Twenty visits on day one. One million visits within 24 hours. Twenty million visits within a week. And, 396 million hits in less than a year. That leap of traffic brought the "actor in the chicken suit" lasting fame. According to Adweek magazine (www.adweek.com/aw/ national/article_display.jsp?vn u_content_id=1000828049), Burger King (BK) initially released SubservientChicken. com to 20 friends of ad agency employees and seeded it in a few chat rooms. Traffic grew spectacularly in early April 2004 as Web surfers delighted in the antics of a man-sized chicken hiding behind a sofa, dancing the jitterbug, or playing dead in response to those and 400 other commands. Viewers quickly clicked the Tell a Friend link to send the message: "Finally, somebody in a chicken costume who will do whatever you want. Check it out."

Created by the Crispin Porter + Bogusky agency, Subservient Chicken took top honors at the London-based 2005 Viral Awards (www. boreme.com/boreme/funny-features /viral-awards-2005.php) in the categories of Most Infectious North American Viral and Most Creative Use of Technology. The agency targeted 18- to 45-year-old men who spend a lot of time online as the audience for BK's then-new TenderCrisp Chicken Sandwich. They followed the underground introduction of the Web site with a minimal media campaign: three, 30-second TV ads, one print ad, and a second Web site, ChickenFight.com (now inactive).

Although the company doesn't release specific sales information, a BK spokesman told Adweek that sales of the sandwich increased an average of 9 percent per week during the first month. Over the following year, BK executives declared the campaign "a success," resulting in increased sales of the sandwich. Perhaps the vagueness of the data indicates that you can't always count your viral chickens even after they've hatched.

Part III
Exploring Online Marketing Basics

The 5th Wave   By Rich Tennant

In this part . . .

Here's the real hub of this book. Once you have an effective Web site, how do you drive traffic to it? This section covers the essential components of online marketing, using word-of-Web techniques to let your target market know your site exists and why they should visit it. With 47 million competing Web sites, you need agility, persistence, and patience to grab their attention. Most important, diversify your Web marketing approaches.

Chapter 7 reviews techniques — generally free or cheap — to leverage other online resources to promote your own site, as a form of marketing ju jitsu. From talking up your site on chat rooms, message boards, blogs, and social networks to conducting the absolutely required inbound link campaign, you can select online-only techniques for site promotion. Like everything else that's Web-based, these techniques evolve as the Internet changes.

E-mail is one of the most effective of those online-only techniques. Chapter 8 covers best practices for breaking through the e-mail flood with messages and newsletters that generate business without becoming spam. E-mail techniques range from simple, free signature blocks to expensive, multisegmented newsletter campaigns.

Every Web site has its own special needs. You can pick and choose from the methods in Chapter 9 to accomplish your specific business goals: integration with offline marketing; a gala site launch; real-time, online events; selling internationally; affiliate programs; or online loyalty programs.

People arrive at Web sites in only three ways: using search engines, clicking links from other pages, or typing in a URL after hearing about it or seeing it elsewhere. Search engines are an absolutely necessary part of your Web marketing mix, though not sufficient on their own. Chapter 10 shows you how to optimize your site for search engines to get the visibility you need.

Chapter 7

Marketing with Online Buzz

Chapter 6 covers community-building techniques deployed on your site to encourage repeat visits and/or extend visit time. This chapter covers similar techniques but leverages other resources on the Web instead. Think of it as online jujitsu.

You can inform your target audience — and get folks talking to each other — about your products, services, company, and Web site with such word-of-Web methods as:

- Chat rooms
- Message boards
- Blogs
- Social networks
- Opinion-maker sites
- Press releases
- Inbound links

These techniques, all of which are covered in this chapter, are a mix of viral marketing, consumer-generated content, word of mouth, and online buzz. Don't worry about the terminology. Just mark the ones that seem most useful for your audience and business sector on your Web Marketing Methods Checklist from Chapter 2, which you can also download at www.dummies.com/go/webmarketing.

Word-of-Web methods work better for tightly targeted market segments than they do for mass marketing or volume traffic. Your site should be live and functioning properly before you drive significant traffic to it. At that point, allot about half a day per week for online marketing.

Becoming an Online Gorilla with Guerrilla Marketing

Guerrilla marketing employs somewhat unconventional promotion methods (online or offline) to reach your audience, usually at low cost. These methods often take more imagination and energy than money. However, when executed with surprise and flair, they can bring a steady supply of prequalified new traffic to your site.

Spending time and money on these or other online guerrilla marketing techniques is worthwhile for any business site, with the exception of minimal, business card sites or for sites that exist to serve only a preselected audience.

Keys to success

Low-cost, word-of-Web techniques take time. Remember that adage about small business: It's your money or your life. Because some of these techniques can consume a lot of your life, start with only one or two. You can always add more later. There are four simple rules for success:

- ✔ **Follow your fish.** Don't waste time on techniques that don't reach your target audience.

- ✔ **Seven is your lucky number.** That's the magic number of times that people must see your name or Web site to remember it. Guess what? *Seven* is how many times you should appear on any one blog, board, chat room, or network to see results.

- ✔ **Plan your work and work your plan.** You won't be successful if you post a message one week and then disappear for a month. Make your life easier by scheduling marketing activities for one morning a week or half an hour each day.

- ✔ **Keep track of your results.** How else will you know which techniques work and which ones don't? Set up a spreadsheet that shows the name of the site, type of activity, date, and outcome.

Tracking effectiveness can be tricky. Your statistics generally list referrer URLs when someone clicks from another site to yours (more on this in Chapter 14). However, you need to plan ahead to capture the source of calls, e-mails, or URLs typed into the address field of a browser.

Ask your developer to create a list of redirect URLs (for example, www. YourDomain.com/R1) to deploy in different marketing efforts, just as you include department numbers in the return address of a direct mail piece or print ad. You can point these URLs to any Web page on your site, but they will appear in your statistics as the entry page. Also, ask your developer for a list of forwarding e-mail addresses that you can use to track responses from different marketing efforts. For phone calls, set up different phone extensions or simply ask, "How did you hear about us?" Record these variations on your spreadsheet.

Niche marketing

To become a powerful marketing gorilla, fish where your fish are. In other words, target your audience very carefully. Relatively few seniors use MySpace.com for social networking, but they might use chat rooms on healthcare sites. If you have a B2B site for oceanographic equipment, there's no point in blogging realtors — unless they lease underwater property. The Internet audience is so large that even a small niche can be profitable.

Think rifle, not shotgun. You can no more afford to spread your word-of-Web time and efforts too thin than you can afford to spread your advertising dollars. Target one market at a time, build traffic by using one or two of the guerrilla techniques described in this chapter, and then move on to the next market. Your competitors' online buzz activities can also give you a clue about what's effective.

Even if you select only one word-of-Web method, try to show up on several sites multiple times, whether they're blogs, directories, chats, or message boards. A critical mass of online appearances lends your site credibility.

B2B guerrillas

Absolutely, you can use online guerrilla techniques for B2B marketing. Many purchasing agents, buyers, engineers, and distributors constantly search the Web for new products and services.

It's a good idea to know the sales cycle in your industry because people with different job descriptions have different roles. They prefer different marketing techniques, visit different sites, and receive recommendations from different peers. At the risk of over-generalization, engineers like technically focused message boards or blogs where users discuss product features, preferably on sites with technical credibility. Purchasing agents gravitate toward directories listing many suppliers, visit price comparison sites, and review sites that rate vendors' performance. An executive who approves spending generally appreciates recommendations from peers who discuss the impact of installing a new tool or software.

For more information about guerrilla marketing, see www.gmarketing.com or review the latest trends in the world of buzz and consumer-generated marketing at www.nielsenbuzzmetrics.com/cgm.asp.

Buzzing with Chat Rooms and Message Boards

By participating in existing *chat rooms* (simultaneous, online conversations with multiple people) or *message boards* (messages posted and read at any time), you can spread the word subtly. Companies and individuals often use chat rooms and message boards on other Web sites to promote films (from the *Blair Witch Project* to *Snakes on a Plane*), to publicize musicians and bands, or to direct participants to other Web sites, such as videos on YouTube.com.

TIP

You might already be familiar with specific Web sites from your own surfing. If not, use some of the directories in Table 7-1 or search online for chat rooms and message boards that attract your target market. If you sell only locally, look for boards and chats in your geographic area.

Facebook bitches

Table 7-1	Chat and Message Board Directories
Company	*URL*
About.com	http://search.about.com/fullsearch.htm?terms=message%20boards
Chatmag.com Directory	www.chatmag.com
Construction Web Links	www.constructionweblinks.com/industry_topics/specifications__technical_data/specifications_and_technical_d/technical__forums/technical__forums.html
dmoz Boards	http://dmoz.org/computers/internet/on_the_web/message_boards
dmoz Chat	http://dmoz.org/computers/internet/chat
Google Groups	http://groups.google.com
MSN Groups	http://groups.msn.com
MSN Chat	http://chat.msn.com
Network World Tech Forums	www.networkworld.com/community/?q=forum

Company	URL
People's Choice Chat Directory	`www.chatterhead.net/chat-list.html`
Yahoo! Groups	`http://dir.yahoo.com/computers_and_` `internet/internet/chats_and_forums`

Talkie-talk on other sites

When starting your search for chat rooms or message boards, I recommend visiting a number of these sites and then winnowing down your participatory selection to two or three. Log in and observe for a few days to get a sense of the audience and the postings first.

Then when you're ready to start posting, keep the following points in mind:

- ✔ Use your job title or company name to establish your credibility as an expert in the field, offering opinions or suggestions supported by your experience.

- ✔ Rather than pontificate, try to end with a question or concern that invites others to respond.

- ✔ Always conclude with a signature block that has all your contact information. Include a marketing tagline for the product or service you want to feature. (See more about signature blocks in Chapter 8.)

After you find a few possible chat rooms or message boards, post about once a week for several months. Use one of your redirect URLs and/or a different e-mail address for each site to gauge whether your effort is paying off. Over time, you'll probably find one or two good sites to stick with. When they stop being effective, switch locations or tactics.

Moderated chat rooms, which are monitored by an individual, might schedule guest "speakers." If you're an expert, contact the moderator offline to volunteer to become a speaker. After you've answered questions on your business area — whether it's interior decorating, computer repair, scrapbooking, dental care, or genealogy research — people might visit your Web site for more services.

You can start the posting process by asking a few employees or friends to post on a selected board or chat. That's how Burger King initiated the viral marketing campaign for Subservient Chicken, which I describe in Chapter 6. Some online promotion companies provide this service for clients (BzzAgent.com, Tremor.com, Streetwise.com).

More jujitsu. If you put a message board or chat room on your Web site, submit it to as many of the directories in Table 7-1 as possible. The listing can drive more traffic to your site and help improve your search engine ranking.

Netiquette

Many chat rooms and boards have rules about what you can post. Read them. In most cases, overt solicitations for products or services aren't welcome.

Don't pretend to be someone else when you participate in a chat room or message board. Certainly, you can use a nickname, a distinct e-mail address, or telephone extension to track communications that come from a board or group. But don't pretend to be a licensed hair stylist, contractor, or healthcare professional — you're setting yourself up for charges of fraud or worse. If you pose as a disinterested consumer when you're actually promoting a product, you might be banned from the group. The ensuing loss of professional credibility is not worth it. (There are third-party companies that will do this for you. It's a gray area, but common in entertainment and music industries.)

Instead, invite people to contact you outside the forum or chat room with product-related questions. For example, after giving some objective advice about banner ads, you might conclude with, "E-mail *me@mycompany.com* if you'd like more information about our advertising packages."

Buzzing in the Blogosphere

Blah, blah, blog! On your site and on others, you can build buzz in the more-contemporary incarnation of the message board: the blog. While popular with political pundits and journalists, and with absolute numbers growing rapidly, blogs are not for everyone. You care about blogs only if your target audience uses them.

Deciding whether blogs will work for you

According to a 2006 study by the Pew Internet & American Life Project, only 39 percent of adult American Internet users read blogs and only 8 percent write them. Many of the remaining 61 percent don't even have a clue what a blog is. While the Pew study estimates the number of blogs at about 12 million, it doesn't account for inactive or abandoned blogs, and more than half are personal diaries. Many business people don't have time to write blogs. If they do use a blog, it's as an easier to way to communicate than a message board or bulk e-mail.

The Pew study also detected significant differences in blog use by age. Not surprisingly, more than half (54 percent) of bloggers in 2006 were under 30, roughly evenly divided between males and females. Other studies show that gender distribution changes significantly with age, with females representing 63 percent of bloggers from 13–17, but declining to 26 percent of bloggers over 48. Be very sure that the people you want to reach are blogging. The adoption rate for this Internet innovation, like others, tends to lag behind publicity. By the time blogs reach those over 30 and saturate the Web, the next wave of innovation already will have crested.

With the exception of blogs in the technical, advertising, lifestyle, and entertainment fields, and a few for industry insiders, most blogs are a better vehicle for B2C promotion than for B2B. Follow *your* fish!

Selecting the right blogs

Before you start posting or requesting mention in blogs, it's a good idea to review a number of them. The blog directories in Table 7-2 are a good way to start. For your first filter, try Technorati.com, which claims to rank some 55 million blogs by frequency of use. Select only among the top 10 percent because there's not much point participating on a blog that is viewed by only its writer and a few friends.

Table 7-2	Blog Resources and Search Engines
Name	*URL*
Big List of Blog Search Engines	`www.aripaparo.com/archive/000632.html`
Big List of International Blog Search Engines	`www.aripaparo.com/archive/000654.html`
BlogPulse: Trends from Nielsen	`http://blogpulse.com`
Blog Search Engine	`www.blogsearchengine.com`
Business Blog Consulting (a blog about blogs)	`www.businessblogconsulting.com`
Feedster Blog Search	`www.feedster.com`
Google Blog Search	`http://blogsearch.google.com` or `http://search.blogger.com`
Robin Good's Top 55	`www.masternewmedia.org/rss/top55`

(continued)

Table 7-2 *(continued)*	
Name	**URL**
SiteReference.com Blog Article	`www.site-reference.com/` `articles/General/Using-Blog-` `PR-to-Promote-Your-Site.html`
Technorati Blog Search and Ranking	`www.technorati.com`

When searching a blog directory, search for tags that appear on your list of keywords. (See Chapter 10 for more information on keywords.)

After you have a manageable list of blogs to visit, look at frequency of use, the quality of the participants (are they influencers who tell others?), point of view of the author, and the quality of the dialogue.

Getting the most out of blogs

If you decide appearing in the blog would be beneficial, you have several options:

- ✔ **Comment on an article written by the blogger.** Offer additional information, not criticism. Though you want to be seen as an expert in the field, don't openly confront the blog author, who might simply remove your posts. This is business; keep your ego in check. As with chat rooms and message boards, try not to pontificate. Keep your blog responses short and open ended. Be sure to include a link back to your site.

- ✔ **E-mail the blog owner to ask for a mention in his blog.** Find bloggers who've written about your industry through directories or inbound links. E-mail the blogger with your request, explaining why you like their blogs, and why your news/product/service matters to their readers. Perhaps you can offer a free sample, or at least a link on your site. Thank them for their time, however they respond.

- ✔ **Note blogs that accept paid advertising for future use.** (See Chapter 12.) Some blogs now accept banner ads, sponsorships, or pay per click ads from search engines.

Bloggers often exchange links to each other's sites or blogs. Do it! Links to your Web site from a blog make your site seem relevant and might enhance your search engine ranking. This benefit alone is an important business incentive to blog. As with chat rooms or message boards, monitor your selected blogs and try to comment once a week for several months. Again, use a different e-mail address with each blog to determine which blogs are generating prospects. Click-throughs from blogs to your Web site show up in your referrer statistics.

This isn't rocket science; it's marketing. If it works, keep doing it. If it doesn't, switch to another blog or change tactics.

TIP

If you put a blog on your own Web site, submit it to as many of these directories as possible. Appearing in directories can drive more readers to your blog, encourage links from other blogs, and help improve your search engine ranking.

Buzzing with Social Networks

Are social networks the Web's answer to the human need for community in an isolating technological world? Or merely the latest craze in online connectivity? Social network sites, whether business or personal, encourage participants to interact with others who share their interests or mutual objectives. Table 7-3 lists some of the largest social networks, and resources to find others.

Table 7-3	Social Network Resources and Major Sites	
Name	**URL**	**What You'll Find**
Fast Company	www.fastcompany.com/ magazine/106/open_ social-networks.html	Article on social networking
Friendster	www.friendster.com	Personal social networking site
LinkedIn	www.linkedin.com	B2B network
LinknRank	www.linknrank.com	Directory of social networking sites
Meetup	www.meetup.com	Network for setting up local meetings (great for house-party sales sites)
MySpace. com	www.myspace.com	Personal social networking site
Social Networking Services Meta List	http://socialsoftware. weblogsinc.com/2005/ 02/14/home-of-the- social-networking- services-meta-list	Directory of social networking sites
The Virtual Handshake	www.onlinebusiness networks.com/ directory.html	Directory of business networking sites

Personal social networks

MySpace.com, the most famous personal social networking site, boasted more than 50 million unique visitors in May 2006, exhibiting explosive growth of 230 percent from the prior year, according to comScore Networks. Sites like these make it easy for users to share blogs, photos, video, and audio. There are specialized social networks for all kinds of interests, from gaming (Xfire.com) to college students (Facebook.com). Most networks now offer customized business profiles and paid advertising opportunities.

Personal social networks, with their emphasis on individual profiles, appeal to a young demographic struggling with the age-dependent search for identity. Unless this activity is part of their job, most busy adults don't have time for extensive social networking.

Like blogs, this B2C technique is very useful for those in the entertainment, fashion, and consumer technology fields with an audience of teens and unmarried young adults, from 15- to 34-years-old. If this isn't your audience, devote most of your energy to other marketing methods.

You might post a profile on several of the larger personal sites as a low-key effort, but don't rely on them too much unless you're in one of the key business sectors. Even in these arenas, the marketing value for small- to medium-sized businesses remains uncertain. People have to find your profile, which means getting noticed among hundreds of thousands of others. Sounds like promoting your Web site, doesn't it? Great success stories turn out not to be homegrown, but rather managed by large public relations or advertising companies who invest significant dollars in Web-wide promotion.

In spite of the hype about social networks, this, too, will pass. Like everything else in online marketing, social networks will go through a cycle of acceptance: from cutting edge to mainstream to replacement by the next creative incarnation of the Internet. In the very process of grabbing onto the coattails of change, large masses of people, corporations, and ad agencies inevitably alter the shape and direction that change will take.

By the time the press discovers a hot new trend, its inventors usually have abandoned it. Technology will *always* be ahead of you. Young, hip, creative trendsetters will *always* be ahead of you. If you're chasing that target audience, your marketing must *always* be in motion and your antennae must *always* be tuned to rumors. Good luck!

AMP Concerts, a small promoter of folk, world, and acoustic music concerts in Albuquerque, New Mexico, already had successful e-mail distribution and a Web site (www.abqmusic.com) when it posted a profile in the music section of MySpace at www.myspace.com/ampconcerts. Shown in Figure 7-1, their profile contains standard elements, including a logo, calendar of shows, photos, sections for a blog, contact information, and comments. Read about AMP Concerts' experience with MySpace in the sidebar.

Business social networks

Relying on the theory of *six degrees of separation* (everyone is connected through a chain of no more than five others), B2B social networks such as LinkedIn.com mainly are used for hiring and job searching, introductions to dealmakers, and for *tips* (sales leads), not for marketing.

Both generic business networks and industry-specific ones, like `http://digg.com/business_finance/Real_Estate_Social_Network`, exist. Those sites that accept advertising, however, can be a good way to reach B2B prospects.

Social networking sites usually track the number of times your profile is viewed and the number of comments received. Again, you can use different e-mail addresses to track prospects arising from social networks. Visits to your Web site originating from your profile do show up in your referrer statistics. You can easily cross-promote between your Web site and social network profiles.

Is the latest the greatest?

AMP Concerts has successfully presented folk, acoustic, Americana, and world music in a variety of venues around Albuquerque, New Mexico, since 2000. "I'm not crazy about MySpace for our audience," says founder Neal Copperman.

He went into MySpace on the advice of a singer whose concert he promoted. Maybe it was self-fulfilling prophecy, but Copperman says he hasn't found MySpace worth the effort. "There's some potential, but it's tricky to figure out how to use it." Clearly targeted at those 30 and over — all AMP events have seating, are nonsmoking, and start and end at reasonable times — with somewhat more mature musical tastes, AMP's audience might be older than most MySpace users.

That, too, might account for the relative lack of viewers and comments on AMP's profile.

For advertising purposes, AMP finds it more beneficial to focus on its Web site and e-mail distributed through Yahoo! Groups to more than 1,400 subscribers. Copperman invests his marketing time writing colorful, musically astute content and updating the site. Cleanly designed, the AMP site is handicapped accessible, allows users to book tickets or make donations, and provides centralized information on the Albuquerque music scene.

To see more value, Copperman observes, "I'd really have to spend a lot of time networking with it."

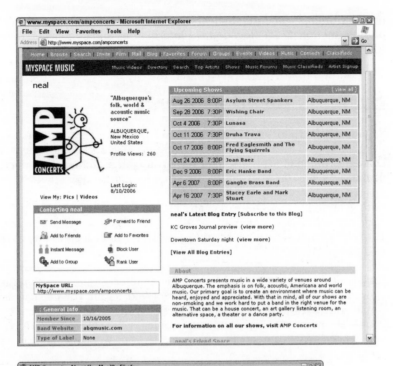

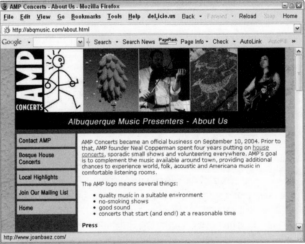

Figure 7-1:
AMP
Concerts
posted its
profile in
the music
section of
MySpace.
com as a
complement
to its Web
site.

Courtesy Neal Copperman. Web site designed by Sue Trowbridge, Interbridge.com.

Buzzing the Influencers

Word of Web includes third-party sites that collect opinions, product reviews, and vendor ratings, or that run online focus groups. Marketing folks talk frequently about the importance of reaching the 10 percent of any audience that charts the course for others. These online "e-fluential" folks can do great good, or great harm, in a chat room, blog, or consumer review site.

With a little forethought, you can take advantage of third-party review sites to promote your product, service, or company. Table 7-4 lists only a few of the hundreds of such sites.

Table 7-4	Sites that Influence Purchases	
Name	*URL*	*Type of Review*
Amazon Reviews (also accessible through Alexa.com to review Web sites)	`www.amazon.com/gp/ help/customer/display. html/002-5030947- 8079226?ie=UTF8& nodeId=16465311`	Product, book, and site reviews
Angie's List	`www.angieslist.com`	Local service company ratings
BzzAgent	`www.bzzagent.com`	Become an opinion-maker
eBay Reviews	`http://pages.ebay.com/ learn_more.html`	Product reviews, vendor ratings
Epinions.com	`www.epinions.com`	Product reviews
GreenBook	`www.greenbook.org`	Directory of market research groups
PlanetFeedback	`www.planetfeedback.com`	Complaint site
Ratings.net	`www.ratings.net`	Product reviews
Shopzilla.com (part of BizRate.com)	`http://merchant. shopzilla.com/ oa/registration`	Vendor ratings
Tremor	`www.tremor.com`	Teen opinion site
Splat! (dmoz)	`www.splatsearch. com/directory/ Consumer_ Information.html`	Directory of opinion/ review sites
Streetwise	`www.streetwise.com/ indexnew.php`	Teen/young adult opinion site

One caveat: Don't do the talking yourself. Internet users have pretty good spin detectors. They can tell whether an actual customer wrote a review or your marketing department did. Instead, ask satisfied customers or clients if they would mind posting their comments on one of these sites, or give you permission to post it in their name.

Posting existing testimonials elsewhere is an easy way to leverage their power. You could offer a small token of your appreciation or a discount coupon to thank good customers for their business and their time.

Buzzing with Press Releases

Unlike the previous categories of online buzz, press releases aren't a form of two-way communication or consumer-generated content. However, they do build interest online when repeated on multiple sites, thus conveying information in a very cost-effective manner. Figure 7-2 shows how a site (AHAnews.com) displays press releases from other sources.

Whenever your company appears on a third-party site or a journalist writes about your site, you gain relevance and credibility from an objective source. You're working on your 15 minutes of fame!

Figure 7-2:
AHAnews.com, a summary news site owned by the American Hospital Association, collates industry news for its readers' convenience.

Courtesy American Hospital Association

Search engines love press releases almost as much as they love blogs. Because they often appear on popular sites, like Yahoo! News and Google News, press releases earn "extra points" with inbound links to your site. Use keywords in the headline or lead sentence to make it even likelier that your rank in search engine results rises.

Of course, you can also post your press release on your own site, perhaps on your Media Room page, along with coverage that you receive.

Online press releases have two audiences:

✔ Like traditional press releases, online press releases run through an intermediary audience of editors or journalists who decide whether to place your headline and link on their site and/or reproduce the information in a print publication.

✔ Many sites now automatically publish press releases from specific distribution sources (that is, they accept an electronic feed) without human review. In this case, your target audience becomes the immediate consumer of your release.

Online readers rarely see the complete release at first glance. They see only the headline and perhaps the *lead* (first line) or a summary. Because you must convince them to click through to the full release, writing an effective release becomes doubly tricky.

Writing an effective release

The principles of writing for the Web, covered in Chapter 4, apply to writing press releases as well. As always, be sure that you:

✔ Keep it short. Four hundred words is a good, maximum length.

✔ Include a dateline with the city and day of release.

✔ Use active voice.

✔ Write an intriguing headline that's no more than ten words long.

✔ Write a lead that hooks your readers and makes them want to read more.

✔ Cover the *who, what, why, where, when,* and *how* basics of journalism.

✔ Conclude with a standard *cut* paragraph (a descriptive paragraph that can easily be deleted for space) about your company.

✔ Spell check and proofread your work.

✔ Test all links before posting. Use as many links as allowed, taking readers to pages with additional detail about the topic of the release, not just to your home page.

✔ Include a contact name, phone number, and e-mail address for additional information.

✔ At the end of your release, type **###** or **-30-** to designate "finished."

Figure 7-3 shows a good press release from the American Dietetic Association at EatRight.org. Note the contact information, dateline, search terms in the headline, and journalism basics in the first paragraph. For additional information on preparing a good press release, try `http://advertising.about.com/od/pressreleases/a/pressreleases_2.htm` or `www.publicityinsider.com/release.asp`.

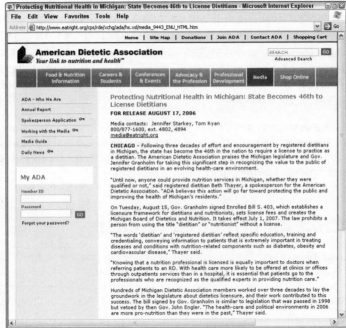

Figure 7-3: This press release from the American Dietetic Association is a good example to follow. They have a creative domain name, too!

Courtesy of the American Dietetic Association

Distributing your release

Because press releases are marketing materials, you must consider your target market. Depending on your topic and audience, a good distribution network might include both online and offline outlets, including:

✔ Web-only sites

✔ Newspapers

✔ Radio, cable, and broadcast TV

✔ Journalists who write about your subject

  ✔ Nontraditional media outlets (for example, text messaging)

  ✔ Publications specific to a particular industry (sometimes called a *vertical market*)

  ✔ General magazines

If you already have a public relations or advertising agency, they can help you with writing and distribution. Otherwise, you can decide whether you're looking for B2C or B2B outlets or both, and whether you want local, regional, national, or international distribution. It all depends on how large a megaphone you want.

While you can distribute a release yourself, especially to local press, it's much easier to select an online distribution network that can target the industry sector(s) you want. You can use the free or low-cost distribution networks listed among the examples in Table 7-5. Rates, formatting, and other requirements vary by network, so you need to select one that fits your budget as well as your needs. Ask whether you can add your own existing list of journalists, trade industry publications, and Web sites that accept press releases. What? You don't have an existing list? Start one now.

Table 7-5	Sample Press Release Distribution Networks and Resources	
Name	*URL*	*Free (Y/N)*
Business Wire	http://home.businesswire.com	N
click2newsites.com (announcements)	www.click2newsites.com/press.asp	Y
eMediaWire	www.emediawire.com	N
Eworldwire	www.eworldwire.com	N
Internet News Bureau	www.internetnewsbureau.com	N
Market Wire	www.marketwire.com	N
PR Free (part of Eworldwire.com)	www.prfree.com	Y (prices vary with service level)
PrimeZone	www.primezone.com	N
PR Newswire	www.prnewswire.com	N
PR Web (part of eMediaWire)	http://prweb.com	N (prices vary with service level)

Schedule your release based on its time dependence and when your target audience will be available to view it. Because many releases arrive in journalists' inboxes through Real Simple Syndication (RSS is discussed in Chapter 13) or e-mail, you might want to schedule date-independent releases as you would a B2B newsletter: Tuesdays or Wednesdays, either early in the morning or midday.

Your release might have a life well after your initial distribution. Print outlets might publish your release anywhere from several days to several months after you distribute it. Be sure the contact information will still be good! For more information about working with the press, check out the Internet Press Guild at www.netpress.org/careandfeeding.html.

Buzzing with Inbound Link Campaigns

Links from other sites to yours not only yield visits from prequalified prospects, but also enhance your search engine ranking. Google, in particular, factors the quantity and quality of inbound links into search engine results. (See Chapter 10.) Good link campaigns are time consuming but valuable for every Web site seeking new business. They're critical for B2B companies, which usually derive more traffic from Google than they do from other search engines.

When you request a link, you have something to offer in return: a link back, which is called a *reciprocal* link.

Some Web sites might charge for links. If they charge what seems like a lot of money, shift them to your paid advertising category. In addition to links from search engines and all the types of sites listed in this chapter, you can obtain free and often nonreciprocal links from these sources:

- ✔ Industry-based business directories.
- ✔ Yellow Pages and map sites.
- ✔ Local business directories.
- ✔ Colleagues.
- ✔ Trade associations.
- ✔ Other organizations you belong to or sponsor.
- ✔ Suppliers, including your Web development company and host.
- ✔ Distributors, clients, customers, or affiliates (ask!).
- ✔ Award, What's New, and "hot/cool" sites, such as CoolSiteoftheDay.com; others are listed in Chapter 6.

✔ Sites to which you contribute content. (See sites like www.mycontent
   builder.com or www.isnare.com for content distribution, or search
   for e-zine directories like www.zinos.com/f/z/author_signup.html
   or www.zinebook.com.)

✔ Sites that list you as an expert (for example, www.prleads.com or
   http://experts.mediamap.com).

✔ Related, but not directly competing businesses.

Evaluating your link popularity

Link popularity, a count of how many sites link to you, measures your visibility on the Web. Links are search engine specific, so only other sites that index
by the same engine appear on the list of inbound links. Start by using one of
the link checkers listed in Table 7-6, or enter *link:www.yourdomain.com* into
the search field of a target search engine. (Some search engines prefer *linkdo-
main:www.yourdomain.com.*)

Table 7-6	Inbound Link Resources	
Name	*URL*	*What You'll Find*
Alexa	www.alexa.com	Link checker and list of related sites for target domain
AllSearch Engines.com	www.allsearchengines.com	Directory of search engines
Arelis	www.axandra-link-popularity-tool.com/screenshots.htm	Link finding and management software (fee)
ClickZ Network	www.clickz.com/showPage.html?page=resources/search_reference/linking	Tips on link campaigns
Link Popularity	http://linkpopularity.com	Link checker for Google, MSN, and Yahoo!
Marketleap	www.marketleap.com/publinkpop	Link checker for multiple engines

(continued)

Table 7-6 *(continued)*

Name	URL	What You'll Find
NeboWeb	`www.neboweb.com/ eMarketing101/ Internet_Marketing_ Inbound_Link_Checker. aspx`	Tips on link campaigns
Newslink	`http://newslink.org/ searchw.html`	List of meta-indexes
WebWorkshop	`www.webworkshop.net/ inbound-links.html`	Tips on link campaigns
Webmaster Toolkit	`www.webmaster-toolkit. com/link-popularity- checker.shtml`	Link checker for multiple engines
Zeus	`www.cyber-robotics. com/index.htm`	Link finding and management software (fee)

You might discover that other sites have linked to yours without your knowledge, which is usually okay. You'll also find that Google usually displays far fewer inbound links than other search engines. That's partly because Google, which indexes itself and dmoz, has tight constraints on sites that it values as inbound links. You find more about selecting links specifically for Google in Chapter 10. Figure 7-4 shows a partial page of inbound links on Google for Snow.com.

You get different results for the number of inbound links by entering the URL with and without www, so try both and compare. Unless your developer forces all URLs to appear one way or the other, your inbound link count might be divided between the two versions of your domain name. This might make your link popularity appear lower than it really is. For more information and a solution, have your developer read the article at `www.netmechanic.com/ news/vol8/promo_no4.shtml`.

Implementing a link campaign

When putting together your link campaign, try for at least 50 inbound links, which you request by e-mail or submit by hand. The more links the merrier, as long as they're from valid sites. Follow these steps:

Screenshots © Google Inc. and are reproduced with permission.

Figure 7-4:
The link report for Snow.com shows inbound links from other, high-ranking sites listed by Google. The upper-right corner displays the total inbound links to this site.

1. **Start your hunt for inbound links.**

   Enter one of your keywords in an engine like Google to see which sites appear at the top of search engine results. Then run an inbound link check for the top two or three sites to get a list of possible targets.

2. **Run an inbound link popularity report on several of your competitors to get ideas.**

3. **Research the sources for free links in the bulleted list in a preceding section, as well as other search engines, business directories, and meta-indexes.**

   Meta-indexes are sites with master lists of directories.

   You can research links while your site is under development, but don't make any requests until the site is live.

4. **Visit each site to make sure it's relevant and that your target audience would visit.**

That way, any traffic referred is prequalified.

5. **Look for directions such as Add your URL to see whether to request a link by e-mail or fill out a form on the target site.**

   You might need to look at the footer or site index to find out how to add your link.

6. **When you're ready, start your link requests. Blind copy 30 or so e-mail requests to save time, using a message like the one in the nearby sidebar. Put your Web site name and link request in the subject line.**

   If you're willing to offer a reciprocal link or if you already have a good, Google page rank or significant traffic, add that to your message.

7. **Submit onsite requests manually.**

   Some sites ask only for the URL; others ask for a page title, description, keywords, contact information, or more.

8. **Do your follow-up homework. Check your e-mail for responses from Web sites.**

   Some responses ask you to confirm that you're a real person by asking you to click a link or e-mail back. Others might request reciprocal links before they post yours. Only a small fraction of your link requests are likely to respond.

9. **After six to eight weeks, check to see which links have posted. Make a second polite request and check again after another two months.**

   If a site still hasn't posted your link after two months, find a substitute.

Unless you request otherwise, most inbound sites link to your home page. If your site is segmented by target market or product, segment your requests for inbound links to match. Provide the URL for the correct internal page rather than for your home page. Most sites post your link on their own Links or Resources pages. From a search engine point of view, links from other content pages usually carry greater value.

Supplying the HTML code makes it easy for Webmasters to copy and paste your link onto a page. The code that follows opens your site in a new window when clicked. The URL after www is the exact landing page where you want visitors to arrive. The text between > and </a> is what appears on the screen.

```
<a href="http://www.yourdomain.com"
        target="_blank">YourDomainName.com or company
        name</a>
```

If the site will take it, offer a graphic logo link as an option in your e-mail request. Ask your developer to write the code. She can give you a file to attach to the e-mail or post a small logo on your site for link purposes.

Link campaigns involve a lot of detail. To keep track, create a spreadsheet to track your efforts, with columns for these details:

- ✔ Site name
- ✔ Appearance URL
- ✔ Submission URL or e-mail address
- ✔ Date of submission
- ✔ URL of page you asked others to link to
- ✔ Whether a reciprocal link or payment is needed
- ✔ Date link was checked

To make your life easier, purchase software like Arelis, which I mention in Table 7-6, or look for a search engine optimization (SEO) consultant or online marketing company to find links and manage your link campaign.

Understanding the difference between nice links and naughty ones

Some search engines count every link, regardless of its source. However, Google and others have criteria for legitimate links. (In Chapter 10, I discuss other criteria that Google uses to establish ranking in search results.)

A "nice" link comes from a site that

- ✔ Is on the same search engine as yours.
- ✔ Shares at least one keyword or search term with yours.
- ✔ Has text content on the page, not just links. It's fine if the text consists merely of one-line link annotations.

There is both a gray market and a black market for selling links to enhance search engine ranking. Avoid the temptation. The links offered probably don't qualify as "nice" in the first place.

Most "naughty" links aren't evil, but they don't do you much good because some search engines ignore them. Avoid the following:

- ✔ *Link farms* that randomly link thousands of sites. Sometimes called *free-for-all* (FFA) sites, these can get you bounced from search engines. (Okay, these sites are close to evil.)

✔ Sites with more than 50–60 links per page.

✔ Web alliances or rings of related sites that exchange links among the members of the group.

✔ Link exchanges that automatically arrange links between two sites instead of allowing two individual companies to establish reciprocity. Because the offered links frequently come from totally unrelated sites, these automated exchanges might be a waste of time. Usually, you must post two links for every one you receive.

Following external and reciprocal link protocol

It's become standard operating procedure to have a page for external links (sometimes called *outbound links*) on your Web site. Often named Links or Resources, this page displays reciprocal links and/or convenient links to sites with additional information.

Google, which incorporates outbound links as part of its algorithm for ranking search engine results, prefers sites whose outbound links demonstrate a broad relation to cyberspace. The better structured your own links page, the better the offer you can make when you request a reciprocal link from others. Try to follow these principles, which are visible on the links page for HeartSmartOnline.com in Figure 7-5:

Sample link request e-mail

Dear Colleague,

I am requesting a link on behalf of YourDomain.com, a new online gallery that focuses on highly collectible and one-of-a-kind pieces by renowned artists and artisans. We offer serious art lovers and collectors the opportunity to acquire unique contemporary art. The site contains artist biographies, an explanation of art media, and a calendar of statewide art events and studio tours.

I believe our site would appeal to the same audience that visits yours. Please consider adding a link to `www.YourDomain.com` on your site. I would appreciate your letting me know whether you are accepting new links, and/or when the link has posted.

For your convenience, I have provided a title, description, and keywords below, as well the code for an HTML text link.

Thank you for your time and consideration.

Signature Block

✔ Limit the number of external links to 50–60 per page. If you have more than that, organize them by topic and start another page.

✔ Put one line of text below each link to summarize its content.

✔ Include some .edu (educational), .gov (government), or .org (not-for-profit) sites among your outbound links, even if they don't link back to you. Adding objectivity and credibility, these links generate good will among your customers and extra value toward Google's search engine ranking.

Links from your site that originate on a regular text page are even more valuable to offer, but they don't draw visitors away from your message and calls to action. Think about internal HTML pages where outbound links might appear without distraction, such as testimonials, success stories, client lists, or lists of retailers.

Generally, you can link to another site without obtaining permission, as long as the other site appears independently. Occasionally, you'll come across a site such as Forbes.com that requires permission. (Use the request form on their site.) This is unlikely, except with large corporations. If you aren't sure whether you can link, look around a large Web site for the media, legal, or public relations sections for directions.

Figure 7-5:
The annotated page of outbound links on HeartSmart Online.com connects users to many .org and .gov sites.

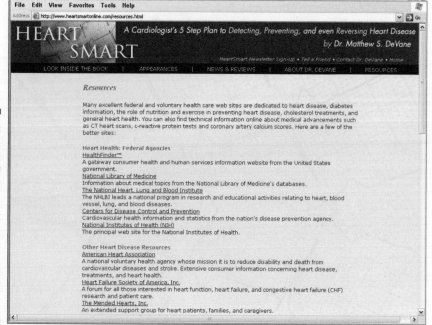

Courtesy Matthew S. Devane

Don't open other sites within a frame on your site without prior permission. (Frames aren't search engine friendly — you shouldn't use them anyway.) Don't in any other way make it appear that someone else's content belongs to you.

Some external sites might refuse to link unless your link page is accessible from the navigation, not just from other pages. That's your call. It's easy to include a Links page in your site index at the beginning of the development process. If the page is an afterthought, decide whether it's worth the cost and hassle to modify the navigation.

Ask your developer to always open external links in a new window, preferably smaller than the main window. That way, your site remains visible on the screen and users can return to it without using the back arrow.

After you start a link campaign, your inbox might fill with requests from other sites asking you to link to them. Evaluate each one strategically for the value the link brings, such as a high Google page rank or your target audience. You're under no obligation to post other links unless you have promised reciprocity.

Be leery of requests from sites that ask visitors to vote on your site popularity, that charge for links, or that otherwise get you in trouble with search engines. Some of these are truly scams, coming back afterwards to ask for payment, like fake Yellow Page bills sent in the mail.

Chapter 8

The Art of E-Mail Marketing

More than 2.5 trillion e-mails flood inboxes every year. Of those, perhaps 70 percent are *spam* (unwanted, unsolicited e-mail), some filtered out and most of the rest deleted without being read. Getting prospects or customers to notice your message in the midst of this deluge takes a bit of doing. Fortunately, you can master some best practices for breaking through with e-mail messages and newsletters that generate business.

Good e-mail messages start with the right From and Subject lines and follow through with good content, links to your Web site, and calls to action. They have a purpose and, in the best of all worlds, are directed to a specific audience. Of course, any e-mails distributed to a group go only to recipients who opt in (specifically and positively say they want to receive your e-mail messages) and comply with the federal CAN-SPAM Act of 2003 (http://ftc.gov/bcp/conline/pubs/buspubs/canspam.htm).

E-mail techniques range from simple, free, signature blocks to expensive, multisegmented, newsletter campaigns, all of which I address in this chapter. You might want to check off techniques you plan to use on your Web Marketing Methods Checklist in Chapter 2. You can download that form at www.dummies.com/go/webmarketing.

Using What You Already Have: Free E-Mail Tools

In the rush to advanced technology, business owners often forget about basic, one-to-one, e-mail marketing tools. That's a shame because these tools are free with services you already have. As I explain in more detail in the text that follows, signature blocks are primarily for branding, blurbs save time offering customer support, and autoresponders help maintain a relationship with prospects or customers. All three are components of good customer service.

Branding with signature blocks

As shown in Figure 8-1, a *signature block* is the e-mail equivalent of a business card or letterhead. A signature block should appear at the bottom of *every* business e-mail you send out. A good signature block includes a marketing tag, all your contact information, and a live link to your Web site.

Jan Zimmerman
Author, <u>Web Marketing For Dummies</u>
Strategic Web Marketing & Site Management
Watermelon Mountain Web Marketing
4614 Sixth St. NW
Albuquerque, NM 87107
t: 505.344.4230
f: 505.345.4128
e: <u>info@watermelonweb.com</u>
w: <u>http://www.watermelonweb.com</u>

Figure 8-1:
A signature
block.

Your company name and marketing tag provide name recognition and branding. The block offers consistent, easy access to all your contact information, including (at a minimum) your phone, fax, street address, e-mail address, and Web site address. Some signature blocks include business hours, a link to a map, and/or a link to a current special offer or event.

Almost all e-mail programs (sometimes called *e-mail clients*), such as Outlook, Outlook Express, and Eudora, allow you to set up a signature block. In other words, signature blocks are free! To set up a signature block, look on the toolbar in your e-mail for a choice like Tools➪Options, or use the Help feature to look up instructions.

Display the Web site address in your signature block as a live link. Most e-mail programs create the link automatically if you start the URL with `http://`.

Letting autoresponders do the work

You've probably received many *autoresponder messages* without realizing it. Autoresponder messages, such as the one in Figure 8-2, are sent automatically in response to an e-mail or as part of the cycle of activity on a Web site. You set up the first type of autoresponder in your e-mail program, usually by creating a Message Rule. (See the Help feature in your e-mail program.) Out of Office messages are perhaps the most common use of this type of autoresponder.

Thank you for submitting your rebate request(s) through Staples Easy Rebates. We have received rebate information for the following product(s):

SANDISK M2 512MB CRUZER

We will begin processing your request(s) shortly. To track the status of your rebate(s), click below:
http://www.stapleseasyrebates.com/staples/Search.do?claimNumber=19841xxxx&email

For easy reference, here is the information you submitted:

Rebate Offer Number(s): 201xxxx
Easy Rebates ID number/Order number: 0780071406223xxxx
Tracking number: 19841xxxx

If you have questions about the Easy Rebates process or the content of this email, please read our Frequently Asked Questions at:
http://www.stapleseasyrebates.com/staples/SplashAction.do?action=FAQ

If you need additional assistance, please send us an email through the Easy Rebates website. This is an automated email system and we cannot respond to emails sent to this address.

Thanks for shopping Staples!

Figure 8-2:
Staples' auto-responder confirms a rebate request and links the customer to additional information.

Web-based autoresponders are often generated when users submit a form or make a purchase. These autoresponder messages are useful to:

✓ Welcome users to a newsletter, perhaps with a coupon for an initial purchase.

✓ Acknowledge a request for information or technical support.

✓ Confirm a purchase.

✓ Indicate that an item is in production or has shipped.

✔ Send a survey for feedback on customer service.

✔ Say thank you and inquire about customer satisfaction.

Because users can't reply to Web-based autoresponders, include a live e-mail address and/or phone number in your message. Simple autoresponders are usually included in a hosting package. Tell your developer what autoresponders you want to send and when. Ask her whether it's possible to personalize these autoresponders with a salutation (Dear __) that draws the user's name from a form or order.

If you need multiple, timed autoresponders, you can use shareware, purchased software, or a third-party provider's Web-based service, like the one at www.ecoursewizard.com. Given the sensitivity to spam, just don't overdo it. See www.thesitewizard.com/archive/autoresponders. shtml for more information on autoresponders.

An e-mailed autoresponder doesn't serve the same function as a Thank You page on a Web site. You still must provide immediate feedback online when users successfully submit a form or place an order.

Speeding response time with packaged blurbs

Blurbs are prepackaged e-mail responses used to respond quickly to customer requests for information. You merely supply a salutation or insert other personalized information. The 80/20 rule applies — 80 percent of the e-mail inquiries you receive cover the same 20 percent of topics. Blurbs that cover 80 percent of your e-mail responses cost nothing more than the time to write them.

Prepackaged blurbs, like the one in Figure 8-3, help you manage your inbox and respond to e-mails within one business day. Save blurbs as drafts in your e-mail program and copy them to a new message as needed. Always include a salutation (Dear __) and an invitation to call or e-mail for additional information.

While you can send blurbs as attachments, recipients are more likely to open and read simple e-mails.

Possible topics for blurbs include:

✔ Items from the Frequently Asked Questions (FAQ) section of your Web site

✔ An abbreviated corporate backgrounder

✔ Copies of recent press releases

✔ Troubleshooting replies to common problems

Subject: Your submission to abuse@comcast.net

Thank you for contacting the Comcast Network Abuse and Policy Enforcement Department.

The email that you have submitted to abuse@comcast.net does not appear to contain a Comcast IP address. The abuse@comcast.net address is only for the investigation of incidents of network abuse regarding Comcast subscribers. We've included some helpful links below for information on reporting various issues. Please review these for future reference to ensure that your submission receives the proper attention.

Please remember the following guidelines for reporting Network Abuse incidents to our department:
1. Provide a brief, general description of the network abuse incident.
2. Include all plain text logs or information relevant to the incident; ensure the logs you're submitting contain:

        a. Date of incident
        b. Time of incident and time zone
        c. Source Internet protocol (IP) address or host name
        d. Destination IP address or host name
        e. Destination port

3. For e-mail abuse i.e. Spam or virus, include full-unmodified header information and content of the email. Header information is a requirement for reporting e-mail abuse. Please note, spam "From:" addresses are usually forged, and not the actual sender's. Even though the address may contain "@comcast.net", it is only by reviewing the full headers that the message can be verified as originating from the Comcast High Speed network.

        For more information on reporting Spam to Comcast:
        http://www.comcast.net/help/faq/index.jsp?faq=SecuritySpam17785

        For more information on reporting Abuse to other ISPs:
        http://www.comcast.net/help/faq/index.jsp?faq=SecurityAbuse17574

        More information on the topic of network security (Spam, virus, etc.):
        http://www.comcast.net/help/faq/index.jsp?cat=Security

Figure 8-3:
This blurb from Comcast was received in response to an inquiry about spam.

If you would like to speak to someone by telephone concerning your submission and how to proceed with it, please call 856-317-7272 and leave a voicemail with your name, and contact information. The Network Abuse and Policy Observance team will respond to all voicemails within 24 hours.

Thank you for your time and consideration in this matter.
Comcast Network Abuse and Policy Observance

Getting the Most Out of E-Mail Messages

Chapter 6 notes, "Marketing is only part of a business, but all of a business is marketing." That includes e-mail correspondence with your customers.

Ignore the marketing value of the messages you send to prospects, customers, vendors, and others at your peril. Your time-critical messages might end up in someone's deleted mail folder, lost, forlorn, and unread. They could be so poorly written that they turn off the recipient, or they could have such large attachments that the recipient's e-mail program discards them as spam.

Only send attachments over 100K to people you know can receive them. Ask before you e-mail. As alternatives, you can post the material on your Web site and send your recipient a link, or (gasp!) fax the documents.

E-mailing like a pro

Here are some other points to keep in mind when composing e-mail messages:

✔ **From line:** The From line is the very first criterion recipients use when deciding whether to open a message. That makes your e-mail address into a marketing decision. Select something that customers will recognize, such as your full name, or a phrase like *CustomerService@yourcompany.com*.

At this point, almost every Web host offers free e-mail addresses with your Web domain name (*@yourdomain.com*), which you should use for branding and name recognition. You can access these addresses directly through your e-mail program or have them forwarded to your regular e-mail account. Your developer or host can help you set these up.

To appear professional, don't display or reply from your regular Internet service provider (ISP) e-mail account (for example, @AOL, @Hotmail, or @Comcast) or send business e-mail with advertisements. Most e-mail programs allow you to define the From address that displays in a recipient's inbox. If you have any difficulty, ask your ISP.

✔ **Subject line:** Recipients use the Subject line as their second criterion in the ruthless game of toss or read. Be succinct and factual; this isn't the place for cute tricks. Keep your subject line to less than 50 characters, which is the maximum length of the standard subject display.

If your e-mail address doesn't include your company name or function, put it in the subject line: *Your Tech Support Reply ABC Products*. If appropriate, put an event name or meeting date in the subject line.

✔ **Message text:** In the text itself, quickly identify yourself, the nature of your relationship with the recipient (or who referred you), and the purpose of your message. Also, keep your messages businesslike in appearance.

Save the fancy fonts and bright colors for your personal e-mail. If you include a small logo, remember that some people suppress images in e-mail. All these directives hold true for autoresponders and blurbs as well as for e-mail messages.

E-mail messages, autoresponders, and blurbs are standard forms of business correspondence. Always check them for clarity, formatting, spelling, and other essentials of good writing. Send them to yourself or others to test that they look right in different e-mail clients. Put the most important information at the top in case someone views messages in preview mode.

It's a good idea to keep separate accounts for your business and personal e-mails. Many people keep a third e-mail identity for newsletters and other correspondence from Web sites they've given their e-mail address to.

Sending bulk or group e-mail

The e-mail techniques discussed so far in this chapter all deal with one-on-one marketing. Bulk e-mail is a free technique that lets you send e-mail to small groups of users who share a common interest.

It's an easy, but rather old-fashioned, alternative to sending a special newsletter to a small subset of your mailing list. Real Simple Syndication (RSS) or text messaging are more contemporary options that I address in Chapter 13. Group e-mail is useful for such things as:

✔ Notifying registrants in a course, conference, program, or other event

✔ Communicating with dealers, distributors, or franchisees

✔ Sending routine service reminders or product recalls

✔ Reminding customers of appointments or item pickups

✔ Distributing information to journalists

✔ Communicating with committees, board members, or employees

✔ Announcing availability of products on back order

The simplest setup for bulk e-mail is to create a *Group* in your e-mail program and add addresses to it. Instead of entering individual names in the address field of the message, you enter the name of the Group. (See the Help feature of your e-mail program for details.)

Because of concerns about spam, some ISPs don't let you send bulk e-mails to more than 50–100 names. To get around this limitation, you can buy inexpensive software to handle bulk mail. Here are a few suggestions to get you started:

Software Name	URL
LmhSoft e-Campaign	www.lmhsoft.com
G-Lock EasyMail	www.glocksoft.com/em
GroupMail	www.group-mail.com/asp/common/default.asp

For more options, search for *group e-mail software*. As a cheaper solution, consider using free Yahoo! Groups (http://groups.yahoo.com) or Google Groups (http://groups.google.com). Unfortunately, both these programs include third-party advertisements in the e-mails that participants receive.

Rolling Out E-Mail Newsletters

Offering deals on the latest digital cameras? Directions for cooking with organic beets and carrots? Perhaps, last-minute tax tips? Suggestions for stain removal? The latest news on the Rockabilly Roller Derby? The buzz on what Carrie told Mary, who left Barry, who used to be with Gary on a soap opera?

Whatever their interests, passions, or buying habits, consumers can sign up for e-mail newsletters to sate their desires. As an e-mail marketer, you must find the people who want your special offers, hot gossip, or the latest news delivered to their electronic doorstep; get them to sign up for your distribution service; and then encourage them to follow through with a click to your site. The informational newsletter from Staffing Advisors (an HR consulting firm) in Figure 8-4 illustrates how a service company can use a newsletter to build relationships with prospects.

Compared to other forms of online advertising, online newsletters have a fairly high, *click-through rate* (CTR), which is the percent of people who see an ad and click through to the Web site. While banner ads routinely draw about 1 percent of viewers to a site, online newsletters average 5–6 percent. To be successful, you need a good newsletter that's sent to the right audience at the right time.

E-mail is on its way o-u-t among the young! If you're aiming at a demographic less than 25 years old, e-mail might be too old-fashioned for marketing communication. For this population, use social networking and blogging (see Chapter 7) or instant messaging and text messaging (see Chapter 13).

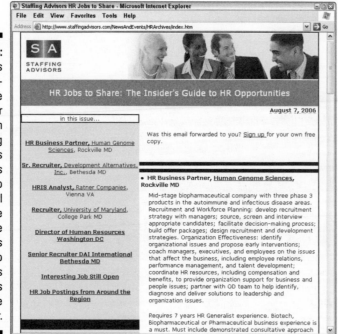

Figure 8-4:
This information-intensive newsletter from Staffing Advisors includes links to additional text online and a table of contents to the left to link readers to sections of the newsletter.

Courtesy Staffing Advisors

Improving the efficacy of your newsletter

The more targeted your newsletter and its audience, the more likely it will be successful. Before creating and distributing each issue of your newsletter, define its objective and its target audience. Is it to make sales? If so, what segment of your customers are interested in the products you display? Figure 8-5 shows a product-driven newsletter from RunBargains.com that targets cost-conscious runners. Each item links directly to its corresponding product detail page with a Buy button. (Men's and women's shoes are on separate detail pages.)

If you're moving a prospect along the sales cycle, for example, you want to provide the information customers need next to make a purchasing decision. Or if you're trying to recover customers you haven't heard from in a while, provide an offer that will bring them back.

Another consideration is whether you eventually want to accept advertising or paid sponsorships for your newsletter. That decision affects your newsletter design and implementation.

Courtesy RunBargains.com

Figure 8-5:
Run
Bargains.
com uses its
monthly
newsletters
to promote
sales items
and other
special
deals.

Watching statistics related to your newsletter objective is just as important as watching statistics on your Web site. If the purpose of your newsletter is branding, track growth in the number of subscribers. If your purpose is sales, measure sales conversion rate and profitability.

A few terms of the trade define what success means. A good newsletter service provides the following statistics on the bounce rate, the open rate, the unsubscribe rate, the click-through rate, and A/B testing. Read on for more information on measuring your newsletter's success.

Bounce rate

Bounce rate is the percent of addresses that aren't deliverable for various reasons. Most services provide a breakdown. Review the list of bounces for typos and poorly formatted e-mail addresses. Some list management services do this automatically before sending, and others test all addresses with a signal to confirm that addresses are valid (a process called *pinging*) prior to sending an actual e-mail. Obviously, the lower the bounce rate, the better.

Open rate

The *open rate* is the percent of *delivered mail* (that is, names sent minus bounces) that readers actually open. You can't guarantee that recipients actually read an e-mail they open, but you can count that it's been opened (clicked on and displayed in the preview box or regular window). The better your From and Subject lines, the higher your open rate. Open rates vary widely by time of delivery, by the size and source of your list, and by industry, as shown in Figure 8-6 for Bronto, an e-mail service provider. You want the open rate to be as high as possible.

Figure 8-6:
E-mail service provider Bronto reports rolling quarterly statistics on open and click-through rates for its clients by industry.

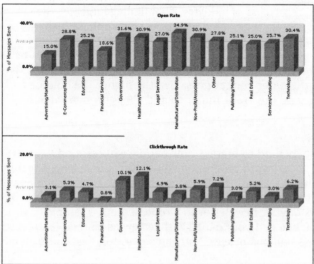

©2006 Bronto Software, Inc. All rights reserved.

Unsubscribe rate

The CAN-SPAM Act requires an option to unsubscribe in all e-mail newsletters. People usually reply by e-mail or click a link to unsubscribe. Everyone on your list should already have opted in, either online or offline. List segmentation by interest area and a *double opt-in process* (subscribers receive an e-mail asking them to confirm their registration by clicking a link; only then are they added to your distribution list) usually reduces the unsubscribe rate, though it may depress your signup rate. Again, this rate varies widely based on the quality of your list. Strive for a low unsubscribe rate.

Click-through rate

The *click-through rate* (CTR) is the number of links to your Web site divided by the number of opened newsletters. To get a higher CTR, make sure you have a good match between your newsletter and target audience, even if it means sending a different message to different segments of your list.

CTR also depends on the quality of your headline, offer, and content, and the number of links you have in your newsletter. Some newsletter services will give you two CTR rates: total clicks and clicks from unique users. Then you can tell how many readers clicked through more than once. Whatever your specific objective, you must drive your readers to your Web site to complete a purchase or to find more information. Strive for a CTR as high as possible.

An intriguing report by Vertical Response (`www.verticalresponse.com/files/www/VREmail-Trends-Q1-2006.pdf`) in 2006 showed that both open and click-through rates start to fall when lists have more than 5,000 subscribers, regardless of industry. That finding indicates the value of using smaller lists, tightly segmented by interest or purchase history.

E-mail lists age rapidly because users often change providers or abandon addresses to avoid spam. Rented and public lists are less effective than your own. Thus, the older your address list, the higher the bounce and unsubscribe rates, and the lower the open and click-through rates.

A/B testing

It's surprisingly hard to predict how people will respond to even slight changes in phrasing on promotional material. *A/B testing,* a technique drawn from direct mail marketing, allows you to analyze different elements of your newsletter to maximize effectiveness. In an A/B test, you send slightly different versions of your newsletter to a representative sample of your audience. Because you can test your e-mail with as few as 25 recipients, testing is feasible even for small businesses. You can separately test these elements:

- ✔ From line
- ✔ Subject line
- ✔ Headline
- ✔ Product selection
- ✔ Offer

Change only one element at a time! If you don't control the variables, you can't distinguish which element accounts for the results you get.

Creating an effective newsletter

Like everything else in Web marketing, creating a good newsletter can take more time than you expect. Allow a learning curve, starting out with a slower schedule than you might eventually adopt.

Your newsletter must comply with the CAN-SPAM Act of 2003, legislation passed by Congress to reduce the burden of spam. Some states have additional antispam laws. As a result of laws — plus better filtering software — the amount of spam actually reaching users' mailboxes seems to have leveled off. Commercial template/hosting services require you to meet CAN-SPAM requirements to retain their own viability.

The From and Subject lines are key to increasing the open rate for your newsletter. In particular:

- ✔ **Don't forget branding.** Include your name, company, product and/or service (whatever readers will most recognize as your brand) in either the From or Subject line. Once established, use the From line consistently.

- ✔ **Entice the subscriber.** Insert a benefit or another reason for opening the message in the subject line. You're more likely to get a response to an e-mail titled *November Savings from Your Company* than one titled *Monthly News from Your Company.* Of course, *Free* always works: *Free 2 for 1 Dinner Coupon Until 9/30.*

- ✔ **Be honest.** Don't trick people into opening your e-mail with a misleading subject line. An accurate subject line is actually a legal requirement.

- ✔ **Create a sense of urgency.** Incorporate time-dependent phrases or other words of urgency to encourage opening your newsletter promptly: the name of the month, *this week*, *now*, *important recall notice*, *exclusive offer*.

- ✔ **Don't overdo it.** Avoid using punctuation in the subject line, especially exclamation points. Don't use all capital letters either; they trigger spam filters.

- ✔ **Keep it short.** Keep the subject line to 50 characters, including spaces.

The length of your newsletter should vary according to its purpose and audience. An informational newsletter, for example, might be longer than one designed to drive customers to your site to buy. Place an internally linked table of contents at the top of a long newsletter to take readers directly to articles of interest.

Just as with your Web site, you have only a few seconds to catch your reader's attention and answer the question: "What's in it for me?" Try to use a headline that grabs attention. Users who scan their e-mail in a preview pane might see only several inches of material on the screen. Keep the most important information at the top, before any scrolling is needed. In other words, shorter is better.

When putting together your newsletter, follow the same design and writing principles that you would use for a page on your Web site (see Chapter 4):

- ✔ **Emphasize your brand.** Include your logo and/or header graphic for branding purposes in a consistent manner.

- ✔ **Use small photos.** Make sure to resize your photos for the Web so they download quickly.

- ✔ **Accommodate subscribers that use text-only e-mail.** Provide vivid descriptions as an alternative to photos because users might suppress image delivery in e-mail.

✔ **Provide relevant content.** Match your content to your audience. You can get better results if you segment a large address list and send somewhat different versions of your newsletter based on interest area or past purchase history than if you try to make one newsletter do everything.

Use teaser lines or incomplete paragraphs with links to the appropriate pages of your Web site. That's far better than putting too much information in the newsletter. In fact, your newsletter should have at least 15 assorted links to your site, some of which are for content or products and some of which are for best practice functions I describe in the upcoming "Following best practices" section.

Links should take viewers as close to the desired call to action as possible. For instance, link a promotion to its product detail page to prompt subscribers to purchase an item. The newsletters in both Figures 8-4 and 8-5 demonstrate these concepts.

Selecting a method of distribution

Options for creating your newsletter are much like those for creating a Web site. Your choice depends on ease of use, cost, the size of your mailing list, and the skills of your support staff. Here's a rundown of your distribution options:

✔ **Ask your Web developer to set things up.** She can design an HTML template that allows you to change content for each issue. Developers can set up your Web site to collect subscribers' e-mail addresses and arrange with the hosting company to provide list management services. Be sure to include these tasks in your RFP (request for proposal) if you want this alternative.

✔ **Use a one-stop solution that offers templates, list management, and distribution.** ConstantContact.com, whose template site is shown in Figure 8-7, offers that type of solution. For small companies, this is generally the easiest and least-expensive approach. These third-party solutions generally require that your developer place a small piece of code on your site that links to your signup page. After that, you handle everything from third-party servers. Examples of other one-stop newsletter sources appear in Table 8-1.

✔ **Purchase HTML Web template software and arrange for list management services on your own.** This solution generally works for larger companies that need more-sophisticated options and have the technical support staff to implement them. Examples of these sources are listed in Table 8-2.

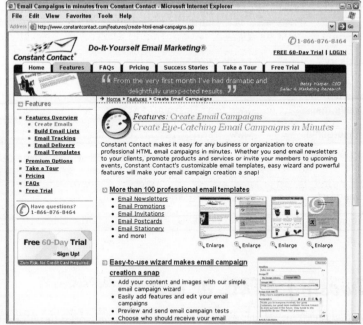

©1996–2006 Roving Software, Inc. d/b/a Constant Contact. All rights reserved. Reprinted with permission from Constant Contact.

Figure 8-7: Constant Contact offers one-stop, template-based newsletters, list management, and distribution.

Table 8-1	Sample Providers of E-Mail Template/Hosting Solutions
Name	**URL**
About.com	http://onlinebusiness.about.com/od/emailmarketing/tp/emailsoftware.htm
Benchmark	www.benchmarkemail.com
Constant Contact	www.constantcontact.com
eNews Builder	www.enewsbuilder.com/ot3/features.cfm
Graphic Mail	www.graphicmail.com
Vertical Response	www.verticalresponse.com

The success of your newsletter is 40 percent due to finding the right audience, 40 percent due to the right offer, and 20 percent due to the design (the newsletter content and appearance).

Table 8-2	Sample Providers of List Management Services
Name	*URL*
Listserv	`http://lists.gurus.com/listserv.html`
Lyris	`www.lyris.com`
Mailermailer	`www.mailermailer.com`
Majordomo	`www.greatcircle.com/majordomo`
Net Atlantic	`www.netatlantic.com/products/mailing lists/index.html`
SparkList	`http://sparklist.com`
Topica	`www.topica.com/solutions/direct.html`

Choosing HTML or text

Because HTML newsletters contain graphics, icons, and different fonts, they're more visually appealing than plain text. Because they're slower to load, some users with slow connections might suppress photos or elect text-only e-mail. Others might block HTML e-mail to protect against viruses. As broadband use expands, HTML newsletters are becoming more prevalent. Your best bet is to offer both and compare the open and click-through rates for the two versions.

Following best practices

E-mail represents an increasing percentage of online advertising spending. With that emphasis, e-mail companies have studied best practices to get a high CTR while complying with all the legal requirements of the CAN-SPAM Act. Be sure to do the following ("required" designates a legal obligation):

Best practices that you're legally obligated to follow:

✔ Include your company's street address — not a PO box — and phone number in your newsletter.

✔ Include a link or live e-mail address to unsubscribe or opt out. You have ten days to remove opt-out addresses from your lists.

✔ Provide a link to your privacy policy. Don't share your lists with a third party unless you give notice to subscribers and obtain consent from them.

Best practices that create a customer-friendly or quality newsletter:

- ✔ As always, proofread everything, including the From and Subject lines, and test all links.

- ✔ Send preview copies of both HTML and text copies to yourself and others.

- ✔ Tell people how often the newsletter will arrive and when.

- ✔ Provide a place for subscribers to indicate their name, areas of interest, job title, or type of newsletter they want (for example, event or sale announcements, discounts, product news), especially if you have more than one newsletter. However, require only a few fields in this subscriber profile; too long a signup form discourages subscribers.

- ✔ Include a link that allows subscribers to change their profiles easily.

Best practices for marketing purposes and growing the list:

- ✔ Send your e-mail only to the people who have agreed to receive it. When feasible, use a double opt-in process (which I discuss in more detail in the previous "Unsubscribe rate" section).

- ✔ Include a link to forward the e-mail newsletter to a subscriber's friend or colleague.

- ✔ Provide a direct link to the Subscribe page for people who've received a forwarded e-mail. This is especially important as a call to action in a newsletter sent to a rented list of e-mail addresses (rental list). The meta-purpose of a newsletter sent to a rental list is to get those names on *your* list.

- ✔ Right above the subscription form on your Web page, restate your privacy policy and benefits of subscribing, such as advance notice of new products or sales, or tips for product use.

- ✔ Post sample newsletters on your Web site for potential subscribers to preview.

- ✔ Save testimonials that praise your newsletter. Get permission to post them on your subscription page.

- ✔ Send a welcome message to new subscribers; include a coupon (promotion code) if appropriate. Remember to update your online store with the promo code and its start and end dates.

Deciding on timing and frequency

Companies have researched the best day and time for newsletter distribution, and results fluctuate by industry, time of year, audience, and size of list. The data for Q1 2006 from one e-mail provider, eROI, is shown in Figure 8-8.

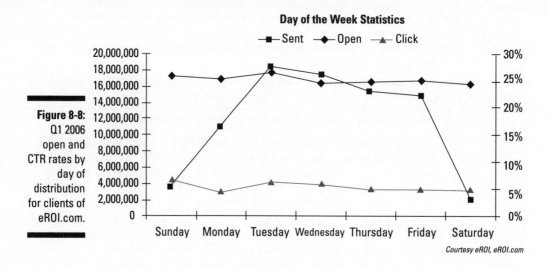

Courtesy eROI, eROI.com

Figure 8-8: Q1 2006 open and CTR rates by day of distribution for clients of eROI.com.

Here are some frequency guidelines for B2B and B2C newsletters:

- ✔ **B2B:** In general, B2B newsletters do best on Tuesdays and Wednesdays. Distribute them early in the morning so that they're near the top of the inbox when workers arrive or at midday when workers often try to catch up on e-mail.

  No across-the-board averages matter more than your own experience. Review your own site statistics for the most popular time of day and day of the week for visitors to your site. (See Chapter 14 for more on Web statistics.)

- ✔ **B2C:** B2C newsletters typically get higher open and click-through rates before or after the workday — if people are logging in from home. Because the highest volume of e-mails are sent Tuesday through Thursday, you might find a higher open rate for B2C e-mails sent on Friday or over the weekend, simply because your message has less competition. Experiment to see what's best for you. Remember, many people research purchases from home on the weekend but wait until Monday or Tuesday to make their actual purchase from work.

The ideal frequency of mailings depends on your audience and the purpose of your newsletter. Recipients don't like being flooded with messages from a single source unless they receive time-critical news (for example, drug alerts for physicians).

Only you can decide whether you should be mailing daily, weekly, monthly, quarterly, or semiannually. If you segment your list, you can send out newsletters often but reduce the number going to any particular group of recipients.

Your audience is always the most accurate source of information. Ask them what frequency they want. Sites with more information on trends in e-mail use and additional resources are listed in Table 8-3.

Table 8-3	Newsletter Resources	
Name	**URL**	**What You'll Find**
About.com	`http://onlinebusiness.about.com/od/email marketing`	E-mail resources
Bronto	`http://bronto.com/solutions/resources`	Trend analysis, e-mail resources
Direct Marketing Association	`www.the-dma.org/channels/internet.shtml`	E-mail resources
DoubleClick	`www.doubleclick.com/us/knowledge_central`	Trend analysis
EmailLabs	`www.emaillabs.com/resources/index.html`	E-mail resources
eROI	`http://eroi.com/roi_resources.htm`	Trend analysis, e-mail resources
Federal Trade Commission	`www.ftc.gov/bcp/conline/pubs/buspubs/canspam.htm`	CAN-SPAM Act
Vertical Response	`www.verticalresponse.com/files/www/VREmail-Trends-Q1-2006.pdf`	Trend analysis

Finding Subscribers for Your Newsletter

As soon as you begin planning your Web site, you should start collecting e-mail addresses. Begin with your e-mail address book: friends and family, your banker, accountant, attorney, investors, business advisors, vendors, members of local media, government officials, or other community leaders. Those in the media or government positions are obligated to communicate with the public.

As a matter of courtesy, ask the folks listed above, and any others that you add to your newsletter list, to opt in by clicking a confirmation link within your newsletter. It's helpful if the confirmation link takes the user to a screen that allows options for selecting types of e-mail (such as HTML or text) and/or choosing interest areas, just as you ask new subscribers to do.

Your e-mail address list is gold! Building a list of e-mail addresses is critical to recovering your investment in an e-mail newsletter program. Be sure to back up your address list along with other valuable files and store a copy offsite.

Mailing to customers and prospects

After you add the e-mail addresses as described in the preceding section, review your list of customers and prospects to make sure you have permission to e-mail them according to the list that follows. You might use contact management software — like ACT! (which is available at www.act.com) — or perhaps you have an Excel or other database file for print mailings.

The CAN-SPAM act allows you to send at least one e-mail to individuals who have a preexisting business relationship, such as one of these:

✔ Existing customers and clients who've purchased within the past 13 months

✔ Dealers and distributors

✔ Prospects who have requested information

✔ Respondents to a questionnaire or survey

✔ Members of professional organizations to which you belong

You must make a strategic marketing decision whether to request approval with an opt-in confirmation e-mail or to send the first issue of your newsletter with the option to unsubscribe.

Keeping your address list up-to-date

Starting a newsletter is a great opportunity to clean out and update your e-mail address list. Any e-mail addresses that have been in your database for more than a year are suspect, on the surface. Here are some ways to keep your address list up-to-date:

✔ Send a bulk e-mail to everyone in your database asking for opt-in e-mail confirmation and then delete addresses that are no longer valid.

✔ If you have a list of print addresses without e-mail, send a prepaid business reply postcard announcing your newsletter. Be sure to request opt-in permission and e-mail information on the reply card, and/or provide a click to sign up online.

Most providers of e-mail services segregate undeliverable e-mails addresses before sending your first messages, or they record them as bounces. That keeps your newsletter list up-to-date, but your base contact list might now be out of sync. You might need to delete undeliverable e-mail addresses from your source file as well.

Maintaining and grooming your list is an ongoing process. Between mailings, add new names to your list and review blocked or otherwise undeliverable ones.

What about e-mailing to that carton of business cards you collected at trade shows and networking events? If you didn't get permission to add them to a newsletter list when you acquired them, you must send a confirmation link or postcard to obtain an explicit opt-in.

Collecting new names

You can collect new e-mail addresses offline at networking events, trade shows, and whenever you have live customer contact. Verbally ask permission to send a newsletter, noting the date, event, and response. Or post a sign above the business card collection bowl saying something like "Get the latest product news and special offers! We'll add your e-mail address to our newsletter list." Sweeten the pot by also drawing from those names to receive a prize. When speaking at an event, provide a newsletter signup form asking for names and e-mail addresses.

Of course, another important place to request e-mail addresses is at your brick-and-mortar store, especially at checkout. If you aren't equipped to add an e-mail address at the register, put out a fishbowl or guestbook. And consider offering customers something free for signing up.

Take advantage of other opportunities on your Web site to collect e-mail addresses:

- Request an e-mail address when offering visitors a free case study or white paper to download; offer newsletter signup as a check box.

- Place a newsletter opt-in check box on the same form customers fill out when purchasing online.

- Put a newsletter opt-in check box on any submission form: contact us, tech support, demo, sales call, or request for quote.

Ask your developer to collect these e-mail addresses automatically in a database that you can access easily. They probably can be added to your list only if the developer has integrated the list server. If you're using a third-party solution or if the onscreen forms are e-mailed to you from the Web site, you must upload these addresses manually to your newsletter list.

Of course, there's an art to the newsletter signup form as well. Try to get more than an e-mail address, but make most fields optional. If you have a B2B company, the user's job title and company name are valuable, as well as the urgency of the need. For a B2C company, specific areas of product interest are helpful to know.

Growing a list of qualified addresses is an essential objective for any site that intends to use e-mail marketing. Make it easy for site visitors to sign up from every page by placing the call to action in the navigation. You might choose to display a simple e-mail text box or a link to a second page where there is room to display options, ask for additional information, provide a reminder of your privacy policy, and summarize the benefits of signing up. Try to word the signup navigation link to convey benefits — for example, `Sign Up for Savings` or `New Product News`.

Renting e-mail subscribers

Legitimate e-mail list brokers rent opt-in lists of both B2B and B2C audiences. These lists generally consist of magazine or e-zine subscribers, members of organizations, or people who participate in surveys and free offers in exchange for providing their e-mail. A small sample of the hundreds of list brokers is listed in Table 8-4.

Table 8-4	Sample Sources for E-Mail Address Lists	
Name	**URL**	**Paid or Free**
Ad-Site.com	`www.ad-site.com/eMailLists.php`	Paid
Business Email Lists	`www.businessemaillists.com/directory/b2b-email-newsletters.asp`	Paid
Email Marketing Blitz	`www.email-marketing-blitz.com`	Paid
L.I.S.T. Incorporated	`http://www.l-i-s-t.com/email_lists.asp?type=2`	Paid
Name-Finders	`http://namefinders.com/email_lists.html`	Paid
VentureDirect	`www.venturedirect.com/html/xactmail_emailmarketing_targetmarket.htm`	Paid
Google Groups	`http://groups.google.com/groups/dir?lnk=hpbgc`	Free, includes UseNet

Name	URL	Paid or Free
Jayde's List of Lists	`http://directory.jayde.com/ search?a=0&query=email+ lists&search=search`	Free
L-Soft CataList	`www.lsoft.com/lists/ listref.html`	Free
Tile.net	`http://tile.net/lists`	Free
Topica	`http://lists.topica.com`	Free
Yahoo! Groups	`http://groups.yahoo.com`	Free

Do *not* use lists from friends or businesses whose users weren't notified that their names could be sold, exchanged, or rented — or from disreputable brokers who offer names at a bargain rate. All you buy is trouble at a discount price.

It's worth searching for a highly targeted list. Some brokers specialize in B2B versus B2C or in certain vertical industry segments. The more targeted the list, the more you'll pay per address, just as with any other advertising audience. Estimate your costs at 10 cents per name, but prices might range from pennies to 25 cents or more. You must usually rent a minimum number of names.

In general, rental lists have lower open and click-through rates than you'll get from your own, highly prequalified list of names, so don't be surprised if success rates are half those for your own list. Run the numbers to be sure that your expected return will offset the cost of list rental and newsletter preparation. Because of the cost, you might want to do A/B testing (which I discuss earlier in this chapter) with your own list first to make sure you're sending out the best possible newsletter.

As an alternative to rental lists, you can e-mail or post a message to people who have voluntarily signed up on free public lists, including the old UseNet groups, a collection of old message boards dating back to the early days of the Internet. Google now maintains it (`http://groups.google.com/ support/bin/static.py?page=basics.html`).

While these lists are generally of much poorer quality, you don't have much to lose. Every once in a while, you might find a technical audience or people highly dedicated to a particular product.

Table 8-4 includes other places to search for lists in your subject area. If you use a free list, be sure to review the rules for allowable content. Some lists constrain the content or form of e-mails sent to members. Information about each list is available online. For more general information about how to select a mailing list, see Name-Finders at `www.namefinders.info/dmr`.

Working with a list rental house

When you rent a list of e-mail addresses, it truly is *rent.* You don't get the names. Instead, you deliver your HTML and text e-mail newsletters to the rental house. The rental house confirms that your newsletter meets its requirements, adds code to links to track open rates and CTR, and sends out a trial blast to you and several others (called *seed names*). You select the day and time for the actual e-mail blast.

When you request a particular audience, the mailing house sends you a *data card* (a page describing the detailed demographics, source, and available sorting criteria) for each possible list that meets your needs. Data cards can be a little hard to interpret, so ask plenty of questions. In addition to minimums and cost per name, you might be charged for each subselection or sort you request (for example, by zip code, gender, age, time since last purchase, and so on). Some companies also charge a transmission fee and/or a setup fee. All charges and minimums vary by broker and by list. Negotiate. When you're ready, the company will send you an *insertion order* (a form used to place an advertisement) to sign.

Besides your seed names, the e-mail house asks you for everyone who has been permanently removed from your list — to eliminate from theirs. If you want to avoid any possible duplication, you can also send names with matching profiles to remove from the list(s) you're renting. Why pay to send the same newsletter to someone who has already received it? Generally, rental houses mail to more than the number in your contract to allow for undeliverable addresses. If the number sent ends up below your contract, they do make good on request.

One of your objectives is to convert rental names to your subscribers. At the top of the newsletter you're sending to rental names, incorporate a linkable invitation to join your list. Make other text changes to accommodate the fact that these recipients, unlike your own, carefully gathered names, might never have heard of your company, products, or services.

Allow a week or more to establish an account before doing your first blast with a particular broker. That gives you time to work out any kinks in your newsletter, formatting, links, or list. After the blast, track your open rate, CTR, and other criteria. Compare them to the results of your own list. Remember that people usually need to see your brand seven times to remember you!

Third-party template newsletters can't be sent to rental houses because their newsletter code is not self-standing. You (or your developer) need to create new HTML and text versions, or you will have to pay the mailing house to create them for you.

A newsletter program can serve as an independent marketing vehicle, or it can carry another marketing effort on its back. For instance, Jack-Tar, an award-winning restaurant in coastal Massachusetts, uses its newsletter (shown in Figure 8-9) to promote a loyalty program aimed at the locals.

REAL WORLD

Appetizing e-mail

Opened in January 2004, Jack-Tar is a seaside restaurant in Marblehead, Massachusetts. Owners Andrew Kramer and Matthew O'Connor realized they couldn't survive on summer tourists alone — too many other restaurants had foundered on the very same shoals.

An independent enterprise with a relatively small marketing budget, Jack-Tar initially promoted itself with public relations and print ads in the local weekly.

A year later, the company launched the Admirals Club, a loyalty program with a menu of rewards based on when and how often customers dine. Determined to attract local residents during the off-season, the Admirals Club needed a cost-effective vehicle to reach prospective members. From the beginning, the restaurant has collected customers' e-mail addresses, so an e-mail newsletter made sense.

The company uses Constant Contact, a one-stop e-mail service provider, to send out a welcome e-mail and quarterly newsletters, which feature special promotions and menu items. The Admirals Club mailing list now has close to 1,000 subscribers, with an open rate of 43 percent and a CTR of 10 percent. About 70 percent of patrons sign up for the loyalty program. By 2006, Jack-Tar had already won multiple dining awards and reached profitability — a remarkably rapid achievement for any small business.

Figure 8-9: The newsletter from Jack-Tar, a Massachusetts restaurant, is targeted toward local customers, offering discounts as part of its loyalty program to bring back repeat diners.

Courtesy Jack-Tar American Tavern

Chapter 9

Staying Ahead of the Online Marketing Wave

- -

In This Chapter

▶ Coordinating offline marketing

▶ Planning a site launch

▶ Arranging online events

▶ Selling internationally

▶ Building an affiliate network

▶ Rewarding loyal customers

- -

Are you trying to integrate your Web site with a brick-and-mortar presence? Do you need to establish awareness of your business within your local community? Interested in exporting to Europe or Asia? Or perhaps you're looking for affiliates to refer customers to your Web site, or you're interested in matching your competition with a loyalty program that encourages repeat purchases.

Pick and choose among the elements in this chapter when your site has special needs like these. Within each category, techniques range in cost from free guerrilla marketing to expensive investments. These options might affect profit margins or require back-office support for the marketing effort.

If you select some of these methods for your Web marketing plan, mark them on the Web Marketing Methods Checklist from Chapter 2. You can download the form at www.dummies.com/go/webmarketing.

Marketing Your Online Business Offline

You have to market your domain name as much as you market your business. Most of the techniques described in this section cost nothing beyond what you already spend for graphic design and printing. Simply make sure your designer includes your URL in all graphics.

Ask your designer to provide a style guide, including capitalization and spacing, for your logo and logotype in various formats, including the following:

- ✔ Black and white
- ✔ Color
- ✔ Horizontal layouts
- ✔ Vertical layouts
- ✔ Square layouts

Also, make sure you include contextual appearance in your style guide. Establish a convention for key elements as they will appear in different situations. For example, decide whether your domain name should appear as `YourDomain.com`, `Yourdomain.com`, `yourdomain.com`, `yourDomain.com`, or `Your Domain` without the extension.

For trademark purposes, your logo and logotype must appear consistently. If you expect significant press attention, post acceptable formats online on the media kit or press pages of your site. If you've filed for trademark, place the superscript ™ to the upper right of your logo or logotype. Once granted, use ®.

Stamping your URL on everything

It goes without saying that your URL appears on your letterhead and business cards, just as it does on your signature block for e-mail. Remember to include your URL on individual documents, too, such as PowerPoint presentations, proposal footers, and white papers. Whenever you reprint other stationery items, include your URL on:

- ✔ Fax cover pages
- ✔ Presentation folders
- ✔ Order forms
- ✔ Invoices and receipts
- ✔ Warranties
- ✔ Shipping labels and packing slips
- ✔ Personalized sticky notes or notepads

The next time you print product packaging, add your URL to clothing labels, container labels, shipping cartons, boxes, shopping bags, printed tissue, ribbon, wrapping paper, caps, lids, wine corks, wrappers, ice cream sticks, and any other form of packaging you use. Wherever you place your name, include your URL. Don't forget your company vehicles, bumper stickers, and signs. Several ideas appear in Figure 9-1.

Figure 9-1: Packaging and promotional ideas cover the map. You can brand almost anything with your domain name.

Clockwise from top left: Packaging lid on coffee can courtesy Rowland Coffee Roasters. Screensweep courtesy Fone.net. Can cooler courtesy NetIDEAS, Inc. Carbiner clamp courtesy Mesalands Community College. Candy wrapper courtesy Certified Folder Display Service. Cork coaster courtesy New Mexico State University.

Look at any material you use for sales and marketing. Make sure that every item includes your URL — from catalogs, product literature, spec sheets, and other marketing collateral to instruction inserts, manuals, press releases, and corporate backgrounders. All those impressions help recipients remember your Web site.

Giving swag, bling, and freebies

Businesses spent an estimated $18 billion on promotional items and gifts in 2005, in hopes of keeping their names — and URLs — in front of clients and prospects, according to the Promotional Products Association International.

You, too, can get in on the action by including your URL with the ubiquitous, toll-free phone number on pens, pencils, T-shirts, hats, mouse pads, mirrors, mints, magnets, mugs, and more. Figure 9-1 has examples of several promotional items with URLs. You can order these items — customized with your company's URL, of course — from thousands of companies that sell promotional merchandise online (a few are listed in Table 9-1) or from a local vendor, or you can make your own at CafePress.com.

Table 9-1	Sample Companies Selling Promotional Items
Name	**URL**
4imprint	`www.4imprint.com`
Branders	`www.branders.com`

(continued)

Table 9-1 *(continued)*

Name	URL
CafePress.com	www.cafepress.com
ePromos	www.epromos.com
Gimmees	www.gimmees.com
Logo-Lites	www.logo-lites.com
NM Commission for the Blind	www.totespromote.com
Promotional Items	www.promotionpotion.com
Promotional Products Directory	www.justpromotional products.com
Promotional Rubber Bands	www.aerorubber.com/promo.htm

The cost of promotional items adds up quickly, especially for a business that needs relatively small quantities. Search for companies that provide a mix of branded items to make up the minimum order. Be sure to include the cost of promotional items and gifts in your annual marketing budget.

Think about how many items you need, how you'll distribute items — at trade shows, as thank-you or holiday gifts, as leave-behinds at a sales call — and the target audience. A plumber's URL and phone number on a potholder or flyswatter makes sense because household items are likely to be around when a plumbing emergency occurs. It wouldn't be appropriate, though, for B2B clients, where office products such as screen sweeps, flash drives, stress balls, pens, or mouse pads are a better fit.

To connect your URL to pleasant memories, give branded gifts with positive associations, such as golf balls and tees, binoculars for sports or concerts, silicon covers for iPods, or co-branded college/team/fraternity/sorority items.

Getting your name out at offline community events

Participating in community events is a great way to promote your business, particularly if you

✔ Have a local office or brick-and-mortar store.

✔ Have a local market.

✔ Want to increase presence for your online-only business within the community.

✔ Need to build credibility with local press.

✔ Seek local employees, investors, or franchisees.

You're after visibility, not anonymity, so wear gear with your company name, URL, and logo for branding. If your employees participate in such events as a run for the cure, a membership drive for public TV, and/or as hosts of one of Alex's Lemonade Stands, have them all wear branded T-shirts or hats. Remember to promote your presence at the event on your Web site, in a local press release, and on local calendar Web sites.

Most community events are inexpensive guerrilla marketing techniques, although you can expect to pay big money to have a stadium named after your Web site! Only your imagination and your target audience limit the range of community events. A local, social networking site might support a high-school soccer team; a site catering to the gay community might partici-pate in Pride parades. Other events to consider are

✔ Speaking engagements

✔ Seminars or training sessions

✔ Participation in United Way or other charitable giving campaigns

✔ Runs, walks, and parades for various causes

✔ Sports team sponsorships with your logo and URL on team shirts

✔ Participation in a Habitat for Humanity, food bank, community cleanup, or other project

Including your Web address in offline advertising

There is no added cost for including your URL in any offline advertising — radio, TV, print, or billboard. The base cost, of course, might be significant.

If you have multiple offline advertising activities, ask your developer to create a simple extension for your URL. Redirect that URL to the page with the item you're promoting, like Dell computer does for its TV ads at www.dell.com/tv. This technique allows you to compare the number of people who reach your Web site from offline ads to other Web traffic. Many people know that the extension isn't needed, but the redirect URL gives a rel-ative estimate of which offline campaigns bring the most traffic.

Going Live: Coordinating a Site Launch

The term *go live* applies to making your site visible online to the world, moving it from a development location to one that is publicly accessible. It can take 24–48 hours for a new site — or one moved to a different host — to become accessible as regional servers point to it. Build this time lag into your schedule, knowing that you might be "dark" for several days during the transition. If you are staying with the same host (with the same IP address), your developer can replace your old site with a new one in a matter of minutes.

Launch refers to a media event that draws online and offline publicity to your site. A launch effort makes sense in the following scenarios:

- ✔ You're opening a completely new business.
- ✔ You have an existing brick-and-mortar business with significant name recognition.
- ✔ You have stakeholders or investors who need or expect public recognition for the opening of the new or redesigned site.
- ✔ You have an innovative application or use new technology on a start-up or redesigned site.
- ✔ You have a good story to tell.

If you can, wait several weeks after taking a site live before driving significant traffic or scheduling a launch. Leave yourself time to retest the site, fix last-minute bugs, tweak text and product photos, and ensure that the server can handle anticipated traffic.

Launches are often tied to external events, such as a trade show, announcement of funding, or the start of a shopping season. Like offline events, your cyber ribbon-cutting might involve coordinated

- ✔ Press releases and online/offline conferences
- ✔ Well-promoted, live, kickoff events online
- ✔ Special offers and discounts for a specific time period
- ✔ Promotions for the first visitors
- ✔ Direct mail and/or e-mail campaigns
- ✔ Announcements on chat room, message board, and social network sites
- ✔ Announcements on calendars and event sites
- ✔ Placement of kiosks in your brick-and-mortar store
- ✔ Partnerships with nonprofits or suppliers to copromote your site

✔ Announcement tag lines in your e-mail signature block

✔ Online and/or offline advertising

Don't run a countdown clock or announce the date your site will open. When it comes to Web site development, anything that can go wrong, will go wrong. It might be hard to recover if your site isn't up and running well on your announced opening date.

Producing Online Events

Well-promoted, live, online events draw prequalified traffic to your site. Guest chats, author interviews, concerts, or Webcasts and Webinars (both of which are described in Chapter 13) can help you acquire leads, conduct market research, and obtain e-mail addresses as viewers sign in.

For instance, Lawyers.com operates an impressive schedule of online chats for consumers at `http://community.lawyers.com/chat/list.asp`. Microsoft publicizes its online demonstrations at `www.microsoft.com/events/webcasts/upcoming.mspx`.

Use all forms of promotion to let people know about your online event:

✔ Announce your event in many places on your Web site.

✔ E-mail announcements of the online event, and send a reminder e-mail to those who have preregistered.

✔ Find trade-related sites to announce your event.

✔ Find event sites that appeal to your target audience, such as `http://events.myspace.com/index.cfm` for live online music.

✔ List your event page in dmoz at `http://dmoz.org/cgi-bin/add.cgi?where=Arts/Music/Concerts_and_Events/Internet_Broadcasts`.

✔ Post your event on calendars maintained by trade associations, culture networks, and other event aggregators, such as `www.wisconline.com/info/promote.htm`.

✔ Use a third-party, online event registration service like Cvent.com to help promote your event.

✔ Use paid advertising or PPC (pay per click) ads to inform people of your events.

You can extract additional mileage from advertising if you produce events on a regular schedule, such as the first Thursday of each month. This might also encourage repeat visitors.

Marketing Internationally Online

It is the *World* Wide Web, after all. In barely ten years, the Web has gone from a U.S.-driven, English-dominated medium to a virtual riot of languages and international users. Global-Reach.biz estimates the population of English-speaking Internet users has dropped from 80 percent of 50 million users in 1996 to only 27 percent of 1.1 billion users in 2005, as shown in Figure 9-2.

Even though the U.S. has the largest absolute number of Internet users (152 million in 2006), the Internet market is fairly saturated. China, India, and Latin America, on the other hand, are poised for continuing growth. As you select target markets abroad, remember that online shopping behavior also varies by country.

Figure 9-2: Global Reach has tracked the growth of Internet users by language for ten years.

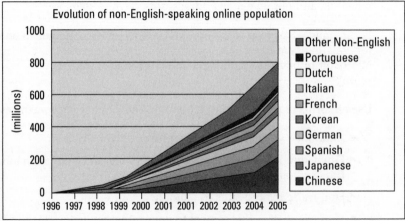

© Global Reach, a Neutralize (tm) (**)(tm) Search Engine Marketing Property.

The Swedish and Danish, for instance, are the busiest European shoppers, according to InSites Consulting, with 70 percent of users buying online, while only 44 percent of southern Europeans buy. On the other hand, the French, English, and Germans buy roughly once a month, compared to a European-wide average of seven to eight purchases a year. Users in Belgium and the Netherlands buy only five times a year.

Selling internationally

Research the consequences of selling internationally with care and select foreign markets consciously and strategically. Selling abroad can be very lucrative — or very foolhardy! For international market research or information about exporting, seek assistance from one of the government resources in Table 9-2.

Table 9-2	International Resources	
Name	*URL*	*What You'll Find*
American Translators Association	www.atanet.org/ onlinedirectories/ individuals.php	Directory of translation services
Babel Fish	http://babelfish. altavista.com	Free translation site
Business.com	www.business.com/ directory/advertising_ and_marketing/ strategic_planning/ global_marketing	Directory (paid) of international marketing companies
Direct Marketing Association	www.the-dma.org/ international/ links.shtml	Directory of international marketing resources
FreeTranslation	www.freetranslation. com/free/web.htm	Free translation site
Global Reach Internet Statistics	http://global-reach. biz/globstats/evol. html	Statistics on international use by language
InSites Consulting (Belgium)	http://www.escape- reports.com	Statistics on European Internet use
Markets Directory	www.marketsdirectory. com/intcompanya-z- alpha.htm	Directory of international marketing firms
Multilingual Search	www.multilingual- search.com	Forum and news on multilingual search engines
SEO Chat	www.seochat.com/c/ a/Search-Engine- Optimization-Help/ Multilingual-Sites- and-Search-Engines- part-1	Constructing multilingual sites
Small Business Administration Office of International Trade	www.sba.gov/oit	Exporting resources

(continued)

Table 9-2 *(continued)*

Name	URL	What You'll Find
U.S. Department of Commerce/U.S. Commercial Service	`www.export.gov`	Exporting resources
Yahoo!	`http://dir.yahoo.com/ Business_and_Economy/ Business_to_Business/ Translation_Services`	Directory of translation services

Analyze costs carefully when setting prices for international shipment. While shipping to countries like Canada, the largest U.S. trading partner, is fairly straightforward, costs might be higher than you expect. Allow for additional handling costs, from filling out customs forms to collecting payment. Especially when first going online, many companies ship only within the U.S. to avoid such problems.

Back-office implications for international marketing might also affect your budget and staffing. Consider the need to handle

✔ Customer and technical support in many time zones and languages

✔ Packaging and instructions in multiple languages

✔ Payments in different currencies

✔ Higher fraud rates on credit cards, especially from Eastern Europe, Africa, and Russia

✔ Different legal requirements for privacy, intellectual property, and consumer protection

If exporting directly seems daunting, explore such alternatives as international distributors, strategic partnerships, or sales representatives, like Thunder Scientific does at `http://thunderscientific.com/contact_us/ international_sales_reps.html`. You might also consider an alliance with a U.S. company that is already selling in your target market.

Unless you already operate multinationally, open one international market at a time, and sequence countries based on the size of the target market online and difficulty of market penetration. Absorbing requirements, costs, and promotional needs is much easier one country at a time. Without a doubt, Canada is the easiest trading partner for small U.S. companies to start with.

Promoting your site internationally

After you've decided to market internationally, consider the level of promotion needed to achieve your revenue targets. Changes to your Web marketing plan range from the simple to the sophisticated.

Think global, but market local. Localization is the key for any successful international marketing effort, online or offline. A fully integrated approach involves cultural as well as linguistic sensitivity, with awareness of local holidays, events, traditions, foods, religion, and color significance. (See Chapter 4.)

Search online for companies that specialize in international online marketing, translation services, and/or international SEO (search engine optimization). In addition to localizing your site, you might need to make technical adjustments to the HTML code for your site. The resource sites in Table 9-2 are a start.

At a minimum, do the first two items in the following list, and then as your global needs expand, add more sophisticated activities:

✔ Indicate which countries you serve by using a map, drop-down list, flags, graphics, or other languages as Fisher-Price does in Figure 9-3.

✔ Submit your site to country- and language-specific search engines, such as those listed in Table 9-3.

Figure 9-3: Fisher-Price makes it obvious that the company has multiple international sites.

Image of Fisher-Price website page used with permission of Fisher-Price, Inc., East Aurora, New York 14052, a subsidiary of Mattel, Inc. Fisher-Price and the Fisher-Price logo are registered U.S. trademarks of Mattel, Inc.

✔ Remove slang or colloquial phrases that nonnative English speakers might not understand.

✔ Translate your home page into the target language of the country you want to serve. Remember, there's a difference between British and American English.

✔ Completely translate your site into the target language(s) and customize it for local needs, adding local contacts. This is less critical for B2B companies, particularly technical ones, where English serves as the international language of business.

✔ Conduct online and offline marketing campaigns in the target country and/or target language. Google AdWords and many press release services, for example, let you specify the countries in which you want your material seen.

Table 9-3	Some International Search Engines	
Name	**URL**	**Country**
Alta Vista	www.altavista.com/web/res_country	Directory of Alta Vista international engines
Ananzi	www.ananzi.co.za	South Africa
Apali!	www.apali.com	Spain
ArnoldIt.com	www.arnoldit.com/lists/intlsearch.asp	Directory of international search engines
Asia-Links	www.asia-links.com	Asia
China Search Engines	www.searchengineguide.com/pages/Regional/Countries/China	Chinese search engine directory
Francité	www.i3d.qc.ca	France
Google International	www.google.com/language_tools?hl=en	Directory of Google international engines
Homer	http://homer.ca/search/canadian.htm	Canadian search engine directory
Mexico Global	www.mexicoglobal.com	Mexico
MOSHIx2	www.moshix2.net	Japan (in English)
Phantis	www.phantis.com	Greece
Porto Express	www.portoexpress.com/search.htm	Portugal

Name	URL	Country
Search Engine Colossus	www.searchengine colossus.com	Directory of international search engines
Search NZ	www.searchnz.co.nz	New Zealand
SearchingIreland	www.searchingireland.com	Ireland
Search.ch	www.search.ch	Switzerland, Germany
Yahoo! International	world.yahoo.com	Directory Yahoo! international engines
Zoek.nl	www.search.nl	Netherlands

Beware of free translation services, even those listed in Table 9-2. Automated translation has significant limitations, so you want to try it out first with any paragraph from your Web site. Translate from English into another language and then translate back to English. This exercise is usually good for a laugh, but also a reminder that there's nothing like a skilled human translator to prevent a linguistic *faux pas*. Even large companies err: Think about Chevy trying to sell its *Nova* model automobile in Mexico — *no va* means *doesn't go* in Spanish.

Some international search engines accept only sites that have registered domains in that country. You can register a one-page site in another country and link (not redirect) it to other pages on your English site.

Generating Leads with an Affiliate Program

An *affiliate program* is an online referral system that offers a commission to the source of the lead. When prospective customers click through on a link or close a sale, the originating site receives a payment. While often used by product companies, affiliate programs can be equally valuable for cross-referrals among service providers. They can be a wonderful source of leads, but they can also turn into one giant aggravation.

The grandmother of affiliate programs, Amazon.com Associates, is worth reviewing as a model (http://affiliate-program.amazon.com/gp/associates/join). For information about other affiliate programs, see some of the sites in Table 9-4.

Table 9-4	Affiliate Program Resources	
Name	**URL**	**What You'll Find**
About.com	`http://onlinebusiness.about.com/od/affiliateprograms`	Affiliate information
AffiliateGuide	`www.affiliateguide.com`	Affiliate directory
Affiliate Programs Directory	`www.affiliate-programs-directory.com`	Affiliate directory
Affiliate Programs.com	`www.affiliateprograms.com`	Affiliate directory
Amazon	`http://affiliate-program.amazon.com/gp/associates/join`	Amazon associate program
Commission Junction	`www.cj.com`	Affiliate hosting
eBay	`http://affiliates.ebay.com/best-practices`	Affiliate information
HowStuffWorks	`http://money.howstuffworks.com/affiliate-program1.htm`	Affiliate information
iDevDirect.com	`www.idevdirect.com/index.php`	Affiliate software
Internet Retailer	`www.internetretailer.com/article.asp?id=16248`	Affiliate marketing survey
LinkShare	`www.linkshare.com/affiliates/offers.shtml`	Affiliate hosting
MyReferer	`www.myreferer.com`	Affiliate hosting
SimplytheBest	`http://simplythebest.net/affiliates/`	Affiliate information

Considering your options

Although this section focuses on using affiliates as a lead source, you can affiliate with another site as well. For instance, authors might affiliate with Amazon and/or Barnes & Noble to earn a commission on the sale of their books, instead of selling them directly. A search engine marketing company might affiliate with an online newsletter service, a press release distribution service, a copywriter, and/or a Web developer as a way of formalizing recommendations.

Figure 9-4 shows the affiliate offer page for eZpZemail.com. If you check out the directories in Table 9-4 or the client lists on affiliate hosting sites, you'll find many other examples.

Figure 9-4: eZpZemail offers an affiliate program with a commission for generating leads. The same page includes an excellent list of directories to which eZpZ submitted its program.

Courtesy EZPZ, LLC.

Marketing with an affiliate program is a business decision. Consider the following questions when deciding whether an affiliate program makes sense for your business:

✔ **How will you define a transaction?** Pay per click (PPC)? Pay per action (PPA)? If PPA, what constitutes completion? When a sale closes? When a lead requests more information? Is a transaction counted only when it's from a new customer or from repeat customers, too?

✔ **How much will you pay per transaction?** Obviously, PPC rates are much lower than PPA rates. The amount you pay needs to be proportional to the value of the transaction. A company can't pay more than a few cents for clicks on a $10 item, but a referral that results in a client for a CPA might be worth much more. Will you offer a higher commission to better-performing affiliates? For new customers? Rewards for performance?

✔ **How many affiliates do you want?** Your software selection might depend on whether you expect dozens, hundreds, or thousands of affiliates. The more affiliates you want, the more marketing might be involved in recruiting them.

✔ **Will you establish and enforce policies about affiliates' competing with your site for PPC or e-mail advertising?** Natural search ranking? Use of trademarks? Banning affiliates that use spam, pop-ups, or spyware?

✔ **Do you have the support staff to communicate with affiliates on a regular basis, perhaps with a blog?** To answer affiliates' questions and make payments? Affiliates usually receive commissions monthly, as long as the amount due reaches a certain minimum level.

✔ **When you figure the commission and implementation expenses into your cost of sales, what happens to your break-even point?** Your profit margin? Will the projected increase in volume generate enough revenue to exceed the costs? Would an affiliate program produce better results than a high-priced PPC campaign?

Starting your affiliate program

After you've answered the questions in the preceding section, research software or third-party hosting sites to manage the signup, tracking, and commission-calculation processes. Several third-party sources are listed in Table 9-4, but many more are available through a simple search. First, though, check your own storefront package if you sell online. Many storefront providers offer an affiliate module, and often, it's wiser to accept the limitations of the module than to try for an ideal solution. Installing software on your own server is usually more complicated, and generally, only companies managing large, multitiered affiliate programs opt for that alternative.

Your Web site needs a page that describes your program and an application form. You might have to modify your navigation and site index to inform viewers of your affiliate program. As usual, it's easier to set up an affiliate program from the beginning than to add it later!

If you're looking for the greatest number of affiliates, promote your program by listing it on many affiliate directories, including those in Table 9-4. Your program must be competitive to attract potential affiliates who are shopping around for multiple revenue sources.

Keep in mind that affiliates that come from directories might not be the world's best lead generators or best-behaved site owners. Because sites that sign up might be completely unrelated to your company's interests, they might yield relatively low-quality leads. So instead of posting passively on directories, recruit affiliates yourself. Search for a few dozen companies that share a client base but offer complementary products. E-mail or snail mail the owners an invitation to become an affiliate, stressing the benefits and low risk involved.

Establishing Loyalty Programs Online

Those ubiquitous little tags we hang on our key chains are loyalty programs. Frequent flier miles and gift cards are loyalty programs. Those stamped, "frequent buyer" cards are loyalty programs. They all owe their popularity to these embarrassingly simple marketing maxims:

- Eighty percent of your sales come from 20 percent of your customers.

- It costs one-third more to sell an item to a new customer than to sell the same item to an existing one.

- Repeat customers spend one-third more than new customers per year.

- It's five times more profitable to sell to an existing customer than to a new one.

- Repeat customers are more than twice as likely to refer a new customer.

Rewarding customers and keeping their business

Whichever maxim you believe, retaining customers is important for every business. Of course, you have to start with good customer service, quality merchandise, and perceived value. But in the cutthroat competition of cyberspace, it doesn't hurt to give people one more incentive to return. That's what a loyalty program does. Nearly one-quarter of U.S. online retailers already have a loyalty program, according to the e-tailing group's 2005 Merchant Survey, with another 43 percent considering one.

Rewards might be points earned toward a free gift, a discount on future purchases, free shipping, an entry in a drawing, first access to new or exclusive products, or whatever is appropriate for your target market and business.

Loyalty programs face many of the same issues as affiliate programs (described in the previous section). In particular, think about how much you can afford to offer as a loyalty award. Also, when you include the cost of awards in your cost of sales, consider what happens to your break-even point and profit margins. If you're in the enviable position of being the sole supplier of a unique product, maybe you don't need a loyalty program — quality and service are enough for repeat business.

Setting up a loyalty program

The complexity of the program you offer determines the solution you need. The points program at TriathlonLab.com (`http://triathlonlab.com/store/customer/pages.php?pageid=3`) is clearly more complicated than an e-mailed promo code from Guaranteed Fit Tango Shoes for 15 percent off future purchases (`www.guaranteedfittangoshoes.com/scripts/akmod/repeatcust.asp`).

Some loyalty programs require a paid membership, while others are free. Your target audience and marketing strategy determine whether you should offer a discount for price-oriented consumers or another motivator.

You can sign up with a third-party loyalty site, like those in Table 9-5, to track purchases and provide awards. The simpler solution is often a loyalty module from your existing storefront provider. It might not be very flexible, but it can be enough to get started.

Table 9-5	Loyalty Program Resources	
Name	*URL*	*What You'll Find*
Entertainment Corporate Marketing Solutions	`www.entertainment.com/pmd/custom/online.html`	Hosts online loyalty programs
the e-tailing group	`www.e-tailing.com/research/merchantsurvey/index.html`	Research on e-tailing trends
Loyalty Lab	`http://instorecard.com/default.asp`	Hosts online loyalty programs
Online-Rewards	`www.online-rewards.com/index.html`	Hosts online loyalty programs
Webloyalty	`www.webloyalty.com/partnerad.asp`	Hosts online loyalty programs
About.com	`http://retailindustry.about.com/od/loyaltycrm/a/uc_msa1.htm`	Article: "Choosing the Right Kind of Loyalty Program"
CIO Insight	`www.cioinsight.com/article2/0,3959,1458960,00.asp`	Article: "Trends: Loyalty Programs"

Name	URL	What You'll Find
USA Today	www.usatoday.com/money/ smallbusiness/columnist/ abrams/2006-04-14- creating-loyalty_x.htm	Article: "How to Create Customer Loyalty"

Once again, post a page on your site that explains your rewards program, such as the one for MontanaLegend.com, shown in Figure 9-5 and described in the nearby sidebar. Some programs require a separate signup screen, while others automatically enroll members whenever someone establishes an account to make a purchase.

You also might need to modify your navigation and site index to include your loyalty program. Like affiliate programs, this option is easier to implement when included in your plans from the start.

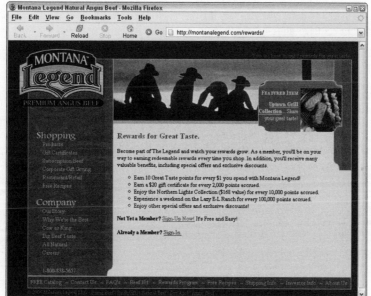

Figure 9-5: MontanaLegend.com offers a generous loyalty program to repeat buyers of its premium, natural Angus beef.

©2006 Montana Legend, LLC. All Rights Reserved.

Keep it simple! You might not need the complex tiers of awards that third-party loyalty programs offer. With each order, Mama's Minerals ships a "Mama's Dollars" coupon with a promo code for a 5 percent discount on the buyer's next online purchase (www.mamasminerals.com/mamasdollars.html). No fancy accounting or software needed!

Montana legend loyalists

Montana Legend's CEO, Keith Lauver, enthusiastically credits a recently introduced loyalty program with tripling repeat retail business from 20 percent of customers in June 2005 to 60 percent in less than a year. A wholesaler of Angus beef to restaurants nationwide since 2000, Montana Legend went online with its B2C site in 2005.

When the number of repeat customers seemed low, the company initiated a loyalty program through LoyaltyLab.com. Since December 2005, customers have earned points toward a free collection of steaks and a free weekend at the company's founding cattle ranch, the Lazy E-L. (Refer to Figure 9-5.) The software also lets the company create exclusive specials for loyalty members. Both the points and the specials keep customers coming back.

Lauver finds the loyalty program much more successful than the e-mail campaigns he tried, especially for tracking purchases, points, and awards. The company also markets through search engines, affiliates, and ad networks.

The site design and copy play to what Lauver calls "the romance of the cowboy" and customers' desire "to connect to the sources of their food." As he points out, it costs a lot to acquire a customer. Keeping them as a customer is most important, he says. That's exactly what their loyalty program does.

Chapter 10

Mastering the Secrets of Search Engines

• •

In This Chapter

▶ Understanding how search engines work

▶ Making search engines happy

▶ Linking up with Google

▶ Getting noticed by Yahoo!, MSN, and other search engines

▶ Mastering meta tags

▶ Seizing specialty search engines

▶ Retaining rank in search engine results

• •

*P*eople ultimately arrive at Web sites in only three ways: by using search engines, clicking links from other pages, or typing in a URL after hearing about it or seeing it elsewhere. As DalmoWorks (www.dalmoworks.com) found in its June 2006 survey, search engines are an integral part of the Web experience. These statistics show why search engines are a necessary part of your Web marketing mix. They also illustrate why search engine marketing alone isn't enough. (Respondents could name all the methods they use to find Web sites.)

According to the DalmoWorks survey, here's how people find Web sites:

   88% followed a link from another site

   85% used a search engine

   65% got a suggestion from a friend

   63% found a site in printed material

   58% found a site in a Web directory

   36% found a site in a signature file

32% saw the address on television

28% used a link from a book

29% located sites in other ways

Source: DalmoWorks.com

With competition from more than 47 million active Web sites in 2006 (about half of all the registered domains), you might think you need a miracle to be found in search engines. As you know from your own experience, a site that doesn't appear in the first page of results is practically invisible. This chapter replaces the miracle with some hard work — and some realistic expectations.

Designate search engines as a technique to use on your Web Marketing Methods Checklist from Chapter 2. (You can download a copy of this form from the book's companion Web site at `www.dummies.com/go/webmarketing`). Rather than try to achieve top ranking on all search engines for all keywords, put a reasonable level of effort into search engine marketing and allow time for other online methods as well.

Which Search Engines Do You Need?

Here's a piece of good news. If you go to the Search Engine Relationship Chart® at `www.bruceclay.com/searchenginerelationshipchart.htm`, you can see that only three sites — Google, Yahoo!, and MSN — generate the results seen on all primary search engines. You need to submit only to those three, plus dmoz (Open Directory Project) at `www.dmoz.org/add.html`, which feeds thousands of small, specialty search engines. The timeline version shows how these relationships changed as companies acquired or allied with one another.

Ignore any spam e-mail promising submissions to hundreds or thousands of search engines. You don't need them, and the process might actually harm your standing in the primary search engines. Also, delete all those e-mails guaranteeing #1 search engine rankings. No legitimate search engine optimization (SEO) company makes such a claim. It's *always* possible to generate a #1 ranking on a keyword that's rarely used.

Ranking by itself doesn't yield profits. You can make money only when a search engine delivers qualified visitors to your doorstep.

Go to each of these URLs to start the submission process by hand.

✔ **Google** feeds six other engines:

`www.google.com/addurl/?continue=/addurl`

✔ **Yahoo!** feeds two other engines:

`http://search.yahoo.com/info/submit.html`

✔ **MSN** is independent, feeding only HotBot:

```
http://search.msn.com/docs/submit.aspx?FORM=WSDD2
```

The Google brand network, which was responsible for nearly 50 percent of all searches in the Nielsen//Net Ratings July 2006 survey, is your choice for a B2B audience. ChangeWave Research reports nearly 80 percent of professionals use Google as their primary search engine. In keeping with their reputation as portals to other services, Yahoo! (24 percent of searches) and to a lesser extent MSN (10 percent of searches), are used by consumers, especially for news and information.

All the other search engines split the remaining 16 percent of some 5.6 billion searches in the U.S. in July 2006. That's why submitting to thousands of search engines doesn't mean much. It does make sense, however, to focus on 10 to 50 specialty search engines used by your target market.

You'll find much more on this topic in *Search Engine Optimization For Dummies,* 2nd Edition, by Peter Kent (Wiley Publishing).

Building a Search-Engine-Friendly Site

Search engines apply sophisticated algorithms to produce relevant results quickly. As smart as they might seem, computers are dumb. To produce good data, they need good input. A well-structured, search-engine-friendly site allows search engines to crawl or spider your site easily. Up to half of all sites are so badly structured that search engines never "see" them in the first place.

It's much easier to plan a search-engine-friendly site from the beginning or during redesign than to retrofit it.

Sites structured with frames or dynamic pages from databases give search engines indigestion. On the other hand, footers, a site index, and XML feeds are like dessert; search engines eat them up!

By looking at their portfolios and lists of services, you can tell whether developers are familiar with techniques for search engine friendliness. If not, ask them to read this section of the book and visit the resource sites. If they can't or won't do that, you might want to ask an SEO company to assist — or find another developer.

Search engine jargon

It helps to master the terminology you'll see on search engine resource sites or in articles:

- **Spiders, crawlers, or robots (bots)** are automated programs used by search engines to visit Web sites and index their content.

- **Search engine optimization (SEO)** is the process of adjusting Web sites and pages to gain higher placement in search engine results.

- **Natural or organic search** refers to search results produced by a search engine's algorithm (rules) when indexing unpaid submissions.

- **Paid search** results are determined by the amount a company pays to appear in sponsorship banners at the top of a page, in pay per click (PPC) ads in the right margin, or in some cases, at the top of the list of search results. Chapter 11 covers such paid techniques.

- **Search engine marketing (SEM)** combines both natural and paid search activities.

Site structure

Many articles on SearchEngineGuide.com or SearchEngineWatch.com in Table 10-1 discuss search-engine-friendly structure. They also cover techniques for using JavaScript and cascading style sheets (CSS) that won't make search engines burp. Requirements for friendliness change over time as technology and search algorithms improve.

Table 10-1	Search Engine Resources	
Name	*URL*	*What You'll Find*
AllSearchEngines.com	`www.allsearchengines.com/complete.html`	Search engine directory
Digital Point	`www.digitalpoint.com/tools/suggestion`	Keyword suggestion tool
Digital Point	`www.digitalpoint.com/tools/keywords`	Keyword tracker and keyword ranking tool
Internet Public Library	`http://ipl.sils.umich.edu/?unresolved=/ref/index.text.html`	Search engine directory
LLRX.com	`www.llrx.com/search_engines.html`	Search engine specialty directory list

Name	URL	What You'll Find
Overture	`http://inventory.overture.com/d/searchinventory/suggestion`	Keyword selector tool
Pandia Search Central	`www.pandia.com`	Search engine news
Refdesk.com	`www.refdesk.com/newsrch.html#type`	Search engine directory
Search Engine Guide	`www.searchengineguide.com/marketing.html`	Search engine articles, blog, marketing
SearchEngineWatch (ClickZ)	`www.searchenginewatch.com`	Articles, tutorials, forums, blogs, SEO articles, and tips
WebPosition	`www.webposition.com`	SEO, submission and page rank reporting software, optimization suggestions
Wordtracker	`www.wordtracker.com`	Keyword suggestion tool

Keep in mind that search engines can't read the following information on your pages:

- ✔ Words within images or graphics or multimedia files like Flash. The graphics in your header are usually not a problem.

- ✔ Content in *frames* (which is an old-fashioned method of programming that places multiple Web pages within one page).

- ✔ Content on *dynamic pages* (pages that are composed on-the-fly from a content database — like some storefront catalogs).

Splash pages

A *splash page* is a graphic-intensive or multimedia home page that delivers a nice "Wow!" Your developer might make money creating one, but that doesn't help you any. Unless you're a design or entertainment company, a splash page might earn you nothing but aggravation from your target audience.

Splash pages might cost you dearly in search engine ranking because they can inhibit a crawler's ability to index your site. It's far better to move your multimedia to another page on your site where users can choose to view it, rather than force them to spend time on something they don't want. If you insist on a splash page, try the following to soften the impact:

- ✔ Be sure there is a highly visible link to Skip this intro in the upper-right corner, or elsewhere high above the fold.

- ✔ Incorporate an ALT tag *(hover text)* for the splash image that's roughly equivalent to the first paragraph of text on the home page.

- ✔ If possible, put a paragraph of text above the Flash or graphic image.

- ✔ Convert your splash page into an entry page by including a navigable footer and/or main-level navigation.

- ✔ Name the splash page something other than your main URL. Submit the home page, rather than the splash page, with content as the primary URL for search engines.

URL construction

As your developer builds your site, she assigns names to your pages. It's an easy task on small sites, but sites with thousands of pages become overwhelming. Instead, developers often use content management or storefront systems that automatically generate URLs for dynamic pages pulled from databases, such as product catalogs. Unfortunately, search engines are better at crawling static pages; they might have trouble with or ignore dynamic pages.

Include different keywords in URLs for different pages, instead of using arbitrary file names. For instance, a URL for a bakery site might read: www.Yourbakery.com/storefront/fresh_breads.htm

The length of a URL doesn't matter to a search engine, but the symbols in it do. Compare the number of characters — other than dash (-), underscore (_), letters, or numbers — in the "bad" and "good" versions of URLs in the examples that follow. To avoid problems with search engine crawlers, limit symbols like ?, %, or = to no more than three! Many systems also generate unusable URLs when they initiate an onsite search or session identification number, which is sometimes called a *token*. Compare these URLs:

```
www.badproductURL.com/cgi-
          bin/shop.pl?shop=view_category&category=bolts%20carriage&sub_categ
          ory=&group=2&wholesale=
www.goodproductURL.com/browse.cfm/4,396.htm
www.badcontentURL.com/regional/web/content.jsp?nodeId=160&lang=en
www.goodcontentURLcom/incentives/taxcredit_1_2_2.htm
```

```
www.badsessionID.com/index.htm?&CFID=1180599941&CFTOKEN=37702390
www.goodsessionIDcom/gp/yourstore/ref=pd_irl_gw/002-9876543-1234567
```

Surprisingly, some of the worst violators of this rule are very expensive, enterprise-level content management systems for large, database-driven Web sites. For shame! Those software manufacturers should know better.

Fortunately, there are several solutions to this problem. The most common is called the Apache Mod Rewrite. Ask your developer to visit `http://httpd.apache.org/docs/1.3/mod/mod_rewrite.html` to convert these plug-ugly URLs on-the-fly into ones that are search engine friendly. Also, review `http://www.sitepoint.com/article/search-engine-friendly-urls` or search for other solutions. Using footers, a site index, or a sitemap can also help.

Footers

Place a linkable footer in HTML text at the bottom of every page of your site. It's extremely helpful to search engines, especially if your navigation appears as graphic elements. At the same time, it's helpful to humans, who can navigate to another section without scrolling back to the top. Include copyright, street address, phone, and a linkable e-mail address, too. While you display the same information on your *Contact Us* page, the easier you make it for users to find contact information, the better. The underlined text in the example that follows represents links. The date in this footer changes automatically.

This site last updated Aug 28, 2006   ©2000-2006 HotShot Co.

Street Address | City, State, Zip   E-mail Us or call 800-123-4567

Home | What's New | Local Business | Properties

Resources | About Us | Site Index | Contact Us

For simplicity, ask your developer to put the footer into the cascading style sheet (CSS).

Site index and sitemaps

A *site index,* like the one for SantaFeArtsandCulture.org, shown in Figure 10-1, is a linkable outline of your Web site. If your Web site follows the outline you wrote during the development process, this index will look almost the same.

Site indexes should allow access to at least the third tier of internal pages so users needn't hunt for pages. Indexes are critical for large, information-intensive sites and for sites that don't have well-formed URLs.

Figure 10-1:
This linkable index allows users easy access to items, like the Mayoral Forum, that appear on the third tier of the site.

Courtesy New Mexico CultureNet

Search engines use the site index as a path for their robots, eventually reaching all the internal pages listed there. If you have a large site, ask your Web developer to convert your site index to a sitemap in XML and submit it to Yahoo! and Google. *Sitemaps* allow search engines to identify dynamically generated pages as well as static ones.

A Real Simple Syndication (RSS) feed for your Google Sitemap automatically notifies Google when your site content changes. RSS is excellent for a large site, or for one with a constantly updated product or information database. Give the links in the following list to your developer if he isn't familiar with this process:

✔ Information about Google Sitemaps:

```
www.google.com/support/webmasters/bin/answer.py?answer=34654
www.google.com/support/webmasters/bin/topic.py?topic=8467
```

✔ Information about RSS feeds for Google Sitemaps:

```
www.google.com/support/webmasters/bin/answer.py?answer=34656
```

✔ Information about Yahoo! Sitemaps:

```
www.antezeta.com/yahoo/site-map-feed.html
```

✔ Free Sitemap Generator for Google, Yahoo!, and MSN:

`www.xml-sitemaps.com`

✔ Resource for Sitemap Generators:

`www.vbulletin.org/forum/showthread.php?t=100435`

Optimizing for Google

Google accounts for nearly 50 percent of all searches. With its dominance of the search engine landscape, Google makes its own rules for ranking sites in search results and changes them often. Some changes result from its own continuing research or from competitive pressures. Google also shakes things up to prevent large, well-funded companies from dominating results permanently or to counteract the dynamic of people gaming the system to enhance search engine results.

Site relevance, as a human being would determine it, guides Google's approach to search results. This approach puts extraordinary pressure on sites to obtain inbound links from related sites. In theory, a site that is well designed from a human perspective and well connected with other sites does well on Google. That's the theory anyway. The following sections detail some best practices to help you compete against all the other sites struggling for the same visibility.

Set reasonable expectations for your search marketing efforts. Your goal is to get some page of your Web site listed for some search terms that real people really use. You *don't* need to have every page appear on page one results for every keyword. Decide which search terms are the most critical for you, especially if you have limited time to devote to SEO and no funds to hire someone to help.

Dealing with the Google sandbox

Call it a timeout. Call it isolation. Call it a *sandbox,* as developers do. Whatever you call it, Google usually doesn't index sites with new domain names for up to six months after the site goes live. The delay allows time for development and avoids wasting search resources on fly-by-night sites, but it can be very frustrating if you have a site that needs to be active by a certain deadline.

Type your URL into the search box at `www.google.com`; if your site appears in the results, Google has indexed it. If not — and it's been more than a few months since you originally submitted — resubmit your URL at `www.google.com/addurl/?continue=/addurl`.

Buying ads from Google AdWords (PPC) can provide a presence on Google until your site is indexed. However, there's an inexpensive solution to start the Google clock ticking. Have your developer post a two-page Web site fairly quickly after you buy the name. Write several paragraphs about your products or services for the home page and prepare a second page with contact information and a little bit about the company. Add some search terms and a good page title. Then submit your preliminary site to Google at `www.google.com/addurl/?continue=/addurl`.

To be especially productive, start collecting e-mail addresses to notify subscribers when the site is open. It helps to offer a thank-you promotion for early signup. JohnnyCupcakes.com's alert page in Figure 10-2 collects addresses for its e-mail newsletter. This particular page, which is used while a new version of the site is under development, works equally well for a completely new Web site.

Even if you have an existing site, it might take a few weeks for Google to fully index a redesigned site. Usually, you see your home page first, and other pages follow over time, depending on the size of the site. Because Google now indexes constantly, you don't have to wait for a fixed period. In any case, it will take at least four to eight weeks for your link requests to bear fruit, so your Google search engine ranking might rise more slowly than you'd like.

Figure 10-2:
This New Site Coming announcement for trendy clothing designer Johnny Cupcakes replaces a meaningless Under Construction message with a useful marketing tool — collecting e-mail addresses.

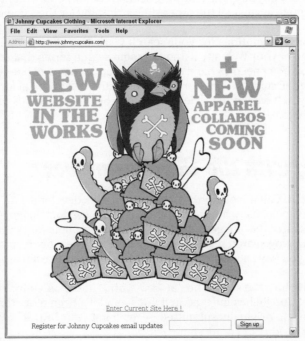

Courtesy http://www.johnnycupcakes.com

Improving your Google PageRank

Google's top secret! Google ranks pages for Web relevance or importance on a scale of 1 to 10, with 10 being the best. To see the PageRank for your site, or any other, you must download and install the Google toolbar from the URL listed under Google Resources in Table 10-2.

Table 10-2	Google Resource Links
What You'll Find	*URL*
Add site instructions	www.google.com/support/web masters/bin/answer.py?answer=3 4397&ctx=sibling
Crawl statistics information	www.google.com/support/web masters/bin/answer.py?answer=3 5253&query=crawl%20statistics &topic=&type=
Domain preference tips (with/without *www.*)	www.google.com/support/web masters/bin/answer.py?answer= 34481&ctx=sibling
Google Maps	http://maps.google.com
Google-friendly site tips	www.google.com/support/web masters/bin/answer.py?answer=4 0349&ctx=related
Google product list	www.google.com/options/
Guide to index search statistics	www.google.com/support/web masters/bin/answer.py?answer=3 5256&query=crawl%20statis- tics&topic=&type=
PageRank information	www.google.com/technology/ index.html **and** www.google.com/ support/webmasters/bin/answer. py?answer=34432
Sitemap information	www.google.com/support/web masters/bin/answer.py?answer=40 318
Submission guidelines	www.google.com/support/web masters/bin/answer.py?answer= 35769

(continued)

Table 10-2 *(continued)*	
What You'll Find	**URL**
Instructions for submitting content	`www.google.com /submit_content.html`
Toolbar download	`http://toolbar.google.com/?promo=mor-tb-en`
Webmaster tools overview	`www.google.com/webmasters/sitemaps/docs/en/about.html`
Webmaster Central	`www.google.com/webmasters`

The PageRank appears when you hover over the PageRank index in the toolbar, as shown in Figure 10-3. Google and Firstgov.gov (the Federal government portal) get 10s, but not many other sites do. The rankings aren't linear. Each point is roughly 10 times as "relevant" as the number below it.

Google toolbar   Page rank info

Figure 10-3:
The Google toolbar shows PageRank with both graphics and text. Ranking is by page, not by site.

Screenshots © Google Inc. and are reproduced with permission.

Google PageRank sometimes varies erratically from day to day, or even hour to hour. If your site rank seems either unusually high or low, or suddenly falls to zero, click the Reload button on your browser or check again in a few hours.

The PageRank equation is a closely held secret. More than the simple link popularity described in Chapter 7, Google's PageRank appears to be affected by the following criteria, among others:

- Links from related sites with high Google PageRank appear to generate extra value.

- Links from .edu, .gov, and .org Web sites appear to generate extra value.

- Links from blogs and press releases appear to generate extra value.

- Text surrounding inbound links is preferred; this favors annotated or contextual links and pages with fewer than 60 links per page.

- Links from link farms and other poor, inbound link sources diminish PageRank.

- Outbound links to other high-ranked, relevant sites — that is, sites that share at least one other search term — generate extra value.

- The size and complexity of your site seems to affect PageRank. Information-intensive sites seem to do better, although Google doesn't index the "deep Web" (information in databases) contents of academic or trade journals, phone books, or other databases.

- A Google sitemap generates extra value, while badly structured sites might diminish PageRank.

- Sites that use *black-hat techniques* (unethical) might not only be diminished in rank, but banished.

- Older sites tend to have higher rankings than newer ones, so be patient.

- Sites with newer content tend to have higher rankings.

- Visible title and ALT tags with search terms have more influence than other meta tags.

- Contents of surrounding pages generate extra value if related.

- Using search terms in subheads, navigation, and links is valued, because Google analyzes the difference in font size, style, color, and placement.

- Site traffic, both visitors and page views, can be rated for quantity and quality.

Finding Google-qualified inbound links

Start your search for inbound links with Google, as described in Chapter 7. Type **link:http://www.*sitedomain*.com** in the search box for competitors' sites and for sites that appear at the top of Google results on shared search terms. As you go through the list, target those with a PageRank of 5 or over for your requests.

Not all Web developers have the skills or staff to handle SEO or to manage a custom, inbound link campaign for good Google ranking. If this is too time consuming to handle inhouse, look for an SEO company to assist.

Your Web developer is still key to developing a well-structured, clean site with a footer, a site index, good URLs, and a sitemap. She must also avoid the things that Google doesn't like: hidden links, hidden text, *cloaked pages* (readers see one page, search engines see another), or sneaky redirects. For more information, refer to the pages for Google-friendly sites and submission guidelines listed in Table 10-2.

Making adjustments for Google dances

When Google adjusts its algorithm, sometimes called a *Google dance,* the SEO community shimmies. Like a game of musical chairs, some sites gain in search engine results, and others lose when the music stops. You might notice changes early if you regularly check your site standing in Google or if you get a newsletter from one of the search engine resource sites listed in Table 10-1.

If you lose position, don't panic. Use the Google resource links in Table 10-2 for crawl statistics information and the guide to index search statistics to gain some insight on what has happened to your site, specifically. Read what you can about how to re-optimize your site or what additional types of links to find. Make adjustments and resubmit to Google manually, with a new sitemap, or via RSS.

Optimizing for Yahoo!, MSN, and Other Engines with Meta Tags

Unlike Google's emphasis on inbound links, most search engines rely on internal consistency among site content and keywords to produce search engine results. Yahoo!, an early Internet pioneer, started in 1994 as a directory of the Web, rather than as a searchable index. A *hierarchical directory* is organized by fixed subject area, like the Yellow Pages or books on library shelves, rather than arranged on-the-fly by relevance in response to a search request.

Using human editors to review and assign sites to categories, Yahoo! quickly became one of the most popular destinations on the Internet. Over the next ten years, Yahoo's paid program for directory inclusion began to fall out of favor, and it acquired its own search engine technology. (See Chapter 11 for more information on the paid directory.)

Alexa.com still ranks Yahoo! as the most visited site on the Web, valued more for its portal services, such as e-mail and news, than for its searches. However, many people remain loyal to Yahoo!, with millions of consumers using it as their home page.

Yahoo! can't be overlooked in the search engine sweepstakes that generate results from meta tags. Essential in the early days of the Web, a long set of *meta tags* provided a structured description of a Web site for directory purposes. Meta tags appear at the beginning <head> of the code on each Web page to provide information to browsers and search engines. Most meta tags are no longer necessary, but three retain some value: the title, page description, and keyword tags.

As search algorithms improve, even these meta tags carry less importance for ranking purposes. However, they can provide an edge in some cases, and they help you structure content in a practical way.

It's easy to see meta tags for any Web site — just view the source in your Web browser. In Internet Explorer, simply right-click a Web page and select View Source (or View Page Source, in Firefox). Alternately, use the browser toolbar. Choose View⇨Source in Internet Explorer (or View⇨Page Source in Firefox). The meta tags should appear near the top of the separate window, as shown in Figure 10-4.

Title page

Page description tag

Figure 10-4:
Title, page description, and keyword meta tags for the catering page of Fairytale Weddings' site.

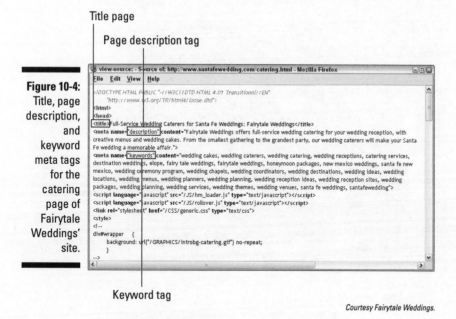

Keyword tag

Courtesy Fairytale Weddings.

Using meta tags

Because meta tags are in transition, limit how much time you spend on them. If tags for a page relate to its content, they're more likely to yield benefits in search engines.

Effective tags include keywords, but you can't optimize one page for all the keywords that apply to your site. Instead, repeat no more than the same four keywords (or search terms) in several locations on a page. Optimize another page for another four keywords. If you do this correctly, some page of your Web site will appear in results for most search terms that are commonly used.

Title meta tags

Probably the most important tag still in use, the *title tag* appears above the browser toolbar when the site is displayed. Figure 10-5 shows how the title tag used in Figure 10-5 appears on the screen. Note that various terms from the keyword tag shown in Figure 10-4 appear in the headline and links, as well as in the title tag.

Title tag appears here

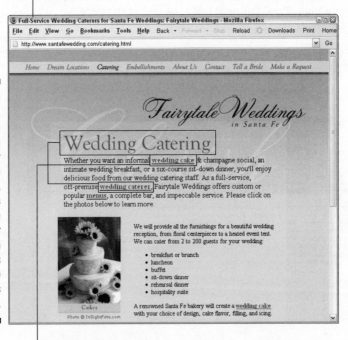

Figure 10-5: The title tag, Full-Service Wedding Caterers for Santa Fe Weddings, appears above the browser toolbar on this Fairytale Weddings page.

Terms from Keyword tag

Courtesy Fairytale Weddings. Photographs © 2006 Insightfoto.com

Years ago, when site navigation was more of a problem, the title tag often repeated the page name, much like the header in a book shows a chapter title. This is no longer necessary, and page names like About Us are meaningless for search engines. Instead, insert one or more of your selected keywords in the title tag.

Because different search engines truncate the title tag at different lengths, place your keywords first, followed by the company name — not the other way around. Your company name appears so many places on your site that it won't matter if it's trimmed off. Limit this tag to 7–9 words, perhaps 50 characters including spaces.

Page description meta tags

All or part of the page description tag is usually the source for the text that appears in search engine results, as you can see in Figure 10-6. Yahoo! search results for the term *santa fe wedding catering* yield the Fairytale site in second and third positions. One result pulls the search term only from the page description tag shown in Figure 10-4; the second entry also pulls a phrase including *wedding catering* from the first paragraph of text. Again, different search engines truncate this tag at different lengths, ranging from 150–256 characters including spaces. Use your four, optimized search terms in the description, placing them as close to the beginning as possible while keeping the text readable.

The page description tag is a marketing opportunity. If you're clever, include a call to action or a teaser in the description to encourage a searcher to click search engine results to your site.

Figure 10-6: A portion of the page description meta tag for the catering page of Fairytale Weddings appears in Yahoo! search results for the term *santa fe wedding catering.*

©2006 Yahoo! Inc. YAHOO! and the YAHOO! logo are trademarks of Yahoo! Inc.

Keyword meta tag

The keyword meta tag in Figure 10-4 shows the list of relevant search terms for this page. Again, different search engines might truncate this tag at different lengths. Place the four keywords you elect to optimize at the beginning of the tag; put your company name and least important terms at the end. And here are a few other things to keep in mind:

- Limit the list of search terms to 30 at most; shorter is better. You can spread out other search terms on other pages.

- Keyword phrases are more useful than single words. It's next to impossible to earn a page 1 appearance on most single words.

- Commas are no longer needed to separate search terms, but they're helpful for you to read what you've done. Search engines will consider reversing the order of words within a phrase, or will scramble words among terms, to find possible combinations. This can be especially helpful for regional sites where you want to specify location and type of business, such as *manhattan delis, manhattan restaurants, manhattan coffee shop, manhattan dining.*

- There's no need to include articles (*a, an,* and *the*) or prepositions (*to, from, by, on,* and so on).

- Use all-lowercase words to encompass all forms of capitalization. If you capitalize a word in the keyword tag, capitalization is required for a match.

- Plurals include singulars, as long as they're formed from the same root without changing spelling. For example, a search for the term *plants* includes the term *plant,* but a search for the term *companies* does not include the term *company.* The same principle holds true for gerunds and past tense.

- Phrases with spaces include the same term without spaces. For example, a search for the term *coffee shop* includes the term *coffeeshop,* but not vice versa.

- If it's essential that a multiword phrase is kept together for identification, put quote marks around it. For example, "*days of our lives*" or "*santa fe*".

- When establishing results, sites with keyword phrases that exactly match the entered search request *(query string)* generally precede those where other text separates the words within the search request.

Google rarely uses the keyword tag; even some other engines now ignore it. Instead, they derive important keywords by the frequency with which they're used (as long as they aren't abused) and by their location on the page. The keyword tag is useful, however, as a way of tracking which pages you optimized for which search terms. Otherwise, you'll probably need to build another spreadsheet.

Choosing good keywords

Selecting the right keywords for your site is more art than science. The best search terms are ones that people actually use — and ones on which there's limited competition. At least give yourself a chance to appear on page one. Phrases are almost always better than single words, except in highly specialized applications with their own terminology.

Everyone's brain works a little differently. You might think the search terms you'd use are so obvious that everyone else would use the same ones. It isn't so. Ask random friends or customers what search terms they would use to research something like tires or to find your Web site. You might be surprised.

Finding words

When choosing keywords, start by reverse-engineering competitors' sites and sites that appear in the first three positions on obvious search terms. View the source for their pages and make a list of the keywords they use. Brainstorm other terms from your text. Then use this list as input for one of several tools that identify good search terms and suggest alternatives.

Don't use search terms that aren't relevant to your site. Companies have won legal cases against sites that use trademarked terms in their keyword list, hoping to divert traffic from the trademark owner's site. If you're an authorized dealer for a trademarked product, review your distribution agreement. It generally specifies where and how you can use trademarked terms. As for *supercalifragilisticexpialidocious*, forget it, Mary Poppins. It already appears on 235,000 pages.

Using keyword tools

Overture has a free keyword tool at `http://inventory.overture.com/d/searchinvetory/suggestion`. After you enter a likely search term, Overture returns the estimated frequency that the term has been queried in the last month across all Yahoo! properties. The tool also suggests related terms.

The frequency with which search terms are used varies by season, holiday, news, and entertainment events.

Wordtracker offers a somewhat more sophisticated tool at `www.wordtracker.com`. After you go through the process on the site, you receive a report that looks like Figure 10-7.

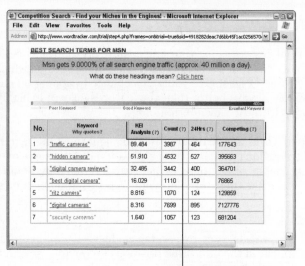

Figure 10-7:
The results
from Word-
tracker's
free trial
display the
value of
keyword
suggestions
on MSN for
the starting
term
camera.

Value of keyword suggestions

Courtesy Wordtracker (Rivergold Associates)

Here's a breakdown of the information on this report:

✔ **Count:** In the Count column, Wordtracker displays the number of times a term has been queried in the past 90 days across *all* search engines. (Wordtracker extracts this data from MetaCrawler and Dogpile meta-search engines.)

✔ **24 Hrs:** In the 24 Hrs column, it estimates the number of times a term is likely to be queried within the next day.

✔ **Competing:** The Competing column in Figure 10-7 lists the number of Web pages that share that search term on your target search engine.

✔ **KEI Analysis:** Wordtracker derives its own Keyword Effectiveness Index (KEI) rating for each term. The higher the KEI, the more likely your site can end up on the first page of search results.

Wordtracker and Overture generally vary in the frequency numbers they return. Partly, that's because Overture reports all variations of a term in its count, while Wordtracker estimates each variant separately (singular/plural, past tense, with or without spaces). And partly, it's because the two tools work from a different database of searches, collected over different time frames, and from different audience profiles.

As with just about every statistic on the Internet, don't worry about the absolutes. It's the relative values that matter. The relative frequency of use of different terms is far more important than the actual number.

The KEI value still doesn't tell you whether these terms are appropriate for your audience or whether *your* audience would actually use them. That's where the art — and some marketing judgment — come in. You can use Wordtracker's free trial, or rent the software for about $8 per day. Rental is worth it. The free trial gives results only for MSN. With the rental version, you can select Google, Yahoo!, or other engines, and you can upload an entire list of words instead of entering them one at a time.

Always test suggested keywords by entering them back into a search engine. Every once in a while, you'll be surprised to find that a keyword yields a completely different type of business than yours.

Some Web developers can help with this element of SEO, but many can't. Look for assistance from copy writers experienced in optimizing text for the Web or from SEO companies.

Page optimization

Unless you're a huge company, optimize your site only for the search engine that your audience is most likely to use. If you already have a site, check your traffic statistics (see Chapter 14) to see which engine generates the most traffic.

Search engines usually specify their preferences on advice pages for Webmasters, or you can find them in the search engine resource sites in Table 10-1. Follow these tips for keyword placement to prime your pages:

- ✔ Use keywords in your page URLs.

- ✔ Use them as terms in the navigation. (This doesn't help if your navigation consists of graphic elements.)

- ✔ Include the same four primary keywords you selected for optimization in the first paragraph of text for that page. That's the only paragraph most search engines scan.

- ✔ Use the same four keywords in the ALT tags. These tags appear as a small text box when a user hovers over a graphic or photo. Descriptive ALT tags make Web sites accessible for the visually impaired, but you can usually work in one or more of your terms.

- ✔ Use keywords as part of the link text, rather than the phrase click here.

- ✔ Some search engines use cues from the HTML code to distinguish text that appears in headlines or subheads; they're usually a different size and/or color. If keywords appear in those headlines or subheads, you might get "extra credit" in some engines.

✔ Have your developer put the meta tags at the very top of the source code.

✔ Text should be the first page content that search engines see. If a photograph appears to the left, right, or above the first paragraph of text on the screen, have your developer rearrange the source code so that the text appears first in the code.

Don't sacrifice human readability and comprehension when trying to use search terms. People come first — they buy; search engines don't. Because you're probably the person responsible for reviewing, if not writing, the copy, you're responsible for assessing keyword use. Your developer usually doesn't get involved, though an SEO company certainly will.

You might read about *keyword density* or *keyword ratio.* These terms refer to the percentage of keywords versus the total text on the page. As long as you avoid nasty techniques such as *keyword stuffing* (the excessive use of keywords on a page), you should be okay. If the keyword ratio approaches 20–25 percent, most search engines get suspicious. You don't have to measure! It's next to impossible to write text densely stuffed with keywords that also makes sense to a human being. If you write good copy, you're fine.

Avoid using any other black-hat techniques, such as *magic pixels* (1–x–1–pixel links that can't be seen) or *invisible text* (keywords written in the same color as the background). They will get you dropped from search engines. If you write an informative Web site that's useful to people, you don't need black magic for SEO. You'll have all the magic you need.

MSN takes paid search results from Yahoo!/Overture but now uses its own technology to index the Web. Their algorithm doesn't seem as accurate as other search engines and tends to reward home pages in the results.

Using the Open Directory (dmoz)

The Open Directory Project (called *dmoz,* which stands for *directory.mozilla. org*) began in 1998 in reaction to difficulties in getting listed in the Yahoo! Directory. It is an attempt to maintain a comprehensive, human-reviewed directory of the Web. Volunteer editors at dmoz assess Web sites for quality and content and confirm or deny their assignment to a category.

dmoz (`http://dmoz.org`) feeds its results to Google, other members of the Google family, and to thousands of smaller, subject-area directories all over the Web. (In fact, you'll find opportunities to submit to dmoz through most of those directories.) Originally, a dmoz entry was critical to getting listed in Google. That has changed as Google's own crawler superseded what dmoz could accomplish. Still, a dmoz entry can result in getting picked up by many, smaller search engines and might contribute to a higher Google PageRank.

Drawbacks to dmoz

Human reviewers can see value in your site without worrying about URLs, frames, images, or multimedia. dmoz editors might reject sites that lack unique content, don't function correctly, or are obviously spam. The dmoz human factor delivers a Cyber Housekeeping Seal of Approval, so to speak.

Unfortunately, some topics have such a backlog of submission requests that editors run months, if not several years, behind. There have been complaints about variability in editorial skills, lost or tossed submissions, accusations of favoritism, and worse. In spite of all that, dmoz continues to operate with a cadre of volunteers, claiming more than 4.8 million indexed sites in a recent report (http://research.dmoz.org/publish/chris2001/odp_ reports/report_200607.htm). Google, by the way, last noted about 25 billion pages in its index.

Even after your site is listed in dmoz, you might have to wait several months for other sites to pick it up. Is it worth bothering? Yes, but probably not worth bothering a lot.

Submission process

Submission is simple. Drill down through categories (shown in Figure 10-8) and subcategories at http://dmoz.org to find the best fit for your site. Your site can appear in only one category of dmoz. As a shortcut, see where your competitors are listed. When you've arrived, click the Suggest URL link. Fill out the form with your URL, the site title (use your title tag) and site description (use your page description tag). That's it. Then wait.

Submit only your home page. If your site hasn't appeared in the dmoz directory after two or three months, submit it again — and again — and again.

dmoz takes patience. Depending on the category, the editor, and the size of the backlog, it can take more than two years to get your site indexed.

Suggest URL link

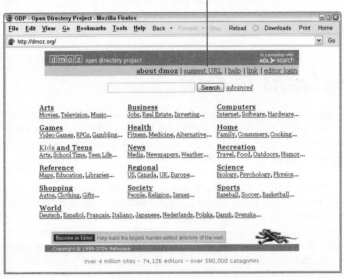

Figure 10-8:
Start a dmoz submission by drilling down until you find the best subcategory for your site. Then click Suggest URL in the top navigation.

Copyright 1998-2006 Netscape. Used with permission.

Submitting to Specialty Search Engines and Directories

Just because you've knocked off Google, Yahoo!, MSN, and dmoz doesn't mean you're done. Now it's time to locate specialty search engines and directories that your target audience uses. Take advantage of the search engine directories listed in Table 10-1 or simply search for directories and search engines by subject.

Use the Google Toolbar or Alexa.com to quickly assess the PageRank and traffic for these specialty search engines. Bother with only engines that appeal to your target audience and that seem to be maintained.

You'll find it easier to track your search engine and directory submissions if you create a spreadsheet corresponding to the one you build for link requests, as described in Chapter 7. A few directories and search engines accept e-mail applications, but most have an online form similar to the one at dmoz, or one slightly more complicated.

You don't have to worry about submitting to meta-search engines such as MetaCrawler or Dogpile because you can't! These search engines compile results from the other primary search engines. Don't confuse meta-search engines with *meta-indices,* which are directories of other directories.

In addition to vertical market, industry-specific, and application directories or search engines, include some essential generics:

- Yellow Pages and white pages (See Table 10-3.)

- Maps and local directories, especially if you have an office or brick-and-mortar storefront (See Table 10-3.)

- General business, trade association, and professional membership directories (See Table 10-4.)

- Directories for images, audio, video, and/or multimedia, if appropriate (See Table 10-5.)

If your Web site uses any of the elements in the bulleted list that follows, submit to the appropriate directories:

- Blog, chat, message board, or social network directories. (See Chapter 7.)

- International search engines. (See Chapter 9.)

- Public calendars and live event directories. (See Chapter 9.)

- Shopping search engines, like Froogle or Shopzilla. (See Chapter 11.)

- Directories of technology-based sites for vlogs, podcasts, and messaging. (See Chapter 13.)

Table 10-3	Some Basic, Free Directories	
Name	*URL*	*Submission URL*
Alexa.com	www.alexa.com	www.alexa.com/data/ details/editor?type= contact&url=
Amazon Maps	www.a9.com	http://a9.com/-/ company/help/ webmasters.jsp
Amazon Yellow Pages	www.amazon.com/ gp/yp	http://a9.com/- /company/help/ webmasters.jsp (*Note:* No charge, but Amazon.com account with credit card required)
AnyWho	www.anywho.com	http://www.super pages.com/about/new_ chg_listing.html

(continued)

Table 10-3 *(continued)*

Name	URL	Submission URL
Google Local Business Center & Maps	`http://local.google.com`	`https://www.google.com/local/add/login`
InfoSpace	`www.infospace.com/home/yellow-pages`	`http://my.super pages.com/spweb/portals/customer.portal`
Verizon SuperPages	`www.superpages.com`	`www.superpages.com/about/new_chg_list ing.html`
Yahoo! Local & Maps	`http://local.yahoo.com`	`http://search marketing.yahoo.com/local/lbl.php`
Yahoo! Yellow Pages	`http://yp.yahoo.com`	`http://dbupdate.infousa.com/dbup date/yahoo1.jsp`
YellowPages.com	`www.yellowpages.com`	`http://store.yellowpages.com/post` (renew annually)

Table 10-4	Some Free Business Directories	
Name	URL	Submission URL
B2B Guide	`www.bocat.com`	`www.bocat.com/b2b/submitsite1.htm`
B2Business	`www.b2business.net`	`www.b2business.net/cgi-bin/portal/add.cgi`
Business Directory Pages	`www.directory-pages.com`	`www.directory-pages.com/botw-web-directory-submis sions.htm`
ComFind.com	`www.comfind.com/directory`	`www.comfind.com/directory/addsite.htm`

Name	URL	Submission URL
CompletePlanet	`http://aip.completeplanet.com`	Submit individually
IndustryLink	`www.industrylink.com`	`www.industrylink.com/cgi-bin/list_01.asp`
Jayde B2B	`www.jayde.com`	`http://submit2.jayde.com`
MacRAE's Blue Book	`www.macraesbluebook.com`	`www.macraesbluebook.com/PAGES/free_lst.cfm`
Manufacturers' News, Inc.	`www.mniguide.com`	`www.mniprofile.com/new`
ThomasNet	`www.thomasnet.com`	`www.thomasnet.com/advertising/free_listing.html`

Table 10-5	Some Audio, Video, Image, and Multimedia Directories	
Name	**URL**	**Submission URL**
iTunes Music Store	`www.apple.com/itunes`	`https://phobos.apple.com/WebObjects/MZLabel.woa/wa/apply`
Fagan Finder	`www.faganfinder.com/img`	Submit to individual directories
Google Images	`http://images.google.com/`	`www.google.com/accounts/ManageAccount` (upload through Google Account)
Google Multimedia Directory	`www.google.com/Top/Arts/Animation/Anime/Multimedia`	Submit through dmoz: `http://dmoz.org/cgi-bin/add.cgi?where=Arts/Animation/Anime/Multimedia`

(continued)

Table 10-5 *(continued)*

Name	URL	Submission URL
Google Video	`http://video.google.com/`	`www.google.com/accounts/Manage Account` (upload through Google Account)
MusicMoz	`http://musicmoz.org`	`http://musicmoz.org/add.html`
Multimedia Search Engines	`http://searchenginewatch.com/showPage.html?page=2156251`	Submit to individual directories
Scala.com	`www.scala.com/multimedia/search-engines-directories.html`	Submit to individual directories
Singingfish	`http://search.singingfish.com/sfw/home.jsp`	`http://search.singingfish.com/sfw/submit.html`
Yahoo! Audio	`http://audio.search.yahoo.com/`	`http://search.yahoo.com/mrss/submit?`
Yahoo! Images	`http://images.search.yahoo.com/`	`http://search.yahoo.com/mrss/submit`
Yahoo! Video	`http://video.yahoo.com`	`http://search.yahoo.com/mrss/submit`

Maintaining Your Ranking

After you've achieved a good, search engine ranking, you don't get to snooze. First, another company is going to fight for that position. Second, things are forever changing. Inbound links come and go, and search engines tweak their algorithms or buy another company's technology. You need to be vigilant to maintain your ranking.

You must update content on your site to remain appealing to search engines, as I discuss in Chapter 6.

Checking your ranking

For most small sites, a quarterly review of search engine ranking, link popularity, and link requests is fine. If you read about a Google dance, have a large site, or run a significant SEO effort for natural search, you might want to run reports more often.

Here's a closer look at how to perform these tasks:

- **Check your search engine ranking:** You can use the link for index search statistics in Table 10-2 to check your ranking on Google. That might be enough, depending on your user base. Or purchase software such as Web Position (http://webposition.com) or Search Engine Tracker (www.netmechanic.com/products/tracker.shtml) to check your standings automatically for multiple keywords on multiple search engines.

- **Run a link popularity report to be sure that your inbound links are solid:** You might find that about 25 percent of sites disappear over a two-year period. If you discipline yourself to request ten new inbound links every quarter, you'll do fine.

- **Review your spreadsheets for link requests and directory/search engine submissions:** If your site isn't found on a requested location after three months, resubmit. If your site still isn't posted after two requests, replace the request with a new one, except for dmoz.

Resubmitting your site

If everything's fine, there's no reason for you to resubmit to search engines. If your search engine ranking drops for no reason, rerun the report a few days later to confirm the results. Resubmit to the four main engines.

If you change or add new pages to your site, submit one of those URLs to your four primary search engines. That triggers a re-spidering of your site. Better yet, send a new sitemap to Google and Yahoo! or ensure that the RSS feed for your sitemap is working.

To keep the workload reasonable, spread out the task of optimizing additional pages for different keywords. Tweaking text, adding longer product descriptions, revising meta tags and ALT tags, or rearranging the placement of keywords on a page all gradually improve search engine ranking.

Thunder Scientific Corporation (shown in Figure 10-9), a manufacturer of humidity measurement equipment, software, and accessories for more than 40 years, believes in the value of SEO. As described in the nearby sidebar, Thunder Scientific finds search engine optimization to be a cost-effective technique for online B2B marketing.

Figure 10-9:
Thunder
Scientific
uses search
engine
optimization
to reach its
B2B market.

Courtesy Thunder Scientific Corp.

SEO for success

A leading manufacturer of humidity measurement equipment, Thunder Scientific developed its second-generation Web site several years ago. Like many technical companies, its market is narrowly focused on engineering users. Thunder targets standards laboratories and the aerospace, military, pharmaceutical, and industrial manufacturing sectors, both nationally and internationally.

Struggling to obtain first-page position on its own, Thunder turned to a search engine optimization company to help select search terms,

optimize its new site for search engines, and obtain greater search visibility, especially in certain international markets. Thunder's site now boasts customized search terms and meta tags on multiple pages.

After it attained the visibility it wanted, Thunder found that quarterly monitoring and re-submissions were enough to maintain search position. The company couples SEO with trade shows, print ads in trade publications, and quarterly email newsletters.

Part IV
Spending Online Marketing Dollars

The 5th Wave   By Rich Tennant

©RICHTENNANT

"Guess who found a KISS merchandise site on the Web while you were gone?"

In this part . . .

Unlike most of the techniques in Part III, the advertising techniques in this section cost money.

Pay per click (PPC) ads that appear on search engines are one of the most cost-effective methods of advertising online. They're easily targeted by keyword search; their conversion rate is easy to measure; and they're excellent mechanisms for generating leads and making sales. Chapter 11 covers some rarely discussed strategic and tactical marketing decisions you should make before spending on PPC campaigns.

Banner ads — those ubiquitous and sometimes annoying hyperlinked graphic ads — are more expensive than PPC, with a much lower click-through rate. As you learn in Chapter 12, they, too, have a place in the Web marketer's quiver, particularly for branding.

It costs money to expand broadband usage and to allow multiple communications devices to interconnect. To pay for these advances in technology, publishers open up new advertising opportunities. If you have the need, resources, and time, consider using some of the new advertising methods described in Chapter 13: video blogging, Real Simple Syndication (RSS), online training seminars (Webinars), podcasting, text messaging on cell phones, and Web sites designed for mobile devices.

Chapter 11

Marketing with Pay Per Click Ads

*P*ity all those poor, pre-Web marketers who are stuck with coupons, direct mail, or television to connect customer interest in an ad to customer action that takes place at a later time. By contrast, the Internet enables banner advertisers to reach viewers while they're actively engaged in a related activity on a Web site. Better yet, search engines allow advertisers to supply answers to viewers at the very moment they're asking specific questions.

Pay per click (PPC) ads, which link viewers' search queries to advertisers' answers, first appeared on GoTo.com (which became Overture and is now owned by Yahoo!) in 1999 and on Google in 2000. As shown in Figure 11-1, these text-only ads, which look like classifieds, usually appear to the right of natural search results. You bid to have your ads appear when a user searches for one of your preselected keywords.

PPC differs from old-fashioned advertising in two important ways:

✔ Your ads display only when users are interested enough to enter a chosen search term, resulting in a highly targeted audience.

✔ You pay based on the number of click-throughs you receive, not on the number of times your ad is served or viewed. (Those views are called *impressions* in traditional advertising.)

As a creative marketer, consider using the guerrilla PPC techniques in this chapter as a complement to natural SEO (search engine optimization). Be sure to add PPC to your Web Marketing Methods Checklist from Chapter 2. If you prefer, you can download it from www.dummies.com/go/webmarketing.

PPC ads

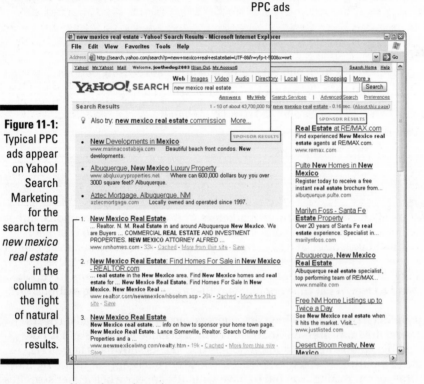

Figure 11-1:
Typical PPC ads appear on Yahoo! Search Marketing for the search term *new mexico real estate* in the column to the right of natural search results.

Natural search results

©2006 Yahoo! Inc. YAHOO! and the YAHOO! logo are trademarks of Yahoo! Inc.

This chapter focuses on the marketing strategy and tactics that apply to PPC programs (also called *cost per click,* or *CPC*), with an emphasis on Google AdWords, Yahoo! Search Marketing (formerly called Overture), shopping search engines, and a few specialty search engines.

For a wealth of additional information on PPC, including detailed implementation directions, check out *Pay Per Click Search Engine Marketing For Dummies,* by Peter Kent (Wiley Publishing).

Devising a Pay Per Click (PPC) Strategy

Under pay per click (PPC) programs, you bid competitively on specific keywords, setting the maximum amount you'll pay each time a viewer clicks through to your site. Except on Google, the ad provided by the highest bidder usually appears at the top of the list of sponsored searches, with other ads appearing in descending order of bid amounts.

Premium sponsored positions appear above the natural results. You can't pay to appear there on Google; appearance rotates and is derived from bid prices. Yahoo! offers those ads through a separate advertising program at varying monthly rates.

Spending on PPC ads, which now generates more than $2 billion in advertising revenue annually, is expected to grow to around $8 billion by 2008, according to *Forbes* magazine. In September 2005, *The Economist* magazine found that "PPC advertising is the fastest growing sector of the advertising industry," accounting for more than 40 percent of all online advertising in the U.S.

The growing popularity of PPC carries downsides as well. As with natural search engine results, your ad usually needs to appear above the fold (on the portion of the page the user sees without scrolling) or in the top five listings to have a reasonable chance of being viewed and receiving a click-through.

The limited onscreen real estate on popular search terms puts small businesses with small pocketbooks at a disadvantage. Scarcity leads to higher prices: The cost of bidding on some popular search terms has become prohibitive for some and unprofitable for others.

In a 2005 report, Jupiter Research found that 87 percent of commercial clicks take place on the natural (not sponsored) search results. Don't rely on PPC to the exclusion of natural search engine marketing.

Comparing PPC to other online advertising

Chapter 12 discusses other forms of online advertising, including banners and newsletter sponsorships. Generally, those ads use a traditional payment model that sets a cost per thousand impressions (CPM), as described in the nearby "PPC terms to remember" sidebar. Others charge a flat fee, often by the month, regardless of the number of impressions or clicks you receive.

A few use a cost per click (CPC) model, but most *publishers* (Web sites that carry ads) don't like the uncertainty of CPC ad revenue. From their perspective, a high click-through rate (CTR) also depends on the quality of the ad text (the creative) and the offer it contains, both of which are outside of their control. All they can deliver is the audience.

In the online world, an *impression* is counted whenever a page containing your ad is downloaded (served). You'll be charged for the impression even if your ad is so far below the fold that no one sees it. With PPC, you pay only when someone reaches your site.

While you try to target all ads as closely as you can to your desired market, only a PPC ad reaches prospects at the very moment they research an item or issue or consider making a purchase.

PPC ads display the same way on other search engines that receive their feeds from Google or Yahoo! (see BruceClay.com), although some, like AOL Search, display only the top few PPC ads in the feed.

Using content ad partners

Google's AdSense program (see Figure 11-2) or Yahoo!'s Content Match display your ads on other non–search engine sites. While those ads are supposed to appear only if related to nearby content on the partner sites, it isn't always so. In that sense, they function more like branding ads. These contextual ads are identified by source on the partners' pages, but they don't always appear in the same location as they do on the originating search engine.

You can intentionally use content partners for branding purposes, which is fairly inexpensive because the CTR on content-based displays is usually much lower than what you receive on search result pages. Recognizing that the viewers on AdSense sites are "less qualified" prospects than those on its own search displays, Google allows you to bid a lower amount for content-derived clicks.

If you're doing sales-oriented ads, you might want to avoid using generic content partner sites. Instead, use Google's site-based or demographic display options, as described in the following section about Google, to review and select specific sites.

Yahoo! currently pays its Content Match partners more per click than Google pays, with rates varying based on the amount of traffic a site receives. If a site on which you'd like to advertise is a Yahoo! partner only, you need to sign up with Yahoo! or advertise directly on that site.

Ads

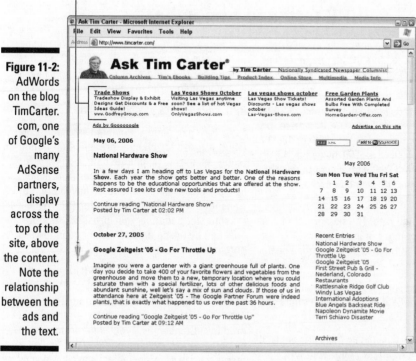

©2006 AsktheBulilder.com

Figure 11-2: AdWords on the blog TimCarter. com, one of Google's many AdSense partners, display across the top of the site, above the content. Note the relationship between the ads and the text.

Planning your PPC campaign

Like any other online marketing technique, you need to set goals and objectives for your PPC campaigns. Here are some questions to consider:

✔ Are you interested in introducing your site (branding it)?

✔ Are you competing for sales on specific goods?

✔ Are you trying to capture the interest of prospects researching major purchases so they come into the store? Or are you selling retail online?

✔ How will PPC fit into your overall marketing plan, including offline activities?

If you're an e-tailer, coordinate your PPC program with merchandising activities continuously to promote your specials, seasonal offers, clearance sales, and new products.

PPC terms to remember

CPC: Cost per click. The actual dollar value you pay. Some people reserve CPC for banners that charge by the click and PPC for sponsored ads on search engines.

CPM: Cost per thousand impressions. Allows you to compare costs from one ad venue, or type, to another. If an ad costs $500 for 10,000 impressions, your CPM is $500 divided by 10, or $50. Because most PPC sites also provide the number of impressions, you can compute CPM for your PPC campaign.

CTR: Click-through rate. The number of clicks divided by the number of impressions. Expect costs for a click-through to be higher than costs for an impression.

Conversion rate: The number of actions taken or purchases made divided by the number of clicks received.

Landing page: The destination page on your site that viewers see when they click your ad.

Paid inclusion: Payment to be listed in a search engine or directory, often for faster review or guaranteed listing. Generally, the search engine or directory charges a flat annual fee or monthly charge per URL, although Yahoo! Express uses a combination of flat fee plus PPC.

PPC: Pay per click payment method.

PPA: Pay per action. Payment is made only when a prospect takes a prespecified action (such as makes a phone call, signs up for newsletter, completes a purchase). Acts almost like a commission. Expect to pay more per transaction unit for PPA than for PPC. That's reasonable, because your prospect has pre-qualified by taking an additional action toward purchase.

ROI: Return on investment. For PPC, refers to the profit made divided by the cost of the PPC campaign. It might be more useful to compute ROI over a whole program than for an individual product. Sometimes, you deliberately lose money or break even on one product (called a *loss leader*) to draw customers into a store, only to make more on sales that follow.

For most businesses, a PPC program is a matter of trial and error. Expect to produce multiple iterations of your ads until you find the combination of ad content and search terms that produces the best results. Consequently, a PPC campaign also takes a commitment to set up and monitor, especially in its early stages — or if it becomes large and complex. Do you have the time?

If PPC seems overwhelming, get your feet wet with Google AdWords Starter version at http://adwords.google.com/support/bin/topic. py?topic=8336. Both Google's Jumpstart program (https://adwords. google.com/support/bin/topic.py?topic=32) and Yahoo!'s Fast Track (http://searchmarketing.yahoo.com/srch/choose.php) offer expert assistance from their staff for a fee. Or call an Internet marketing or SEO company.

If you have a limited budget, pause your campaign at times, instead of running it evenly over time and place. In most cases, you get better visibility and more click-throughs from qualified prospects if you spend more money over a shorter period of time than spending a little bit of money all the time. Use your PPC budget only when it will do you the most good, such as

✔ When you first launch your site for greater visibility and branding.

✔ While you're waiting to get out of the Google sandbox, for link campaigns to kick in, and/or for search engines to spider new pages.

✔ When you add important new products, services, content, or features to your site.

✔ When you can't get first-page traction in natural search results for a particular keyword.

✔ During seasonal campaigns tied to holiday giving (especially December, February, and May) or at key points in your own annual sales cycle.

✔ During the hours in which your target audience is online. (Look at your traffic statistics to see when that is.)

Carrying Out Your PPC Plan

After you've decided to carry out a PPC campaign, you need to decide where you'll spend your PPC budget. Given that Google provided about 50 percent of all searches in September 2006 (according to Nielsen||NetRatings) and Yahoo! controlled another 23 percent, your campaign will undoubtedly include one or both of them.

Choose your PPC venue based on where your target audience searches. Watch your own traffic statistics (see Chapter 14) and the results of your search engine optimization (SEO) campaign in Chapter 10. The source of visitors and the terms they use for natural search is invaluable information about the best sites for your PPC campaign.

Keep in mind that PPC features change often, so check both Google AdWords and Yahoo! Search Marketing on a regular basis. Yahoo! upgraded its search marketing program completely in fall 2006. Google offers its own, quick comparison chart at `https://adwords.google.com/select/comparison. html`, or review the summary of the differences in Table 11-1.

Some find that Google offers more flexibility and tools, as well as reach, and the ability to spread your advertising dollars evenly over time, instead of using them up all at once.

Table 11-1	Comparison of Google AdWords to Yahoo! Search Marketing	
Feature	*Google AdWords*	*Yahoo! Search Marketing*
Audience	80% of all B2B searches	Mostly B2C
Minimum bid	$0.01	$0.10
Bidding flexibility	Automatic discounter charges only $0.01 more than the next highest bid, up to your maximum	Charges the full amount of your bid
Budget period	Daily	Daily
Set display location (Geotargeting)	Yes	Yes
Set display language	Yes	No
Set display time of day	Yes	No
Ranking appearance of ad on page	Combination of bid and quality score	Bid only
Set display position to request appearance only in certain positions	Yes	No, though you can set position indirectly with bid amount
Timing	Ads live almost immediately	3–5 days for review on self-service program
Campaign organization	By campaign/ad group/ad	By keyword
Start-up cost	$5 one-time fee	$50 deposit (may vary with promotions)
Minimum monthly fee	None	None
Premium top display	Rotated based on bid	Bid separately for placement
Multiple ads/keyword	Yes	Yes

Feature	Google AdWords	Yahoo! Search Marketing
Keyword suggestion	Yes	Yes
Displays competing bid amounts	No	Yes
Conversion rate tracking	Yes	Yes
Reporting tools	Yes	Yes
Partner programs for context ads	AdSense	Content Match
Different ad price for content partners	Yes	Yes
Ads on search partners	Yes	Yes
Image ad display on content partners	Yes	Yes
CPM alternative for content partners	Yes	No
Demographic sort for content partners	Yes	Yes
Simplified entry program	Google Starter	No
Online training	Yes	Yes
Professional paid assistance	Jumpstart program	Fast Track program

Bidding within your budget

When you put together your PPC budget, work your numbers backward to set up a budget within your overall marketing plan. Think about how much you can afford to spend and whether you want to spend it all at once or spread it out over a month or year. Each PPC provider has a somewhat different format for estimating bids and results on search terms. The Yahoo! Search Marketing form appears in Figure 11-3.

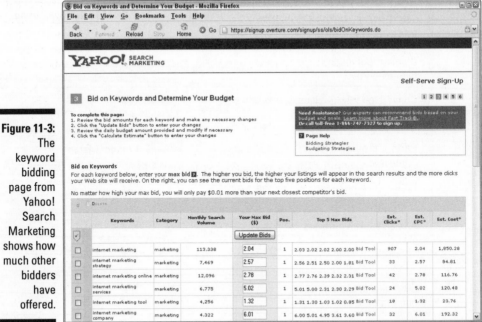

©2006 Yahoo! Inc. YAHOO! and the YAHOO! logo are trademarks of Yahoo! Inc.

Figure 11-3:
The keyword bidding page from Yahoo! Search Marketing shows how much other bidders have offered.

It's easy to break the bank on PPC ads, so try these tips to get the most out of your PPC spending, without getting sucked into the budget-busting barrel of overbidding:

✔ **Don't bid to win the top position.** In fact, anecdotal evidence shows that the top PPC ad might get the most tire kickers. Ads in positions two through four (as long as they're above the fold) might get more serious buyers.

✔ **Improve your natural search engine ranking.** Why waste money advertising on sponsored search if you achieve top results for free? Save your money or spend it elsewhere.

✔ **Set geographic limits.** It's obvious that you would limit the range of your ads if you depend on a local population to attend an event or make a purchase in your real-world store. Setting geographical limits can extend your budget, however, even when you sell nationwide. Look at your sales statistics (see Chapter 14) to see where your past and most lucrative buyers live. Constrain your ads to run in those locations.

✔ **Use your traffic statistics (see Chapter 14) to see which days of the week and times of day your buyers are active.** Constrain your ads to run during those times.

✔ **If you're selling online or have a specific way to monitor viewer activity, set up conversion tracking.** Your programmer needs to place a small piece of code on the Thank You pages after a sale or signup, or on other pages you want to track. Your reports will show what percent of click-through visitors reach that page and how much your campaign has cost per conversion.

✔ **Get ruthless about dropping keywords that don't convert!** This is especially true if you're selling. If your ad is designed for research or driving people into a real-world storefront, you might want to maintain CTR as your key parameter.

✔ **If you're using PPC for sales purposes, don't bid more than an average sale (not single item) is worth.** As a rule of thumb, spend no more than 10 percent of your average sales amount on advertising. If you estimate conservatively that 2 percent of people who click through to your site will buy, you must pay for 50 clicks to make one sale! For example, if your average sale is $100, limit advertising to $10. Divide $10 by 50 to get an average bid of 20 cents per click. Of course, you can bid more on some words and less on others.

You can always break these "rules" for strategic marketing purposes. Paying more to acquire a new customer makes sense if you have a history of turning first-time shoppers into repeat buyers. While it's true that online sales also lead to offline sales — according to some studies, $1 in online sales generates another $2.50 offline — you can't count on that, especially in the beginning.

Selecting search terms

Selecting the appropriate search terms for your ad is much like selecting keywords for SEO. You might find it helpful to use PPC ads for search terms on which you don't appear on the first page of search results. Both Google and Yahoo! offer search term selection tools, as shown in Figures 11-4 and 11-5. The Yahoo! tool counts the uses of a search term, including plurals and past tense, for the past 30 days across all its partners. The Google tool displays a mini bar chart showing the relative number of competitors on search terms and how frequently a term is searched.

As with natural SEO, select targeted search phrases rather than single words. Also, don't select terms that are longer than most users will type in, or that they will find hard to spell. Review Chapter 10 for more suggestions.

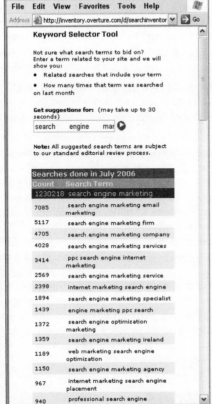

Figure 11-4:
The Yahoo!
Keyword
Selector
Tool counts
the uses of
a search
term for
the past
30 days.

*©2006 Yahoo! Inc. YAHOO! and the YAHOO! logo
are trademarks of Yahoo! Inc.*

If you aren't sure whether to include a search term, use it. It's better to start with too many terms and delete the ones that don't perform; sometimes a term will be successful unexpectedly. You can and should apply keyword ideas you found on WordTracker (see Chapter 10) or other keyword suggestion sites like www.nichebot.com or www.keyworddiscovery.com. Don't forget search terms used by existing users, which are usually available in your traffic statistics. (See Chapter 14.)

As with regular search term selection, not everyone uses the same words when looking for an item. Dialect, region of the country, and certainly different countries use different words to refer to the same thing. Are you selling buckets or pails? Is that a stroller or a pram?

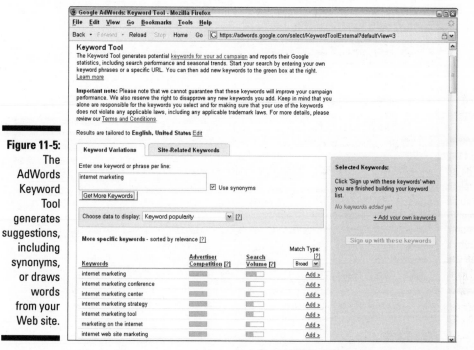

Screenshots © Google Inc. and are reproduced with permission.

Figure 11-5:
The AdWords Keyword Tool generates suggestions, including synonyms, or draws words from your Web site.

Writing a good PPC ad

Remember that adage about advertising? Successful ads owe 40 percent to the offer, 40 percent to the audience, and 20 percent to the creative. If you use the right search engine and select search terms that your prospects are likely to use, you have the audience. Now, viewers need a reason to click your ad rather than your competitors' ads.

Most PPC ads follow a formula of headline, two lines of text, a visible URL, and an unseen landing page URL. Each search engine sets the specific length of each line, but the same general principles apply across all engines. Tips for writing ads are available on Google and Yahoo!, or you can find out how to write a good classified ad at such sites as www.websitemarketingplan. com/small_business/classified.htm. Figure 11-6 displays Google's ad template.

Both Yahoo! and Google have additional rules governing word use, punctuation, qualifiers, proper nouns, and more. Because both review your ads to make sure they comply, read the rules for whichever site you use.

Figure 11-6:
The ad
template
at Google
automati-
cally counts
characters
to keep you
within limits.

Screenshots © Google Inc. and are reproduced with permission.

Headline

Just as with your Web site, you need a headline that grabs attention quickly. Here are some general guidelines:

- Avoid small words that take up space.

- Use words that draw attention, like *new, exclusive, special, now,* and *save.*

- Try to use search terms in the headline and/or in the text of the ad. That might mean writing a lot of different ads!

A small difference in wording might have a big effect on the success of your ad. Try several variations if you don't see a good click-through rate. Google lets you run multiple ads on the same search terms, making it easy to test wording. (Only one of your ads will appear at a time for any one of your keywords.)

Offer

Try to keep your text specific to the purpose of the ad, focusing on user benefits. For sales-oriented ads, the more details the better. Include the price or low shipping costs if they're some of your selling points. Also, think about your audience and what matters to them. You might have several ads for the same product, each oriented toward a different benefit that appeals to a different segment of your market.

These short ads work much better when you deal with only one item or group of closely related items rather than with diverse products. Combining shirts and shoes might work in a print ad, but it's difficult online because users can click to only one destination page.

Just as you did when writing text for your site, stick with active voice, second person — think *you,* not *we.* Also, use a call to action in your offer. An imperative verb, such as *enjoy, savor, relax, play, indulge,* or *earn* gives people an immediate reason to click through. Don't waste any precious characters telling people to click! When users search for something, they want to know "what's in it for me" on the other side of the action.

Landing pages

Generally, you display the same primary URL on all your ads for branding purposes. However, the click on each ad should take users to a destination, or *landing page,* on your site that is directly related to the ad. A good landing page fulfills the promise implicit in your ad, and its content and appearance should be well structured to convert a browser to a buyer. Try to imagine yourself in your viewer's place, looking with new eyes at your site.

Here are some other points to consider for landing pages:

- ✔ To improve the visibility of your ad on Google, it might help to have your search terms or synonyms appear in the text or meta tags of your landing page.

- ✔ If you're selling a single product, the landing page should be the product detail page. If you advertise related sizes or items, go up a level to a sub-category or category page in your storefront that encompasses your offer.

- ✔ You can specify the results of an onsite search as a landing page to get closer to a group of products you advertise.

- ✔ Land visitors where they want to be! Don't strand them on your home page, wondering where to find the product you advertised.

Reviewing reports

If you can afford it, put some extra funds into the first week or two of your PPC campaign so you can see which search terms perform best for CTR and conversion. Watch your results for at least a week to get representative data, especially if some of your terms are rarely used.

Yahoo! and Google both offer reporting tools at various levels of detail, as shown in Figures 11-7 and 11-8. If you have implemented conversion tracking, these reports also show the number or value of conversions and cost per conversion. Remember that PPC is an iterative process. Look at your PPC and traffic reports and make changes based on what you find.

©2006 Yahoo! Inc. YAHOO! and the YAHOO! logo are trademarks of Yahoo! Inc.

Figure 11-7: The Yahoo! summary report provides a high-level overview of your PPC campaign.

Figure 11-8: A Google report for a specific ad within an ad group shows clicks, impressions, CTR, average CPC, total cost, and average position for your ad by keyword.

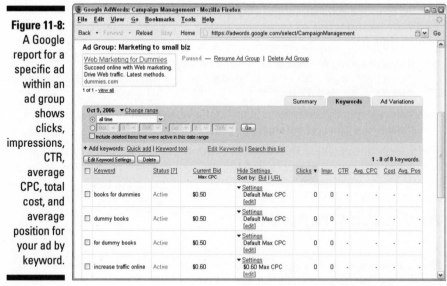

Screenshots © Google Inc. and are reproduced with permission.

Over time, you'll probably discover that a reduced set of search terms works best with a particular ad. Stick with what works until it doesn't. Then refresh your ads with new content and new offers.

Yahoo! Search Marketing Specifics

If you decide to use Yahoo! for paid search, you might want to take advantage of several of the following alternatives to PPC:

- ✔ **Yahoo! Express Submission** is a cross between paid inclusion and PPC. For $49 per year for the first URL, you can submit your Web site to Yahoo!'s natural search engine. In addition, you provide a deposit to pay either 15 cents or 30 cents per click. For many businesses, this is an inexpensive and efficient way to obtain preferred standing in Yahoo! search results.

- ✔ **The Yahoo! Directory** offers paid inclusion for directory placement, which is separate from Yahoo!'s search results. Yahoo! fans still like this yellow-pages-style directory. For $299 per year, Yahoo! quickly reviews and posts corporate sites.

- ✔ **Yahoo! premium sponsors** pay to appear at the top of a specific search results page. These positions are available only to companies also listed in the Yahoo! Directory under Business and Economy/Shopping and Services or Business and Economy/Business to Business. Categories are priced from $50–$300 per month.

- ✔ **Yahoo! Local** is an option for Yahoo! PPC advertisers. It's worth a separate submission effort, especially if you're a PPC advertiser seeking to drive traffic to your brick-and-mortar store or event. Yahoo! offers three different tiers for local advertising: basic, enhanced, and featured placement.

- ✔ **Yahoo! Shopping** and **Yahoo! Travel** are fixed-rate CPC programs, rather than bid programs, with the CPC depending on product category. I discuss them later in the chapter in the "Working with Shopping Search Engines" section. These programs generally yield a higher conversion rate for advertisements in these categories than regular PPC ads do.

You find more information on all these programs at the URLs in Table 11-2.

Table 11-2	Helpful URLS for Yahoo! Sponsored Search
URL	*Topic*
`http://inventory.overture.com/d/searchinventory/suggestion/`	Keyword suggestion tool
`http://searchmarketing.yahoo.com`	Sponsored search home page
`http://searchmarketing.yahoo.com/arp/srch_roi.php`	ROI estimate for sponsored search
`http://searchmarketing.yahoo.com/dirsb/index.php`	Directory submission, $299 per year
`http://searchmarketing.yahoo.com/local/ls.php`	Local sponsored search
`http://searchmarketing.yahoo.com/srch/choose.php`	Sign up for Sponsored Search, Self Serve, or FastTrack
`http://searchmarketing.yahoo.com/srch/cm.php`	Content sites for sponsored search
`http://searchmarketing.yahoo.com/srch/index.php#`	Sponsored search main page
`http://searchmarketing.yahoo.com/srchsb/sse.php`	Express submission $49 annually for first URL + $0.15 or $0.30 per click
`http://smallbusiness.yahoo.com/marketing/sponsorlist.php`	Premium sponsors
`www.low-cost-web-hosting-services.com/articles/Overture_ad_campaign.html`	Article: "Overture Ad Campaign"
`www.ovtd.com/overture_advertiser_count/`	OVTD.com; Count competing advertisers on Yahoo!
`www.advertisepayperclick.com/overture.cfm`	Article: "Overture Marketing"

Google AdWords Specifics

Google AdWords differs from all other PPC companies in one, very important way: The position of your PPC is not totally dependent on what you bid. Instead, it's multiplied by what Google calls its Quality Score, which it uses to measure the quality of your keywords and establish your minimum bids for them.

According to Google, "Quality Score is determined by your keyword's click-through rate on Google, relevance of your ad text, historical keyword performance on Google, the quality of your ad's landing page, and other relevancy factors." From your perspective, this means that deep-pocket competitors can't "squat" at the top of a keyword list by placing a high bid to keep competitors out of contention. A good ad with a good CTR and a good landing page can place your ad in the top four, even if you can't afford the highest bid. Of course, this works for Google, too, by maximizing its return on PPC ads. Google receives more revenue from an ad with a lower bid but a higher CTR than it does from an ad with a higher bid that viewers don't click.

Google offers flexibility not always available with other PPC programs. As part of your campaign setup process, you select for such factors as language, location, delivery (evenly over time or accelerated), position preference, and choice of ad distribution, and whether you want a different bid for clicks from Google's content network. Pages from the AdWords setup process are shown in Figures 11-9 and 11-10.

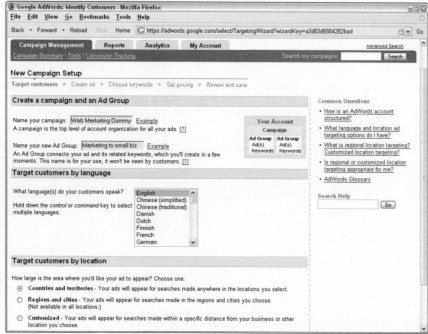

Figure 11-9: Starting a campaign on Google AdWords requires some basic marketing decisions.

Screenshots © Google Inc. and are reproduced with permission.

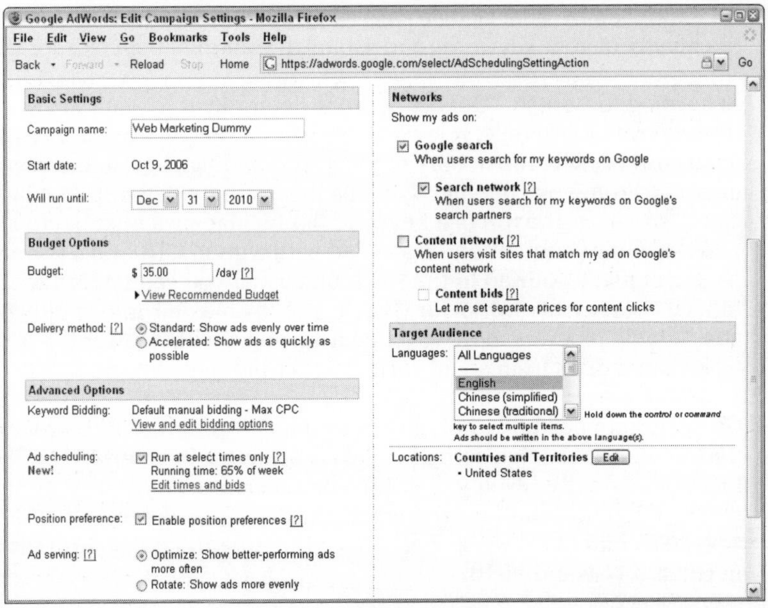

Screenshots © Google Inc. and are reproduced with permission.

Figure 11-10: Additional AdWords screens allow you to establish flexible settings to best serve your marketing needs.

Google offers several options not available through other PPC search engines. Look up details through Adwords.Google.com or view some of the URLs in Table 11-3 to see if they can help you achieve your marketing goals.

Table 11-3	Helpful URLs for Google AdWords
URL	**Topic**
http://adwords.google.com	AdWords home page
http://adwords.google.com/ support/bin/topic.py?topic=8336	AdWords Starter Edition
http://catalogs.google.com/intl/en/ googlecatalogs/help_merchants.html	Google Catalogs
https://adwords.google.com/ select/KeywordToolExternal	Keyword suggestion tool
https://adwords.google.com/support	AdWords Help Center
https://adwords.google.com/support/ bin/answer.py?answer=39454	Video ads

URL	Topic
`https://adwords.google.com/support/bin/topic.py?topic=29`	AdWords glossary
`https://adwords.google.com/support/bin/topic.py?topic=32`	AdWords Jumpstart expert program
`https://adwords.google.com/support/bin/topic.py?topic=8964`	Google checkout
`www.google.com/adwords/learningcenter`	AdWords training center
`www.google.com/adsense`	Earn revenue by displaying Google AdWords on your site
`www.google.com/help/faq_clicktocall.html`	Google Click-to-Call program
`www.google.com/local/add/login`	Google free local and map listing

Here are some Google options to consider:

✔ CPM or site-targeted ads run only on Google AdSense partners, but you can select which partners to use by topic, demographics, or name. You can even exclude specific sites. These ads work well for branding but will probably experience a much lower CTR. Many of these sites also accept image (banner) ads. You can set the CPM rate you want.

✔ Google offers free local marketing for companies that sign up through Google maps. Google has refined these free options to include a brief description, your logo, and a coupon promotion.

✔ Google AdWords can now incorporate a symbol that indicates you'll allow purchase through Google's integrated checkout system. There is no extra charge to participate in the checkout program.

✔ Your ads can designate participation in a new feature, *Click-to-Call,* that lets users dial directly to your sales office through Voice Over Internet Protocol (VOIP) or enter their phone number to get a call back. Again, there is no additional charge for this service.

Working with Shopping Search Engines

Every product seller should consider shopping search engines, such as those listed in Table 11-4. Many users research product features, vendor history, and prices on the Web before making a purchases offline or online.

Table 11-4	Some Other Shopping Search Engines
Name	**Signup URL**
Amazon.com	`www.amazon.com/gp/seller/ sell-your-stuff.html`
Bizrate.com and Shopzilla	`http://merchant.shopzilla.com/oa/ registration`
CNET Shopper	`www.cnetnetworks.com/advertise/ opportunities.html`
Froogle.Google.com	`www.google.com/base/help/ sellongoogle.html`
Half.com	`http://sell.half.ebay.com/ws/ eBayISAPI.dll?HalfSellHome`
MySimon.com	`http://shopper.cnet.com/4002-5_ 9-1008724.html`
NexTag	`http://merchants.nextag.com/serv/main/ buyer/sellerprograms.jsp`
Overstock.com	`http://partners.overstock.com/ cgi-bin/sellInv.cgi`
Pandia Shopping Directory	`www.pandia.com/shopping`
PriceGrabber	`http://www.pricegrabber.com/user_ sales_jump.php`
Search Engines Shopping Directory	`www.searchenginesdir.com/dir/ shopping/index.php`
Shopping.com	`https://merchant.shopping.com/enroll/ app?service=page/PartnerWelcome`
Yahoo! Shopping	`http://searchmarketing.yahoo.com/ shopsb/index.php`
Yahoo! Travel	`http://searchmarketing.yahoo.com/ trvlsb/index.php`

Some shopping search engines operate primarily as directories of vendors, and others offer sophisticated comparison features. For example, if you target the price-conscious consumer, comparison shopping sites are excellent PPC locations. If you're in the hospitality arena, consider Yahoo! Travel (`http://searchmarketing.yahoo.com/trvlsb/index.php`), which has a travel-specific program with CPC fixed by category of service.

Don't pass up *free!* Froogle.Google.com (shown in Figure 11-11) is a must-do for any e-tailer. Google provides specific directions for a free, automated, product feed on its site. (Refer to Table 11-4.) Google also offers free, electronic distribution of catalogs at `http://catalogs.google.com/`.

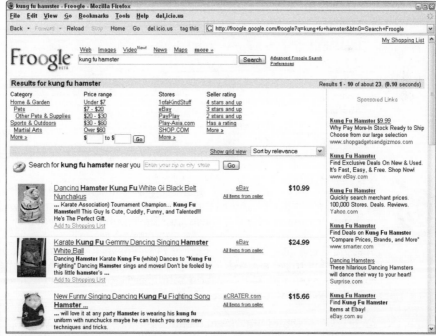

Figure 11-11:
Froogle.
Google.com
is a free,
shopping
search
engine
offering
both
mundane
and unusual
products.

Screenshots © Google Inc. and are reproduced with permission.

Considering Other Paid Directories and Search Engines

Consider some of the smaller search engines, such as MSN or specialty search engines listed in Table 11-5, when you have a particular audience that uses those venues to search for what they need. For instance, if you offer a B2B service, you might want to place PPC ads on Business.com.

Table 11-5	Some Other PPC Search Engines and Directories
Name	**Signup URL**
7Search.com	www.payperranking.com
Business.com	www.business.com/info/advertisewithus.asp
Enhance	https://client.enhance.com/ols/index.do
ePilot	www.epilot.com/ePilot4/AdvertiseWithUs/landing.asp
Kanoodle	www.kanoodle.com/about/advertise.html
Live Search at MSN	http://advertising.msn.com/microsoft-adcenter
LookSmart	https://adcenter.looksmart.com/security/login
Miva	https://adcenter.us.miva.com/Login.aspx
Search123	http://search123.com/sc/advertiser_programs.shtml
SearchFeed	http://home.searchfeed.com/rd/index.jsp

Treat placements on specialty search engines much as you would a banner ad placement. (See Chapter 12.) Ask about page views, visitors, and demographics to decide whether these sites have potential for you.

Some of these smaller venues accept PPC bids as low as one cent or offer free consultation to get started. You might use one of them as a trial site before rolling out your PPC campaign on Yahoo! or Google. Just remember that user behavior varies among search engines.

American Meadows first opened under another name as a Vermont tourist attraction and gift shop in 1981. Long before it went online in 1998, the company had developed a line of seed mixtures and become the number one supplier of wildflower seeds in the U.S., selling primarily through a print catalog. When it decided to go online, the company repositioned itself for national seed distribution and changed its name to American Meadows, as shown in Figure 11-12. The online move was quickly followed by the use of PPC advertising, which increased qualified traffic to its Web site by 120 percent per month.

PPC ad

Figure 11-12:
American Meadows has enjoyed great success from its PPC ads, one of which is shown on a Google search for *wildflower meadow.*

Web site courtesy AmericanMeadows.com. PPC screenshots © Google Inc. and are reproduced with permission.

PPC paid for success

A PPC pioneer, American Meadows (www. americanmeadows.com) started its first PPC campaign with GoTo.com in 1999, when there were perhaps five or six competitors online. Now a large PPC buyer on both Google and Yahoo!, owner Ray Allen found PPC a revolutionary idea, giving a business of any size a reach that was otherwise unattainable.

"From the very first click, I was an avid user," he says. Allen takes full advantage of conversion tracking and relishes the ability to change copy easily in real time. Allen stresses the importance of fresh copy, rather than stay with the same ads. "Look at your competitors' ads. . . . Then write something that competes with what they're offering. This is a great way to pay for only the No. 2 or 3 position, and have No. 1 traffic."

He prefers Google for its "exceptional" customer service staff and ease of use. Running the campaigns himself with up to 5,000 keywords, Allen finds that Google takes less time to manage. American Meadows has dropped its catalog and other print advertising altogether, finding the return on PPC to be far greater. With the catalog now online only, Allen supplements PPC with banner ads on other gardening Web sites. As the company grows, so, too, has its PPC spending, roughly doubling every two years.

"We have new product introductory sales, promotions, even one week sales. . . . This takes work to do all the ads, prepare the site, and then when the sale is over, change all the ads again. But believe me, it works, and almost none of your competitors are doing it."

Chapter 12

Marketing with Paid Online Advertising

In This Chapter

▶ Understanding online advertising options

▶ Making tactical banner decisions

▶ Sponsoring newsletters

▶ Selling through online classifieds

*L*inkable online display advertising, broadly called *banner advertising,* is one of the more expensive methods of online promotion. From a strategic perspective, banner ads work well for branding, often pushing traffic to your site after running for a period of time. *Direct response banners* (those intended to generate an immediate click-through) generally have a lower CTR (click-through rate) than pay per click (PPC) search marketing (described in Chapter 11).

In addition to banners, consider less expensive newsletter and site sponsorships, and online classifieds. Depending on your budget, you might want to explore one or more of these paid advertising options. If so, check them off on your Web Marketing Methods Checklist from Chapter 2, which you can download from www.dummies.com/go/webmarketing at full size.

Compared to the cost of print media, banner advertising — with the added plus of easy tracking — looks like a bargain. Indeed, some of the growth in Internet advertising has come at the expense of print and billboards. Figure 12-1, which shows the allocation of advertising dollars in April 2006, includes only banner ads in its Internet market share. The Internet share would be higher if other types of online advertising were included.

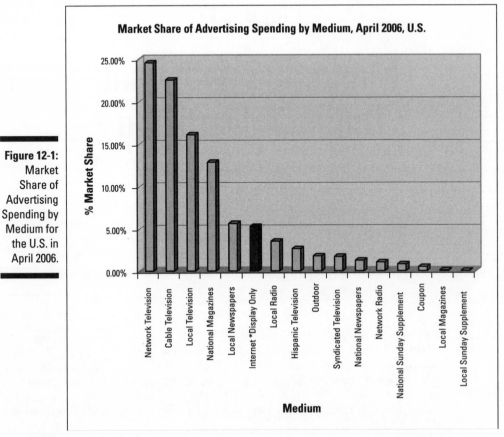

Courtesy Nielsen Media Research

Figure 12-1:
Market Share of Advertising Spending by Medium for the U.S. in April 2006.

Total expenditures for all types of online ads — including search, e-mail, classifieds, and banners — hit a record $7.9 billion during the first half of 2006, according to the Interactive Advertising Bureau (`www.iab.net/news/pr_2006_09_25.asp`).

Understanding Banner Advertising

One of the more complex aspects of online marketing, paid banners are tantalizing and seductive but not always the most cost-effective use of your money. With an average CTR hovering slightly below 1 percent, most banner ads produce only one-third to one-half as many clicks as PPC search marketing.

Figure 12-2 (which you can find at `www.roi-web.com/cost_per_customer_acquisition.asp`) is a graphic reminder that banner advertising is the most expensive of all forms of customer acquisition, exceeding even traditional media.

Figure 12-2:
Banner ads are the most expensive form of customer acquisition; by comparison, customer referrals are free.

$ Cost per New Customer Acquired →

Banner Advertising

Traditional Media Support

Email/Newsletter Sponsorship

Affiliate/Partnering Programs

Paid Per-Click Placement

Opt-In Email

Free Links Negotiation

Search Engine Optimization

Customer Referral

©Rapport Online, Inc. Courtesy Rapport Online, Inc., roi-web

Your developer generally doesn't handle online advertising, although one with a strong background in marketing communications can produce banner and Flash ads. Because you need good *creatives* (ads) to compete in the banner world, go to a pro, especially for rich media ads using Flash, video, or sound. Some networks will create your ads for a price or offer banner-builders onsite.

You can place ads yourself by reviewing online media kits, calling individual Web sites that post ads (called *publishers*), or using one of the networks listed in Table 12-1. An online marketing company or ad agency can also help with your media buys.

Table 12-1	Online Advertising Resources	
Name	**URL**	**What You'll Find**
AdCritic.com	`www.adcritic.com/interactive`	Examples of creative banner ads
Adotas	`www.adotas.com/2006/08/the-ad-network-analysis-adotas-surveys-the-cream-of-the-crop-from-bottom-to-top/2`	Rating of ad networks

(continued)

Table 12-1 *(continued)*

Name	URL	What You'll Find
Banner Co-Op	`http://bannerco-op.com`	Sample banner exchange program
DoubleClick	`www.doubleclick.com/us/knowledge_central/documents/research/dc_bpwp_0605.asp`	White paper on best practices
Google AdWords	`https://adwords.google.com/select/imagesamples.html`	Popular ad sizes used on Google
iBoost Journal	`www.ipowerweb.com/profit/advertising/networks/00003.htm`	Directory of ad networks
iMedia Connection	`www.imediaconnection.com/adnetworks/index.asp`	Resources for online advertising
Internet Advertising Bureau	`www.iab.net/standards/adunits.asp`	List of standard online ad sizes
Web Marketing Association	`www.advertisingcompetition.org/iac`	Internet ad competition
Online Advertising Discussion List	`www.o-a.com`	Discussion list and advertising resources
University of Delaware	`www.udel.edu/alex/dictionary.html`	Dictionary of online advertising terms
Web Reference	`www.webreference.com/promotion/banners/networks.html`	Directory of networks
Webby Awards	`www.webbyawards.com/webbys/categories.php#interactive_advertising`	Internet ad competition

Paid online advertising comes in a variety of forms:

✔ Static banner ads in various sizes, as shown in Figure 12-3

✔ Animated GIF or Flash ads

✔ Other rich media ads involving video or sound

Figure 12-3:
Some common banner sizes are shown on Google, which lets you distribute banners, Flash animation, and video ads to content partners through its AdWords program.

Screenshots © Google Inc. and are reproduced with permission.

✔ Pop-ups, which infamously appear over a page

✔ Pop-unders, which are visible when you close a window

✔ Interstitial ads that appear as user links between pages

✔ Expandable ads that grow to cover more of a page when users hover over them

At the risk of being repetitious, a successful ad owes 20 percent to the creative, 40 percent to the offer, and 40 percent to the right audience. As with PPC ads, be sure to match your offer to your audience. Be careful, also, to link to the correct landing page on your site.

Get inspired by looking at award-winning ads at the competition sites in Table 12-1, which also lists a number of other online advertising resources.

If you're willing to post ads on your site, you can test the waters with a banner exchange program like the one at BannerCo-Op.com. You can also use an exchange program to test one creative against another for efficacy before going to an expensive publisher's site.

Keep in mind that the audience you get through an exchange program will probably not be as targeted as the audience you get through a paid network, and certainly not as targeted as individual sites that you identify yourself.

Making Banner Ad Decisions

You need to make six tactical decisions about banner ads:

✔ How much you're willing to spend

✔ Whether you'll handle the campaign yourself or use a network or agency

✔ Where to advertise

✔ What type of ads you'll run

✔ How to evaluate the return on investment (ROI) of your banner campaign

✔ Whether it's appropriate to use paid advertising in nontraditional venues like video or blogs

Estimating costs

Unlike pay per click ads, charges for most banner ads are either cost per thousand impressions (CPM) or a flat rate per month, quarter, or year. The more targeted the audience, the more you pay. Decide how much of your overall marketing budget to dedicate to paid banner advertising. Drive your spending from your budget, not by costs.

Most sites that accept advertising publish a media kit online. The media kit should include demographics, page views, banner size specifications, and rates. If you can't find it on the site, look for an Advertising link to locate contact information for a sales representative.

A broadly targeted, consumer audience might run only a few dollars per thousand impressions. A prequalified, narrowly targeted market, such as vice-presidents of financial corporations, can have a CPM of $70–$100 or more. Portal sites, which have a low CPM, generally have a very high minimum as well. Highly trafficked sites like the Yahoo! portal, major news outlets, entertainment and sports sites, and other portals are generally too expensive for small businesses.

Various factors affect the rates charged for ads:

✔ Size and type of ad; Flash ads with only a few images can generally run for the same price as static banners

✔ Location of an ad on a page

✔ Number of ads sharing the same space in rotation

✔ Pages of the site on which an ad runs; ads that appear on every page are called *run of site* (ROS)

✔ Length of contract for running the ad

Life is negotiable! A site that has just recently opened its ad program, or is trying to fill empty slots, might cut a deal. Watch for *house ads* — ads for the publisher itself — as a sign of unsold inventory. Sometimes, you can get a publisher to run an ad for several weeks as a free trial. Ask! What's to lose?

Doing it yourself or using an agency

You might pay a premium of 10–15 percent over the cost of direct placement if you use an agency or network to place your ads. The CPM on some ad networks is fairly low, which indicates that the audiences are rather broad. If you plan to run ads on only several sites, you can probably handle placement yourself.

If you intend to run an extensive branding campaign over dozens to hundreds of sites, you'll find it much easier to use a network, which automates placement and reporting. For an intermediate solution, try the Self-Service option at Advertising.com (`www.advertising.com/abt_self_service.php`).

Table 12-2 lists some of the many online advertising networks, or you can explore the network directories in Table 12-1. Confirm that the network you select offers sites within your specific channel of interest or target demographics. Sometimes, a specialty network is a better solution, particularly for B2B advertisers.

Table 12-2	Some Online Advertising Networks
Name	**URL**
24/7 Real Media	www.247realmedia.com
Advertising.com Self-Service Option	www.advertising.com/abt_self_ service.php
AOL Media Networks	http://advisor.aol.com
Blogads	www.blogads.com
Blue Lithium	http://bluelithium.com
Burst Media	http://burstmedia.com
FeedBurner Ad Network	https://feedburner.com/ads/ add-campaign.do
Gorilla Nation Media	www.gorillanation.com
Microsoft CPC Banners	www.microsoft.com/smallbusiness/ online/banner-advertising/detail. mspx
Right Media	www.rightmedia.com/content/right- media-exchange/1
Tribal Fusion	http://tribalfusion.com
ValueClick Media	www.valueclickmedia.com

Deciding where to advertise

If you run an inbound link popularity report (www.linkpopularity.com) on your competitors, you might be able to identify where they're running ads. A banner ad is merely a link in drag, after all.

Look at other ads on a publication site as a clue to whether particular sites are appropriate for your business. Then check their online media kits. If you don't find detailed information about demographics, page views, or the number of ads sharing the same space in rotation, ask. Ask, too, about reporting options and how to track the results of your campaigns.

Rates are usually lowest for run of site (ROS) because ads might appear on many pages that get relatively few viewers. Rates are highest for the home page, which is usually the most highly trafficked page on the site. You might do well to select an inside page at the second or third level. Rates are lower, but visitors to the page might actually be better qualified as prospects for your site.

Generally, publishers won't divulge or predict CTR. That depends too much on the quality of the creative and the value of the offer made in an ad.

Create a spreadsheet showing CPM, demographics, and banner options to compare alternatives more easily.

Choosing banner types, sizes, and position

Bigger is better! Go for leaderboards, large rectangles, and wide skyscrapers (refer to Figure 12-3) if you can afford them. Figure 12-4 (`www.adrelevance.com/intelligence/intel_dataglance.jsp`) shows that advertisers favor larger options, with the single exception of medium rather than large rectangles.

The best positions for ads are on the right side by the scroll bar, as close to the top of the page as possible, but definitely above the fold. Rectangles integrated with page layout also work well. Avoid standard banner ads (468 x 60 pixels) at the top of a page — viewers ignore them.

If you can't afford big ads, take small ones in a better position. Ask about supplying an animated Flash ad rather than a static one. If a publisher's ad server can handle them, small Flash ads will attract more attention than large static ones. If a Flash ad fits within the same file size limits set for a static ad, you usually won't pay more for it.

Want to create several alternate offers but can't afford to buy more than one position? Ask whether you can supply several static ads that rotate in your position. Because there's usually no charge for this, you can compare CTRs to assess the effectiveness of your ads.

You can find free or low-cost software online for creating banners and animated ads. However, many of those ads look somewhat amateurish. If you are spending significant money on your advertising, invest the $80–$100 per ad needed to hire a graphic designer.

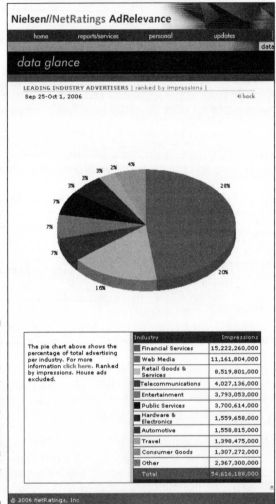

Figure 12-4:
This graph shows how banner advertisers spent their dollars during the last week of September 2006.

Source: Nielsen//NetRatings Ad Relevance Sep. 25–Oct 1, 2006

Companies with highly visual products find banner ads of great value in their campaigns. NewMexicoCreates.org, an online gallery for fine arts and crafts by New Mexico artists, initiated a banner campaign shortly after the site went live in 2006. Figure 12-5 shows a sample of its suite of banner ads; the nearby sidebar explains the ad campaign.

Courtesy Museum of New Mexico Foundation Shops

Figure 12-5:
Examples of
the multiple
banner ads
used in the
online ad
campaign
for
NewMexico
Creates.org.

Evaluating results

At the very least, publishers should provide the number of impressions and the CTR, by ad and by page. Small publishers might provide this only once a month; others might have an online dashboard for viewing results in near real time.

Like Google, some publishers might provide code for conversion tracking. If you run multiple ads that share a landing page, ask your programmer to create a different URL for links from each ad to track the number of visits by ad and by publisher.

Your programmer can place a cookie for tracking a visitor from arrival to purchase. Easier yet, you can manage cross-channel conversion tracking through Google AdWords (`https://adwords.google.com/support/bin/topic.py?topic=230`).

If the functions of your banner and PPC ads are comparable, calculate your ROI for banner ads the same way. However, you might need to measure a banner ad designed for branding by a different criterion. You might want to calculate ROI by individual ad, ad types, publisher, offer, or time period.

Oh boy, banners

NewMexicoCreates.org launched in late summer 2006 with an aggressive promotion plan to make holiday sales. The site, which is an online gallery for unique, handcrafted pieces of art, is a project of the Museum of New Mexico Foundation Shops. MNMF Shops already has experience managing a successful online museum store at www.ShopMuseum.com as a vehicle for its four museums (Museum of Fine Art, Museum of Indian Arts & Culture, Museum of International Folk Art, and Palace of the Governors/New Mexico History Museum).

MNMF Shops also already had a very good idea of the target audience for NewMexicoCreates: women over 45 in higher-income brackets. Its target audience of art collectors, who travel widely, also have sophisticated tastes in apparel and jewelry. Art collectors happen to correlate well with buyers of fine wines and leisure activities.

NewMexicoCreates ran its banners through Google's CPM program on carefully culled AdSense partners, as well as through independent contracts on several thoroughly researched, high-end, regional sites in wealthy markets, and on art sites. Designed in a variety of sizes, the banner ads appeared in multiple formats: traditional Web sites, blogs, directories, and as newsletter sponsorships.

Banners were only part of the integrated promotional campaign, which encompassed search engine optimization, PPC ads, e-mail newsletters sent to inhouse and rental lists, print ads, press releases, and promotional bookmarks distributed through the museum shops.

Considering multimedia banners, blogs, and RSS feeds

Most developers don't have the skills to create ads with video or audio. Go to the same professionals who create audio and visual materials for your site. Because these ads are much more expensive to produce, you might want to limit their use.

You can place banner ads in other places, including blogs (as shown in Figure 12-6) and in RSS feeds. The networks Feedster (www.feedster. com/corporate/advertise.php) and Pheedo (http://pheedo.com/ advertisers) offer options for advertising in RSS feeds.

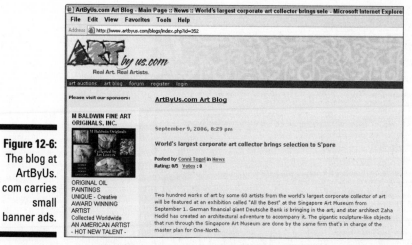

Blog site ©2006 ArtByUs.com. Banner ad ©2006 M. Baldwin Fine Art Originals, Inc. All rights reserved.

Figure 12-6:
The blog at ArtByUs. com carries small banner ads.

Sponsoring Newsletters and Sites

Sponsorships, which garner only 4 percent of online ad spending, are often overlooked as a means of increasing your company's exposure on either for-profit or not-for-profit sites.

While you can promote your products and services in only a subtle manner on not-for-profit sites, you benefit from the goodwill of visitors who appreciate your support for something that matters to them, such as the environment or healthcare research.

This cost-effective advertising opportunity comes in three forms, generally requiring contributions at increasing levels:

- **Newsletter sponsorships:** Offered by the issue or by the month. Advertising might be text (as shown in the newsletter from `www.hin.com/hinwkly.html` in Figure 12-7), graphics, or both. This type of advertising gives you access to a targeted mailing list that is probably not available any other way.

- **Site sponsorship:** Usually, small button ads with different prices based on links and placement.

- **Integrated sponsorship:** Combines both of the previous, with added visibility for company name and logo in other offline media. It works especially well if you adopt a particular not-for-profit related to your business mission as your company's focus for charitable giving.

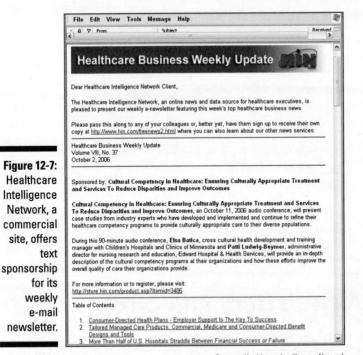

Figure 12-7:
Healthcare
Intelligence
Network, a
commercial
site, offers
text
sponsorship
for its
weekly
e-mail
newsletter.

Courtesy Healthcare Intelligence Network

A 2005 study by Performance Research found that viewers were more likely to consider purchasing from a sponsor (41 percent) than from an advertiser (23 percent).

Advertising with Online Classifieds

According to the Interactive Advertising Bureau (IAB), online classifieds accounted for 20 percent of online ad spending in the first half of 2006. While individuals use classified sites as a grand cyber-swap meet, your business can use them to sell merchandise, services, entertainment, or commercial rentals. (See Figure 12-8 for an example.)

Choose from either free or low-cost independent classified sites, classified sections of MySpace, Yahoo! and other portals, or product-specific classified sites for cars, apartments, and pets. A small sampling of popular classified sites appears in Table 12-3.

Figure 12-8: La Casita lists its bed & breakfast inn in Albuquerque as a vacation rental on Craigslist .org.

Courtesy La Casita Bed & Breakfast: Patrick Joseph Hoffman, William R. Davis

Table 12-3	Sample Classified Ad Sites	
Name	**URL**	**Fee or Free**
Abracat	www.abracat.com	Fee (collates online classi-fieds from many newspapers)
CityNews	www.citynews.com	Fee
Craigslist	http://craigslist. org	Free (with a few exceptions)
eDirection	http://www. edirection.com	Free
EPage Classifieds	http://epage.com	Free
LiveDeal	www.livedeal.com	Free
Mpire	www.mpire.com	Fee (multisite posting)
OnLine eXchange	www.olx.com	Free
Postlets	www.postlets.com	Free (multisite posting)

(continued)

Table 12-3 *(continued)*		
Name	*URL*	*Fee or Free*
ShopLocal.com	www.shoplocal.com	Fee
TraderOnline.com	www.traderonline.com	Fee
vFlyer	www.vflyer.com	Free (multisite posting)
Web Marketing Today	www.wilsonweb.com/cat/cat.cfm?page=1&subcat=ma_Classified	Free (classified ad resources)

Generally designed for local advertising, you must post classifieds on multiple sites for broad coverage. To overcome this time-consuming hassle, three new services listed in Table 12-3 (Postlets, vFlyer, and Mpire) offer easy, multiple postings to many classified sites.

Writing a good classified is an art. Keep the following principles in mind:

✔ Grab attention with the title, using strong, emotional words that pack a punch.

✔ Repeat descriptive text from the title in the body of the ad for maximum impact.

✔ If you're offering a service, include the main benefit in the title.

✔ Don't use all caps.

✔ Avoid excessive use of exclamation points.

✔ Include a picture, if possible.

✔ Tell people what they have to do to get more information or make a purchase (call to action).

✔ Include a link to your Web site, which is good for search engine ranking, too.

✔ To avoid receiving spam, don't post your e-mail address online.

✔ Test different titles and copy to find out what works best.

✔ Write separate ads for different items.

✔ Proofread your ad carefully for correct spelling and grammar.

These principles are a lot like the ones you use for writing pay per click text ads and Web copy. Classified ads also perform better when you write them in active voice and second person (you).

Chapter 13

Capturing Customers with New Technology

*I*s your target audience mostly young, hip, and technologically savvy? Are you an adventurous marketer with a bit of a budget? Most of the technology-driven techniques described in this chapter fit these profiles for audience and advertiser, though not exclusively, and probably not for long.

Two trends drive these new applications: increased broadband access and the search for convergence among multiple communications devices, such as cellphones and hand-held units. As new Internet technology evolves, the marketing applications now on the cutting edge will become mainstream. In the meantime, you have several years to get a jump on your competition.

Here are some of the techniques described in this chapter:

✔ Adding video blogging, or *vlogging,* for branding or generating leads

✔ Using Real Simple Syndication (RSS) as an alternative to e-mail for new content and products

✔ Producing online training seminars to generate leads and enhance branding

✔ Distributing audio podcasts to catch people on the move in a form of radio on demand

✔ Combining text messaging on cell phones with search queries and site promotion

✔ Leveraging your presence with Web content customized for mobile devices

If you decide to use any of these techniques, add them to your Web Marketing Methods Checklist from Chapter 2. (For convenience, you can download the checklist from the book's companion Web site, www. dummies.com/go/webmarketing.) Although they don't have the reach of mass-market advertising, these methods might reach influentials. Early adopters of technology are heavy users of online media but comprise a small percentage of the online audience.

New technologies always enjoy a certain amount of hype. Be cautious about investing in these techniques unless — or until — your target market uses them. Don't get enamored with a technology at the expense of your bottom line.

Adding Video Blogging to Your Campaign

The growth of broadband access plus the advent of inexpensive video recording technology has fueled a surge in video on the Web. YouTube.com symbolizes the growth. This venture-financed company, which opened in February 2005, drew 16 million visits per month less than two years later, according to comScore Media Metrix. Users also post their own videos — often no more than a personal journal — in the video sections of Yahoo!, MySpace, MSN, AOL, Google, and many other sites.

What are vlogs?

Streaming video or video downloads have long been available on individual Web sites. When you combine short video clips with a distribution channel, you have *video blogs,* or *vlogs.* While vlogs imply video on the Web, video clips and even episodes from broadcast TV now appear on cell phones, iPods, and personal digital assistants (PDAs). For marketers, the trick is to tap into the video audience in one of three ways:

- ✔ Advertising on these sites (covered in Chapter 12)
- ✔ Posting your own vlog, perhaps one that is quirky enough to be part of a viral marketing campaign
- ✔ Tapping into the creative potential of your target audience by getting them to post vlogs about your company or products

Combined visits to video sites total more than 100 million per month. Many of these are one-time visits as a result of clicks on links recommended by friends.

Vlog viewers/producers don't represent the Internet population overall. As a group, they're likely to fit the standard profile of early adopters: younger, better educated, wealthier, and more likely to be male. (Overall, women represent about half of all Internet users.)

Vlogging considerations

First, view some vlogs (search the directories in Table 13-1) to get ideas from other businesses. Then decide whether you want to create your own vlog or whether you want vloggers to participate interactively.

Table 13-1	Vlog Resources	
Name	*URL*	*What You'll Find*
del.icio.us	http://del.icio.us/thelastminute/vlogging	Blogs about vlogs
FeeVlog	http://feevlog.com	Vlog service
Freevlog	http://freevlog.org/tutorial	How to make a vlog
Rocketboom	www.rocketboom.com/vlog	News vlog and directory
Singingfish	http://search.singingfish.com/sfw/submit.html	Submit to video and podcast directory
Vidblogs.com	www.vidblogs.com	Vlog host
VLogDir	http://vlogdir.com/suggest.php?action=addlink	Submit to directory of vlogs
YouTube	www.youtube.com/signup?next=/my_videos_upload%3F	Submit to video site

Movie, sports, entertainment, and music sites are obvious candidates for vlogging: Post trailers, teasers, concert samples, or game excerpts. You can also use vlogs for product updates, industry news, or helpful, do-it-yourself, training clips, like ifixipodsfast.com does in Figure 13-1. Its free training vlog builds credibility and links to its Web site for additional products and service.

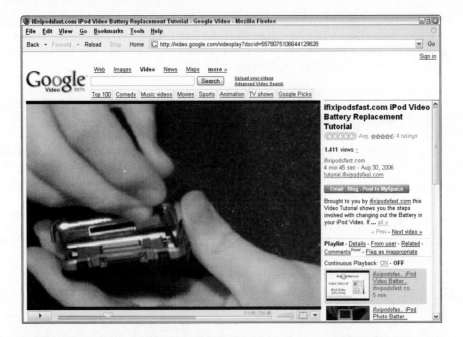

Figure 13-1: ifixipodsfast. com uses a vlog to show people how to replace an iPod battery

Site and video courtesy Blake Paulson/ifixipodsfast.com. Google video screenshots © Google Inc. and are reproduced with permission.

Even if you post the same video on your site, the vlog posting offers an additional pathway for new prospects. As with most online techniques, shorter is better!

Many companies now run vlog contests, inviting users to post video that promotes their product or service. Be careful! When Chevy tried this for its Tahoe SUV, it received many negative commercials complaining about poor gas mileage and environmental damage. That's the risk you run.

Most Web developers don't have the skills to produce vlogs, although they can certainly help you upload them and post video on your site. It's one thing for individuals to produce low-quality video with their digital video cameras, but it's quite another for a business to do so. If you don't feel comfortable producing video yourself, look for film school students, video production companies, or marketing companies that specialize in video. Start with the resources in Table 13-1.

Whether you create your own vlog or recruit responses, pay attention to the demographics of the sites on which you post. As with most online techniques, shorter is better!

Feeding Updates to Your Fans with Real Simple Syndication (RSS)

Have you noticed an orange symbol with concentric arcs (as shown in the margin) on news sites or blogs? It might appear in a browser toolbar, on the right side of the address box for many Web sites, or on individual Web pages. The symbol, which stands for Real Simple Syndication (RSS), indicates that visitors can sign up to receive automatic notifications of new content on that page. (Sometimes, you'll see *XML* rather than *RSS* in an orange box.)

RSS technology has been around since 1999 as a way to distribute (syndicate) content from Web sites. Marketers awoke slowly to its potential for avoiding e-mail distribution problems while expanding access to prospects.

Understanding how RSS works

On their request, RSS notifies users when you change content on your site. In classic marketing terms, users "pull" the information they want instead of you "pushing" it to them. They can sign up or opt out whenever they choose.

RSS involves four steps:

1. Your developer formats content in a special file, called a *feed*.

2. If people want to receive your updates, they add your URL to the list in their RSS reader software, much like bookmarking a site.

3. When you change your content, your feed is updated.

4. The user's reader software visits your site on a set schedule. If the reader finds an update, it posts a message in the user's e-mail inbox or on the reader list in the user's browser.

Users can download free RSS reader software if needed, but readers are already bundled into the latest versions of browsers, e-mail programs, and operating systems, including the newest release of Windows. (If you can see the orange symbol, an RSS reader is already installed.) As users upgrade their computer systems and tools, RSS will become easier to use and more popular.

RSS should be right up your developer's alley. If she has any questions, start with the resources in Table 13-2 for leads to technical information.

RSS is less cumbersome than e-mail. You don't have to manage address lists, and your message won't get lost in a spam filter. From users' perspectives, an anonymous RSS feed protects them from spam, phishing, and identify theft.

The simplest form of RSS gives everyone the same feed whenever anything changes on the site. Individualized RSS (IRSS) lets users specify which changes they want to know about. One person might want to know when you add new shoe models; another might want to know only about raincoats. Because IRSS access can be tracked much like e-mail newsletters, you can respond to your audience's interests more easily.

Table 13-2	RSS Resources	
Name	*URL*	*What You'll Find*
Bloglines	www.bloglines.com	Publish, subscribe, or search for blogs
ContentDesk	http://rssfeeds. contentdesk.com/dir/ addfeed.html?catid=	Submit to RSS search engine
FeedBurner.com	www.feedburner.com	Prepares blogs and other content feeds for RSS
FeedForAll	www.feedforall.com/ index.htm	Create, edit, and publish RSS feeds
Feedster	www.feedster.com	Directory of feeds; news, blogs, podcasts
Feed Validator	www.feedvalidator. org	Checks feeds for correct RSS formatting
NewsGator	www.newsgator.com/ home.aspx	RSS feeder and reader software

Name	URL	What You'll Find
RSS Feed Reader	`http://rssfeedreader.com`	Add others' RSS feeds to your site
RssReader	`www.rssreader.com`	Free reader and publisher software
SiteBuildIt!	`http://rss.sitesell.com/rss-1.html`	RSS basics

Knowing when to use RSS

As of January 2005, the Pew Internet & American Life Project counted 6 million U.S. Internet users with active RSS readers, less than 5 percent of those online. A separate 2006 study by WorkPlace Print Media showed that "88 percent of the at-work audience doesn't even know what RSS is."

Despite these numbers, some 11 percent of e-mail marketers already use RSS feeds, and another 25 percent plan to do so, according to a 2006 survey by Jupiter Research. Most see it as a way around e-mail delivery problems for now augmenting their e-mail efforts.

RSS is best for sites with frequently changing content, such as news, weather, science, medicine, or technical support updates. It's also useful for product sites with large, dynamic inventories, such as event tickets or airline flights.

The RSS audience tends to be younger and wealthier than the average user and technically astute. RSS is well suited to academic or select B2B environments, such as high tech or journalism. As more people become familiar with the concept and as RSS is distributed with new equipment, the user base will grow.

Unlike other technologies in this section, RSS is free, other than having your developer do a little work. If you want something even cheaper, create an RSS feed for your free blog. Because an RSS feed might increase blog distribution and repeat traffic to your site, it might also indirectly improve your search engine ranking.

Developing sales prospects

RSS is an excellent way to let people know immediately when you post new products, sales, or specials. Because people might be more likely to sign up for a feed than for a newsletter, you might convert more visitors to prospects.

Ask your developer to use Individual RSS so you can track what interests your visitors. It's great market intelligence! You might want to create special offers or promo codes for RSS subscribers to monitor involvement all the way through purchase.

Be sure to explain the benefits of signing up for RSS on your site. Of course, submit your RSS feed to the directories and search engines shown in Table 13-2. One note of warning: RSS subscribers might simply look at the feeds without clicking back to the source site.

By keeping your name and Web site in front of users with news feeds, RSS is excellent for branding. Of course, this works only if you update your site frequently, not just once a year!

Delivering Useful Content: Webcasts, Web Conferences, and Webinars

In the instant-gratification world of the Web, you rarely have a chance to interact with prospects or customers for more than a few seconds, let alone minutes. All three Web education methods (Webcasts, Web conferences, and Webinars) allow you 15 minutes or more of uninterrupted user contact. How can you pass that up, especially when you compare the costs of traveling and staging live events in multiple locations.

These content-driven techniques work very well in B2B environments, where you can adapt them for free product demonstrations, market research presentations, and/or teaching sessions in exchange for contact information. They're great for building brand awareness, positioning your company as a leader, and generating sales leads. Don't poison the well with overt marketing or sales pitches.

Segment leads by including a question on the signup form about registrants' levels of interest or decision-making time frames.

Comparing options

Webcasts, Web conferences, and Webinars all run in a browser environment. The combination of increased broadband access and the inclusion of streaming media within browsers makes these methods more attractive.

Webcasts

Generally a *Webcast* refers to a live, video-only, Internet broadcast. Inherently passive, it's delivered from one speaker to many listeners, often 50 or more. Of the three techniques, Webcasts work best in a B2C environment for concerts, lectures, dance, comedy, theater, performance art, sports, events, entertainment, and the actual delivery of educational or training content. Depending on its audience and purpose, you can promote a Webcast like any other online event, as I discuss in Chapter 9.

Web conferences

Web conferences work best with small group presentations that are data or document driven. They support two-way interaction, such as in an online focus group or a presentation near the close of the sales cycle. Conferences generally involve some combination of two-way audio teleconferencing, live desktop-based whiteboards, PowerPoint presentations, and instant messaging or chat software.

Webinars

Webinars are the most-complex format, mixing and matching such multimedia components as a one-way audio conference, video (sometimes a talking head, which is more useful for product demonstrations), PowerPoint or whiteboard presentations, live polls or surveys, and one-way instant messaging for participants to submit questions.

Designed to reach a large number of participants over a widespread geographic region, Webinars generally require a sequence of activities to be successful: promotion, registration, confirmation e-mails, reminder e-mails, thank-you messages, and feedback surveys. Consider these as premium branding and lead generation opportunities.

Deciding how to go about it

Before planning Webinars or Web conferences, participate in a few to see how other businesses use them. (Search some of the sites in Table 13-3.)

Table 13-3	Webcast and Webinar Resources	
Name	*URL*	*What You'll Find*
Conference Calls Unlimited	`http://conferencecall sunlimited.com/web.html`	Commercial Web teleconferencing provider
GoToMeeting	`www.gotomeeting.com`	Commercial Web conferencing provider
HRmarketer	`http://hrmarketer.blog spot.com/2005/01/using- webinars-as-effective- marketing.html`	Tips on promoting and conducting a Webinar

(continued)

Table 13-3 *(continued)*

Name	URL	What You'll Find
Macromedia Breeze	`www.adobe.com/products/breeze`	Flash-based software for Web conferencing
MeetingBridge	`www.meetingbridge.com//home.aspx`	Low-cost Webinar service provider
Mollygard	`www.mollyguard.com/accounts`	Free, basic Webinar registration service
WebEvent Search.com	`www.webeventsearch.com/build.asp`	Submit Webinars and Webcasts
WebEx WebOffice	`www.webex.com/solutions/small_business.html`	Commercial Webinar provider, small business option
WebEx MeetMeNow	`http://meetmenow.webex.com`	Commercial Web conferencing provider
Webinar Blog	`http://wsuccess.typepad.com/webinarblog`	Blog about Webinars

Expect falloff from registration to attendance. Perhaps only 30–40 percent of preregistrants actually show up. Of those, you'll probably find only 5 percent to 10 percent of your registrants are close to sales ready. Step softly in these environments! Use these opportunities to build credibility and trust, establish a relationship, and answer questions fairly.

Here are some tips for planning Webinars or Web conferences:

✔ To increase attendance, focus on high-quality, relevant content. If what you offer is useful and appealing, you'll find an audience.

✔ Your promotion should clearly answer, "What's in it for me?" Be sure to list your live events in Web event directories, as shown in Table 13-3 and discussed in Chapter 9. Consider paid advertising or newsletter sponsorships to promote your Web learning event.

✔ Get more mileage from the effort involved! Archive any of these events on your site and make them easily available on demand. This also saves staff time downstream.

✔ Use one of many survey packages available (StellarSurvey.com, Zoomerang.com, SurveyMonkey.com) to obtain feedback after the event. You might want to share some or all of the feedback with participants in a final, e-mailed, thank-you note. Of course, include contact information for the future.

Unless you have a large company or plan frequent Webcasts, conferences, and Webinars, you probably don't want to purchase and install software. Look for third-party providers to handle the real-time events. Simply search for them or start with the sample companies listed in Table 13-3. Your developer can easily post your archived media on your site, of course.

Delivering Content and Generating Leads with Podcasts

Coined as a term in 2004, *podcasts* are basically radio on demand over the Internet. Like RSS and vlogs, they currently exhibit more promise than practice. According to a Forrester Research report in April 2006, only 1 percent of Internet users listen to podcasts regularly, and another 2 percent have tried them occasionally. About 73 percent say "they've never heard of podcasting and don't care to learn more about it."

Other studies insist that as many as 11 percent of Internet users have listened to at least one podcast. Some exuberant, early predictions estimate 12 million or more podcast listeners by 2010.

Holding the world together, one child at a time

In January 2005, Gretchen Vogelzang and Paige Heninger decided to open MommyCast.com as an informational Web site. Aware that busy moms lack the time to form close, personal ties and need information-on-the-go, they soon decided to start podcasting. By September 2006, they had produced 117 podcasts of 20–30 minutes each — mostly interviews — and 20 music shows.

The pair started out casually, with simple podcasting equipment and "fell into being a business." The most difficult step, they say, was deciding to take MommyCast to the next level, which they have done with a great deal of professional acumen.

They invested in better audio equipment and hired an audio engineer, recognizing that professional podcasts would be more attractive to advertisers and sponsors. It worked. Sponsors now include Dixie and Walt Disney Studios, and MommyCast sells another one or two advertisements per show.

Sponsors like Dixie offer great online exposure, feeding listeners to MommyCast.com. In addition, MommyCast markets through a natural search campaign, inbound links, branded promotional items from CafePress.com, active media coverage, and word of mouth. Consequently, the site registers more than 550,000 monthly downloads and averages 75,000–90,000 monthly subscribers.

They advise other podcasters to "go for it and don't worry about being perfect, right out of the gate."

Before you spend money producing audio programs, make sure your audience listens to podcasts. Initially, the podcast audience skewed young, male, and wealthy, but a recent Arbitron survey shows that the demographics have smoothed out, with women now representing 48 percent of listeners, and users 35 or older comprising 45 percent of the audience. The success of the podcasting site MommyCast.com (described in the sidebar "Holding the world together, one child at a time" and shown in Figure 13-2) confirms the shift. This Internet radio show, "for and by women immersed in motherhood and life," was the first podcast to receive commercial sponsorship.

Figure 13-2:
MommyCast.
com
receives a
stream of
visitors from
its primary
sponsor,
Dixie, as
well as from
other
marketing
efforts.

Courtesy mommycast@gmail.com. Dixie and Make It a Dixie Day are trademarks of Georgia-Pacific Corporation or one of its subsidiaries.

Understanding how podcasts work

The term *podcasting* comes from a combination of the acronym for *portable on demand* and *broadcasting*. Users download digital audio files by using free podcasting software and then listen at their convenience on their computer, iPod, or other portable MP3 player.

Listeners can use Windows Media Player or RealPlayer to hear streaming audio in real time or downloaded files. Other free software is used to transfer files to an MP3 player. Users might download an individual podcast or subscribe via RSS to an ongoing podcasting feed.

To make a podcast, you record your audio content, adding music and effects if you desire. You upload your audio file to your Web site or to another hosting location, such as those in Table 13-4. Then you reformat the podcast for RSS with FeedBurner (see Table 13-2) or something similar. After that, promote your podcast and submit it to directories and search engines.

Table 13-4	Podcasting Resources	
Name	*URL*	*What You'll Find*
Apple.com	`www.apple.com/itunes/store/podcaststechspecs.html`	Production resources, submissions
iTunes	`www.apple.com/itunes/download`	Free podcasting software for Mac or PC
Audacity	`http://audacity.sourceforge.net`	Free sound-editing software
Digital Podcast	`www.digitalpodcast.com/login.php`	Podcast directory you can submit to
Indie Podder	`www.ipodder.org/directory/4/ipodderSoftware`	Free podcasting software for Mac or PC
Marketing Sherpa	`http://www.marketingsherpa.com/barrier.php?ident=29679`	Article: "Practical Podcasting Guide for Marketers"
Odeo Studio	`http://studio.odeo.com/create/home`	Free resources to create and publish podcasts
Podcast Alley	`http://podcastalley.com/add_a_podcast.php`	Podcast directory you can submit to
Podcast Bunker	`www.podcastbunker.com/Podcast/Podcast_Picks/Podcast_Submit_Form`	Podcast directory you can submit to
Podcasting News	`http://podcastingnews.com/topics/Add_Your_Podcast.html`	Podcast directory you can submit to
Podcast.net	`http://www.podcast.net/addpodcast`	Podcast directory you can submit to
PodshowCreator	`www.podshowcreator.com`	Commercial podcast creation, syndication, hosting, and tracking

(continued)

Name	URL	What You'll Find
	Table 13-4 *(continued)*	
Podtrac	`http://podtrac.com/essentials/essentials-meth-measurement.stm`	Free, audience demographics for podcasts
Yahoo! Podcasts	`http://podcasts.yahoo.com/publish`	Resources, directory

Your skills, equipment access, and confidence can help you decide whether to create your podcast yourself or hire someone. Creating podcasts might be outside the comfort zone for most developers, unless you have one who specializes in audio. Developers can, however, help you upload files to your site.

Low-cost, third-party, turnkey solutions might be the easiest way to go. Some are listed in Table 13-4, and you'll find others through a simple search. You can create podcasts by using nothing more than a phone (see Table 13-4) or do high-quality productions at local sound studios.

Audio quality is actually more critical than video quality. Listeners are on their own with your audio content, lacking the supplemental information an image provides — or the distraction factor.

Getting the best results from podcasts

Before you decide to market with podcasts, listen to some (search the directories in Table 13-4) to hear how other businesses take advantage of this technique. To buy ads on existing podcasts, see one of the advertising networks in Table 13-4 or find a podcast that you'd like to sponsor.

If you want to create your own podcast, decide what you're trying to accomplish. Like Webinars (described earlier in the chapter), podcasts are best used for branding, lead generation, and content delivery — not sales. Also, take some time to think about your content. Unfortunately, just reading your newsletter aloud won't work. Audio is completely different from print; it definitely has a performance component. Will you riff on your own commentary? Interview someone? If so, whom? Clients, colleagues, decision makers in your field?

Don't do just one podcast to experiment. These take practice. Try at least a short run of 6–10 episodes of 10–20 minutes each.

After you've created content, promote your podcasts aggressively:

- Feature your podcasts on your site and make them easily accessible by link.
- Submit them to podcast search engines and directories
- Consider distributing your podcast as free content to other appropriate sites on the Web.
- Research bloggers who might continue the topic in print while promoting your podcast.
- Send out a press release in advance of a celebrity guest or special event.
- Track results. You can measure the number of downloads, but it's hard to know whether people actually listened. If you publicize your site on blogs, you can note the number of *trackbacks* (other sites that mention your podcast).

Entering the Wireless World

Mobile marketing, which includes cellphones, PDAs, iPods, and other hand-held devices, offers several options: text messaging (which is also called *SMS,* for *short messaging service*), picture messaging (which is also called *MMS*, for *multimedia messaging service*), and mobile Internet advertising (in which Web content is specially formatted for mobile devices).

A 2006 survey conducted by Harris Interactive's quarterly Mobile Media Monitor illustrates the opportunity. It estimated more than 200 million wire-less subscribers in the U.S., with about one-third using some form of mobile media beyond personal text messaging. Of those, 29 percent were female, 36 percent male. Like other new technologies, use of mobile content skews to the young (18–24), the affluent, and the technologically experienced.

Unlike some of the other technologies, ethnic groups — African American, Asian American, and Hispanic American — use mobile data more often than the general population.

Searching + text messaging

Teenagers have grabbed headlines for communicating with text messages over cell phones, sending answers to everything from final exams to the secret of life. Marketers and search engine companies have been looking for more modest ways to answer questions asked by someone on the road.

Wireless Internet access makes it possible for cell phone users to ask and receive results of search queries in SMS format, which is available on more than 95 percent of all cell phones. A caller enters a text query by using a keyword and zip code or location, such as *Chinese food 47110.* She sends her message to a special, five-digit number for Google (46645), Yahoo! (92466), or 4Info.net (44636). In response, she receives a text message with a list of names, addresses, and phone numbers for Chinese restaurants in that zip code.

The most valuable uses for search-based text messaging occur when time or geographic constraints affect a decision or activity: hotels, tourist destinations, restaurants, entertainment, movie schedules, sporting events, transportation schedules, driving directions, gas stations, appointment reminders, or action alerts.

If your business is in one of these market sectors, search by text is one more incentive to submit your site to city directories and search engines, including mapping and local options. As cell phones incorporate geographic information system (GIS) technology, you'll be able to further narrow your marketing to callers in specific neighborhoods. This type of location-aware technology is more advanced in Japan and Europe than in the U.S.

Initiating a text messaging campaign

Large companies have combined text messaging successfully with other advertising. For instance, users can text message their votes on *American Idol* or respond to a packaging promotion to win a prize. Because cell phone users are often close to making a purchasing decision or an impulse buy, SMS works well for sales messages. Remember that the maximum length is 160 characters, so keep your messages short. For branding purposes, you can sponsor a text service for stock tickers or sports scores.

Many large advertisers, such as McDonald's, send promotional messages or coupons with SMS. Customers usually redeem an SMS coupon by showing their stored text message at checkout.

Companies that sell ring tones, screen savers, wallpapers, games, and other mobile content are some of the biggest users of SMS. Stock tickers, horoscopes, sports scores, emergency services, retail offers, weather, price comparisons, and real estate applications now appear on cell phones and PDAs as well.

Never send unsolicited text messages to customers' cell phones. Depending on an individual's cell phone plan, a consumer might have to pay to receive text messages; in that case, the customer would be furious to receive spam. In Europe, where text-messaging services are more common, cell phone users already complain about this type of spam.

Most text messaging campaigns follow a few, simple steps:

1. Register a 5-digit code that will work on all carriers and have each wireless network approve it. You can choose to restrict an ad campaign to only one or two carriers. You can send messages to e-mail addresses, through a specific carrier's Web site, or with special messaging software.

2. Think of a promotion that invites users "to text" first as an opt-in — for example, a TV, print, billboard, or radio ad that tells customers to enter your number to get a coupon, a free sample, or to enter a contest. You can repeat the offer on your Web site for a cross-media promotion.

3. Measure your responses to assess the effectiveness of your campaign. Compared to other forms of advertising, the costs of text messaging are relatively low and the audience is very targeted. Generic, opt-in rates range from 1–5 percent, with even higher rates when the opt-in program is very appealing.

Text message marketing is outside the standard realm of a Web site developer. Consider using a third-party provider, such as the examples in Table 13-5. They, and dozens of others found through a simple search, provide opt-in subscriber lists, ad distribution, campaign management, and tracking.

Table 13-5	Text Messaging Resources	
Name	*URL*	*What You'll Find*
Bulk SMS	`www.smswarehouse.com/html/bulk_sms.html`	Bulk text messaging provider
DM News	`www.dmnews.com/cms/dm-news/e-commerce/33240.html`	Article: "Going Direct with Mobile Marketing"
dmoz	`http://dmoz.org/Computers/Mobile_Computing/Wireless_Data/Short_Messaging_Service/Software`	Directory of SMS providers
Google SMS	`www.google.com/sms`	SMS for Google search results
HowStuffWorks	`www.howstuffworks.com/instant-messaging.htm`	Instant messaging information
ICQ	`www.icq.com/download/wireless`	Commercial provider SMS and instant messaging

(continued)

Table 13-4 *(continued)*

Name	URL	What You'll Find
Miranda IM	`www.miranda-im.org`	Open source IM software
Simplewire	`http://simplewire.com`	Commercial SMS provider
Wireless Association	`http://www.ctia.org`	Trade association, statistics
Yahoo! Mobile	`http://mobile.yahoo.com/sms/sendsms`	Send text from PC free

Marketing with picture messaging (MMS)

Picture messaging works like SMS but supports graphics, animation, video, or audio. It reaches about half as many users as SMS, but the conversion rates are often well over 5 percent because MMS (multimedia messaging service) reaches such a highly motivated audience.

Stick with simple things for MMS. Consider sponsoring news or data feeds with an ordinary banner. Banner click-through rates on cell phones reach about 4 percent, compared to 1 percent online. Click-to-call options are a nice fit on cell phones.

Developing Web sites for wireless access

PDAs and most cell phones can now access the Web, offering yet another way to promote your site or deliver content such as news, sports, blogs, vlogs, and games. Typically, users must subscribe to a data plan for their cell phone to enable Web browser capabilities.

Some 30 million consumers now use mobile devices for Web surfing, but only a small fraction of cell phone users own the advanced 3G phones designed for video and music; few of those seem ready to pay for premium content.

Most Web sites translate poorly to cell phone and PDA environments. Graphics-heavy sites take a long time to download; text-intensive sites are hard to read. A special, top-level domain (.mobi) indicates a Web site specially designed for visibility on the tiny screen. Until the industry fully settles on standards, however, adoption of this technology will be slow.

New ad formats combining text, video, and the location-based nature of cell phones might be technologically feasible, but that doesn't mean they should be implemented. In-your-face advertising that invades private space might provoke a backlash. Even large companies move tentatively in this area.

Special, third-party providers develop .mobi sites and can help you plan a wireless marketing campaign. A few examples, along with other mobile marketing resources, are listed in Table 13-6. The only limits are your imagination, your budget, and the presence of your target audience.

Table 13-6	Wireless Marketing Resources	
Name	**URL**	**What You'll Find**
Brilliant Blue	www.brilliantblue. com/_landing_pages/ wireless.htm	Commercial provider of mobile marketing
Cellit Mobile Marketing	www.cellitmarketing. com	Commercial provider of mobile marketing
Enpocket	www.enpocket.com	Commercial provider of mobile marketing
Google Mobile Web Search	www.google.com/ mobile/mobile_search. html	Mobile-ready sites
Mobile Marketing Association	www.mmaglobal.com	Trade association
Mobile Top Level Domain	http://pc.mtld.mobi	dotMobi association, . mobi emulator, and list of registrars
Mobile Weblog	www.mobile-weblog.com	Blog about wireless marketing
Palowireless	www.palowireless.com	Wireless resource directory
Simplewire	www.simplewire.com	Commercial provider of mobile marketing, software
Third Screen Media	http://thirdscreen media.com	Commercial provider of mobile marketing

Part V
Maximizing Your Web Success

In this part . . .

A book about Web marketing isn't complete without a discussion of Web analytics and a sketch of the overall environment in which Web marketing occurs.

Chapter 14 discusses using basic Web statistics about traffic and sales to understand user behavior and improve the performance of your site. Combined with financial statistics, you can use Web analytics as part of a cycle of continuous quality improvement to make sure your site (and your profits) spiral upward.

Every Web site exists in a real-world matrix of legal, tax, and regulatory constraints. Because these concerns might affect your profitability and access to prospective customers, Chapter 15 identifies some issues for you to consider. From the CAN-SPAM Act to privacy laws, from Internet sales taxes to intellectual property concerns, you're responsible for keeping your site legal. Remember, any activity that is illegal offline is illegal online.

Finally, Chapter 16 returns to marketing basics as the best way to maintain a vibrant, innovative, and profitable Web presence. Surprise: Good business practices make good Web practices. More than anything, listen to your customers and provide good service. Keep innovating, be creative, and have a good time. When your online business stops being fun, maybe it's time to think about doing something else.

Chapter 14

Improving Results with Web Analytics

*W*eb analytics is the art of using traffic and sales statistics to understand user behavior and improve the performance of your site. In the best of all possible worlds, analytics is part of a continuous spiral of feedback and quality improvement.

Before getting mired in the details of Web analytics, think about your most critical statistics — your financials! If you have a business site, the most important number to know is whether the site is providing a return on your investment. If you aren't making a profit, it doesn't matter whether you have fantastic traffic, a soaring conversion rate, or revenues through the roof.

As part of the planning of your site, talk to your bookkeeper or accountant. While this conversation is obviously critical for a site that sells online, it's equally important for tracking costs on a nonsales site. Unless you have a tiny, brochureware site, ask your accountant to

✔ **Set up your Web site as a separate job in your accounting software.** This will enable you to track costs (and revenue, if appropriate) attributable to the site. In other words, operate your site financially as if you're opening up a new, brick-and-mortar location and need to know how it performs. Your Web site is, indeed, a new cost center and — with some hard work and luck — a new profit center.

✔ **Segregate online advertising expenses from other marketing and advertising costs in a unique cost category.** If you sell online, separate online shipping and handling costs from offline shipping. You need to track whether you're losing money on shipping, one of the most common problems e-tailers have.

✔ **Decide how you'll allocate labor, benefits, and overhead costs to your Web site.** While cost of goods might be obvious, cost of sales is not.

✔ **Figure out how development costs will be amortized over how long a time frame.** Having trouble figuring out return on investment (ROI)? Bookkeepers and accountants compute this for entertainment.

✔ **Become familiar with your site goals and objectives, help measure financial results, and prepare a custom report monthly or quarterly.**

✔ **Review your Web and store statistics software to see what data should be fed into the accounting system.** If you already have an integrated inventory, point of sales (POS), and accounting system, this might be semiautomatic.

Your financials are worth the effort only if you use them. Watch that profit number like a hawk to ensure that your projections are on track — or as an early-warning sign that revenues and expenses are getting out of whack. Act as soon as you identify a problem because it won't solve itself.

Now, and only now, are you ready to use Web analytics to improve your marketing and your Web site.

Tracking Web Site Activity

The basic principle "You can't manage what you don't measure" applies doubly to Web sites. You must know whether your site is losing or gaining traffic; whether visitors boogie away after less than a minute; or whether anyone is bothering to call, e-mail, or buy. Otherwise, you don't have a clue what problem you need to solve, let alone how to solve it.

Fortunately, computers are good at counting. In fact, that's what they do best. All sites need traffic statistics; if you sell online, you also need sales statistics. Unless you have a huge site, you need to pay attention to only a few key statistics, as detailed in the later section, "Which statistics to fret over." You find more information about Web analytics in Table 14-1, which provides a list of resource sites.

Table 14-1	Information Resources for Web Analytics	
Name	*URL*	*What You'll Find*
Emetrics.org	`www.emetrics.org/resources.html`	Articles, events, resources
WebTrends	`www.webtrends.com/Resources/WhitepapersAndGuides/ClickZBestofWebAnalyticsGuide/1069.aspx`	Article download

Name	URL	What You'll Find
Gartner Marketscope for Web Analytics	`www.websidestory.com/public/assets/pdf/white papers/Gartner.pdf`	Article download
Google Analytics	`www.google.com/analytics/conversionuniversity.html`	Google-specific resources
Web Analytics Association	`www.webanalytics association.org/index.asp`	Resources, events
Web Analytics Demystified	`www.webanalytics demystified.com/web-analytics-resources.asp`	Resources, links, worksheets
WebSideStory	`www.websidestory.com/resources/best-practice-briefs/overview.html`	Article downloads
WebTrends	`www.webtrends.com/resources.aspx`	Resources

Ask your developer or Web host which statistical packages are offered for your site. Unless you have a fairly large site or need real-time data, one of the free packages in Table 14-2 should be fine. Review your choices to select the best fit for your needs. Do the same thing with sales analytics (sometimes called *store statistics*), which usually come bundled with storebuilder or shopping cart software. If your developer or Web host tells you that statistics aren't available or that you don't need them, find another developer, host, or storefront package.

Table 14-2	Some Free Statistical Packages
Name	**URL**
AccessWatch	`www.accesswatch.com`
AddFreeStats	`www.addfreestats.com`
Analog and Report Magic	`www.analog.cx` used with `www.reportmagic.org`
AWStats	`http://awstats.org`
eXTReMe Tracking (1 page only)	`http://extremetracking.com/?reg`
Google Analytics	`www.google.com/analytics`

(continued)

Table 14-2 *(continued)*	
Name	*URL*
StatCounter	www.statcounter.com
Web Stats (shareware)	www.webstats2003.com
Webalizer	www.mrunix.net/webalizer

Identifying What Parameters to Measure

When you read articles about Web analytics, you might see the term *key performance indicators* (KPI). KPI differs slightly for each business and Web site. A lead generation site and retail site both care about the most important statistic of all: *conversion rate.* However, requests for quote might be a KPI for a B2B lead generation site. For a retailer, number and average value per sale are more important. Because you calculate conversion rate, you must decide what's essential to measure.

Ignore hits. A *hit* is every little file downloaded as part of a Web page. In other words, every image is a hit; every text file is a hit. Hit rates usually overstate the number of visits to a site by a factor of 10 or 12. As mentioned in Chapter 4, never put a visible hit rate or visitor counter on your site.

The sections that follow address some general Web statistics that are worth attention, but they might not apply to your business. After you decide what really matters, monitor whichever Web statistics best support your needs.

Which statistics to fret over

Of the many, many statistics that are available, the following key parameters provide valuable information for every business. Compare them by month or week, depending on the statistical package you use. Sites with heavy traffic justify review by day, or even by hour. Figure 14-1 shows a typical statistical summary.

Some packages might use slightly different terms but measure the same things. (These definitions apply to whichever time frame you choose.) Here are the key statistics to track:

- **Visits:** The number of distinct *user sessions* that take place; in other words, how many times your Web site is viewed. This is your total traffic to the site. Stat packages might define a new visit after different time periods expire; many users go back and forth among Web sites several times. Most statistical packages delete visits made by search engine spiders or robots because these artificially inflate the number of visits.

✔ **Unique visitors:** The number of user sessions from different computers. (Stats can track users' IP addresses but not who's sitting at the machine.) This number will be smaller than total visits; the difference represents repeat visits, which are extremely valuable. To assess your success drawing people back to your site, you might want to track visits/visitor or repeat visits as a percent of all visits.

✔ **Page views:** The total number of distinct Web pages downloaded — that is, seen on the screen.

✔ **Page views per visit:** The number of pages seen divided by total visits. The more pages seen, the longer the user is on the site and the *stickier* your site is. If more than half your visitors leave before viewing two pages, you have a problem capturing viewers' attentions and interests. This key parameter correlates roughly to time on site. Time measurement can be misleading, however, because it doesn't take into account what happens if people leave a browser window open when they go to lunch or leave at the end of the day.

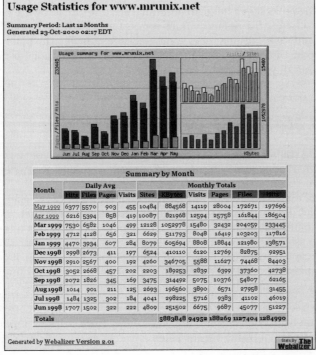

Figure 14-1:
Webalizer, one of the most common, free statistical packages, displays a summary page with visits and pages, as both daily averages and monthly totals.

Usage Statistics for www.mrunix.net

Summary Period: Last 12 Months
Generated 23-Oct-2000 02:17 EDT

Month	Daily Avg				Monthly Totals					
	Hits	Files	Pages	Visits	Sites	KBytes	Visits	Pages	Files	Hits
May 1999	6377	5570	903	455	10484	884568	14119	28004	172671	197696
Apr 1999	6216	5394	858	419	10087	821968	12594	25758	161844	186504
Mar 1999	7530	6582	1046	499	12128	1052978	15480	32432	204059	233445
Feb 1999	4712	4128	656	321	6629	511793	8048	16419	103203	117816
Jan 1999	4470	3934	607	284	8079	605694	8808	18844	121980	138571
Dec 1998	2998	2673	411	197	6524	410110	6120	12769	82875	92951
Nov 1998	2910	2567	400	192	4260	346705	5588	11627	74468	84403
Oct 1998	3052	2668	457	202	2203	189253	2839	6399	37360	42738
Sep 1998	2072	1826	345	169	3475	314492	5075	10376	54807	62165
Aug 1998	1014	901	211	125	2693	196560	3890	6571	27958	31455
Jul 1998	1484	1325	302	184	4041	298225	5716	9383	41102	46019
Jun 1998	1707	1502	322	222	4809	251502	6675	9687	45077	51227
Totals						5883848	94952	188269	1127404	1284990

Generated by Webalizer Version 2.01

Courtesy Cold Spring Harbor Laboratory

✔ **URLs viewed:** How many times each individual page of your site is viewed (downloaded). It's helpful to know not only which pages are popular, but also which ones aren't. The latter might be due to lack of interest or perhaps a lack of contextual links or calls to action that pull someone to that page. This statistic is handy to count Thank You pages for contact forms or other pages that are part of your conversion equation.

✔ **Referrers:** The Web sites or pages that generated a link to your site. Some statistical packages include links between onsite pages in this list. If you have an active, inbound link campaign, you can easily see which links are driving traffic your way. You might also discover links from previously unknown sources.

✔ **Search engines:** Which search engines generated a link to your site based on appearance in natural search results.

✔ **Conversion rate:** This number is calculated as a percentage. The denominator is total visits. You decide on the numerator, whether it's number of sales, number of contact forms, e-mails or calls generated from the site, newsletter subscribers, and so on.

Unless you have a very large site, monitoring statistics monthly or quarterly is usually sufficient. You might check more often when you first open your site and whenever you initiate a specific Web marketing activity.

Most statistical packages have an administrative setup, allowing your programmer to change the default values for certain statistics. If you don't see what you want, ask! For instance, some packages display the page views for only the top 25 URLs. If you have a larger site, set that parameter to display the results for all your pages.

Which statistics to scan casually

The following statistics are less critical but still helpful when you make decisions about your marketing program, site development, or timing of newsletters:

✔ **Time of day:** The time of day people visit lets you know whether they're visiting from work (where they usually have faster Internet access) or from home. Watch for a bulge around lunchtime, which is often a good time to release a newsletter. Unless you're publicizing your site locally only, your hours of use will extend across four time zones. If you're marketing internationally, use will spread out over time accordingly.

✔ **Day of week:** The days of the week also let you know patterns of use, from work or home. Anecdotal evidence shows shoppers browsing from home on weekends and buying on Monday from work. Compare your own patterns of traffic versus sales.

✔ **Browsers and OS:** Most statistical packages can identify browser, version, and operating system. This information is valuable during development because you can infer some characteristics of your user base: The more current these items, the more likely your users also have faster access and higher-resolution monitors. Let this information guide the features you include on your site and the size screen for which your site is optimized.

- ✔ **Length of visit:** Some analytics packages offer length or duration of visit in minutes and seconds (for a sample display). Set a goal to have more than half your visitors stay more than 30 seconds.

- ✔ **Search strings:** Also called *search terms,* these are the words that users entered into a search engine when they found your site. If these terms aren't already in your keyword list, add them. You might also want to use them in your keyword list for PPC ads. Some advanced packages analyze search strings by search engine. Different people use different search engines, and they often use different terms.

- ✔ **Countries:** Whether you're already shipping internationally or thinking about it, watch these statistics. They can indicate either your success penetrating another market or where interest exists.

- ✔ **Hosts or sites:** This is a list of host IP addresses of visitors to your site, sometimes sorted by state. If you're curious about an address that seems to generate many visits, you can find out to whom it belongs. Try clicking the IP address, copying it into the address bar of your browser, or submitting it to the WhoIs database at `www.networksolutions.com/whois/index.jsp` to see who owns it. This data is sometimes used to track someone hacking your site.

- ✔ **Entry pages:** Some packages display how users first arrived at your site. While your home page is almost always the most frequently used entry page, users might enter on other pages: from a bookmark; from a link provided by someone else; by clicking another URL that shows up in natural search engine results; by clicking a landing page URL in an ad, or by entering a promotion-specific URL that you created. This is a quick way to track entries from offline ads.

- ✔ **Exit pages:** The last page that users view can provide insight into when "they've had enough." In some cases, the exit page is a thank-you.

Take absolute numbers for any statistic with an entire shaker of salt. While there are efforts to standardize the meaning of statistical terms, right now, they're still efforts. For example, does a new visitor session start after someone has logged off for 24 minutes or 24 hours? Relative numbers are more meaningful. Is your traffic growing or shrinking? Is your conversion rate increasing or decreasing?

To minimize attention on absolute values, focus on ratios or percentages. Suppose 10 percent of a small number of viewers converted before you conduct a sales-focused ad campaign, compared to only 5 percent of a larger number of viewers afterwards — what does that tell you? (It might indicate that your ad wasn't directed tightly on your target market.)

Even if they let you set a date range, some free stat software packages will display only 12 consecutive months of data. They won't let you review stats for a more useful, 13-month window. That's unfortunate because most sites — even B2B — experience cyclic traffic, especially during the summer and around holidays. For retailers, same-store sales comparing say, May 2007 to May 2008, are critical. If your stat package has this limitation, and you can't select another, download and back up statistics for comparison on your own. You can feed the data into a graphical display through spreadsheet software.

Some statistics are more useful to your developer than to you. Every quarter or so, ask your developer to review such statistics as bandwidth and HTTP status codes, especially for pages not found.

Special statistical needs

If you have a large site with heavy traffic or extensive reporting needs, free packages might not be enough. You'll find hundreds of paid statistical programs through an online search; a few are listed in Table 14-3. Several are fairly inexpensive, but the ones marked "high-end" can escalate into real money. Generally, those labeled "high-end" or "hosted" solutions offer real-time analysis.

Table 14-3	Some Paid Statistical Packages	
Name	**URL**	**What You'll Find**
123Log Analyzer	www.123loganalyzer.com/webtrends.htm	Installed software, low price
ClickTracks	www.clicktracks.com	High-end solution
Coremetrics	www.coremetrics.com	High-end solution
DeepMetrix LiveSTATS	www.deepmetrix.com/livestats/net	Recently acquired by Microsoft
Index Tools	www.indextools.com	Hosted solution
Log Rover	www.logrover.com	Installed software, low price
Omniture	www.omniture.com/products/web_analytics	High-end solution
OneStat.com	www.onestat.com/html/os_pro.html	Hosted real-time solution
Sawmill Lite	www.sawmill.net/lite.html	Installed software, low price

Name	URL	What You'll Find
Site Stats Lite	www1.sitestats.com/home/home.php	Hosted real-time solution
VisitorVille	www.visitorville.com	Hosted 3-D statistics
WebTrends	www.webtrends.com/Products/Solutions/SmallBusiness.aspx	High-end solution

Like so many other solutions for Internet services, stat packages fall into two categories: installed software placed on your server and hosted solutions, which send your traffic data to a third-party site for analysis. Instead of a one-time fixed price, most hosted solutions charge monthly fees based on the number of visits or page views that occur. Paid solutions offer additional options, such as

- More flexible, sophisticated reporting tools and data-mining filters.

- Real-time analysis, compared to the time-delayed display on most free packages.

- Visual displays that make site statistics easier to understand, as shown in Visitorville.com in Figure 14-2.

- Path-through-site analysis, which tracks an individual user from entry to exit in a process called *clickstream tracking*.

- Integration of traffic and store statistics to track a user from entry through purchase.

- *Funnel displays,* which are graphic depictions of the conversion funnels as visitors move through your site.

- Analysis of downloaded PDFs, video, audio, or other files.

- Mapping of host addresses to company names and details. Some services such as WebTracker (http://binomic.com/en-US) specialize in these statistics to show whether competitors visit your site or whether prospects you've met follow up with a site visit.

- Additional details, such as analysis by the page, or by the visitor, as shown on Opentracker's site in Figure 14-3.

- Information about where visitors go after leaving your site.

Whether you need any of this information depends on your KPI, the complexity of your site, the amount of traffic it receives (you must have enough to make statistical analysis valid), and what you would do with the information if you had it. Don't bother collecting information for information's sake. Stop when you have enough data to make essential business decisions.

Figure 14-2:
Visitorville.
com offers
a unique
graphic
perspective
on users'
paths
through the
site
(clickstream
analysis).

© 2006, World Market Watch, Inc. All rights reserved. VisitorVille is a registered trademark of World Market Watch, Inc.

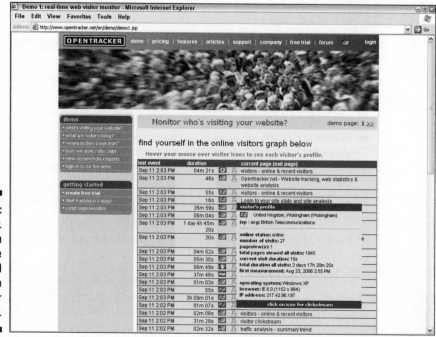

Figure 14-3:
Opentracker.
net lets you
see usage
and
identification
details for
any visitor.

Courtesy Opentracker.net

While it's nice to know industry averages, the only statistics that really matter are yours. Bear in mind that industry statistics are just as prone to error in absolute value as the stats you collect for your own site. Once again, pay more attention to trends and relative values.

Interpreting Sales Statistics

Traffic stats are relevant for all sites, but those who sell online face another challenge. It's just as important to analyze what's happening with a cyber-store as it is for a brick-and-mortar shop. Business owners who integrate their bricks-&-clicks operations through shared point of sales (POS) software, inventory control, and accounting might need to make some changes in their reports but have a framework to start with. For store statistics, pure-play online businesses must rely on software supplied with their storefront package or custom-developed by their programmer.

If you expect significant sales on a catalog of more than a few products, store statistics are critical. When selecting your storefront package or developer, review the statistics you'll receive. If you can't get statistics, look elsewhere for a storefront solution.

Here are a few of the statistics to watch for:

- ✔ Internal store reports, often by item, include the number of active items, items missing images, and store size.

- ✔ In addition to summary sales reports, watch for sales reports broken down by products. Sometimes called a *product tree,* these statistics reflect your store organization, with reports at category, subcategory, and product level.

- ✔ Look for sales reports by average dollar amount, as well as by number of sales.

- ✔ You should have the ability to request order totals for a specific period of time that you define.

- ✔ Sales sorted by day should be available so you can track sales tied to promotions, marketing activities, and sale announcements.

- ✔ Make sure you can collect statistics on the use of promotion codes by number and dollar value so you can decide which promotions are the most successful.

- ✔ If you use special shopping features such as gift registries, upselling, cross-selling, wish lists, or an affiliate program, monitor the items sold and those on reserve for each activity.

✔ Sales sorted by customers, both to allow for future, personalized correspondence and to see how many repeat versus new customers you have, can be useful.

✔ The standard shopping cart abandonment rate is 75 percent. It's important for you to know how many carts were opened, compared to the number of completed purchases. Computation can be tricky if your storefront places cookies that allow users up to 30 days to complete a transaction. Statistics that show the contents of abandoned (and active) carts can give you a clue about merchandising changes that you might need.

✔ If you haven't used an integrated storebuilder solution, you might discover that users often enter a completely different Web site when they link to shopping online (watch what happens to the URL). Only a portion of users who arrive at your HTML site will shift to your storefront, essentially creating an intermediate conversion rate. Be sure you understand how the store statistical package interprets the number of visitors. You will overestimate your conversion rate if your base is the number of visitors who enter the store itself rather than those who arrive at your site.

The sales report in Figure 14-4 is an example of the type of store statistics available.

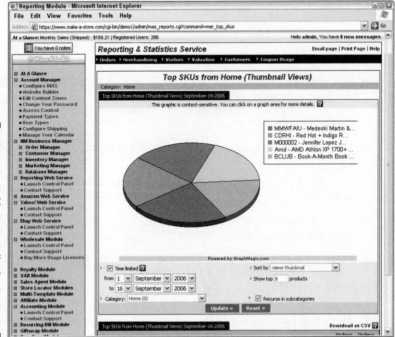

Figure 14-4:
Make-a-Store shopping cart software includes a graphic display of sales by category in its store statistics.

Courtesy MAKE-A-STORE, Inc.

Diagnosing Conversion Rate Troubles

Without a doubt, a poor conversion rate is the key statistic to watch. Depending on the nature of your site, your product or service, and your sales cycle, a reasonable conversion rate will probably fall into the 2 to 5 percent range. Retail sites with less-expensive goods generally see a higher rate than that. If your problem is low traffic, you have lots of marketing options to try.

If traffic is good but your conversion rate doesn't hit the mark you established in your financial projections, you have three possibilities to address: your audience, your Web site, or your business fundamentals, including merchandising. Web analytics can help you determine the source of the problem and the solution. It's the ultimate proof of management by measurement! Here are some sample problems.

Is the conversion problem with the audience?

If you see a fair amount of traffic coming to the site (total visitors), but the conversion rate and repeat visitors are low, you might have the wrong audience. Look at pages per view or time on site. If those parameters are less than three pages per visit and/or less than two minutes, the problem is with either the audience or the Web site. If those numbers are high, you've got the right audience. Check referrers, search engines, search terms, and entry pages to see how people arrive at your site.

 Have you defined your target audience correctly and narrowly? "Everyone over 25 who uses a computer" is not a well-defined market! How successfully are you reaching them? Segment your market into smaller slices and target only one segment at a time. If you're running ads, are they specific enough to what you do? Does the landing page take people directly to the product or service you promote in your ad or strand them on the home page? Are your keywords and text adequately focused to draw your target market?

Fix these problems and watch the results. If these changes don't work, the difficulty might be with the site itself.

Is the conversion problem with the Web site itself?

Web site problems show up in many ways. If you're getting the right audience (high pages per visit and time on site) but users leave without fulfilling the objective you established, you might have trouble with the site itself. Compare the lists of entry and exit pages. Are they close to the same? If so, your visitors might have trouble with navigation.

Inking a deal through analytics

A family-owned, B2B, promotional products company in Wichita, Kansas, Inkspress has been in business for 25 years. Since going online in 2003, Inkspress has seen its revenues expand by 30 percent and forecasts 50 percent growth by 2008. Business was a little slow for the first 12–18 months, says owner Tom Staats, until they figured out their marketing.

Web analytics played a key role from the start. Son Randy Staats, who is also the Inkspress Web developer, explains that the company shopped around to find software that would provide the detail they wanted. After some experimentation, they settled on DeepMetrix LiveStats. Given Inkspress' key performance indicators, the most helpful statistics include which search terms are used, which pages are visited, and the number of new visitors.

They use the results to tweak their site regularly. For the first few months, they checked statistics daily. As Web site revenues increased, they were able to cut back to a weekly review. Randy advises technical users, "With lots of research to help you determine which direction to take, you can do this yourself." He recommends that nontechnical users hire a professional.

Their efforts paid off: Inkspress was voted the #1 Web site by the Promotional Products Association International (www.ppai.com).

Look at the HTTP error codes and browsers used. Have you designed a site that's appropriate for the browser, OS, monitor, and access speed? Ask your programmer to make sure links are working and that there are no *orphan pages* (pages no one can get to). He can recheck syntax and browser compatibility as well.

If the site is functioning correctly, take a look at your text and navigation. Did you include calls to action so users know what to do? Are directions clear? Does the process meet users' expectations for speed and ease of use? Observe people who've never used the site as they figure out how to locate information and complete a transaction, whether a sale or inquiry. Check your onsite search function to see what people are looking for. If they can't find what they're looking for (and what they want fits with what you offer), then you might have navigation, content, or product issues. See what happens after you address these concerns.

Is the conversion problem with business fundamentals?

If your target market arrives at a well-designed, well-functioning Web site and still doesn't convert, you have to go back to basics. Are you offering the product or service they want, at a price they will pay? Your onsite search statistics might tell you whether you need to modify your product or service offerings.

Here are some additional issues to consider:

- ✔ Do you have enough merchandise on the site for selection purposes?

- ✔ Are you positioned correctly against your competition? Do you have a clearly stated value proposition that sets you apart from your competition? Are your expectations correct?

- ✔ Is your viewer researching online but buying offline from you or others?

- ✔ Are you reaching people at the right point in the sales cycle?

    (In either of the two previous cases, you might see multiple visits from the same user.)

- ✔ Are you reaching the right decision-maker? Most B2B efforts close offline.

- ✔ Are you integrating your sales efforts with your Web marketing for follow-through? A Web site can't follow up on leads for you!

Inkspress, described in the nearby sidebar and whose site is shown in Figure 14-5, uses Web analytics to optimize its site in a process much like this.

Figure 14-5: Inkspress. com used Web analytics as one key to their success.

Courtesy Inkspress™

Chapter 15

Staying Out of Legal Trouble

In This Chapter

▶ Asking permission is less expensive than begging forgiveness

▶ Protecting your intellectual property

▶ Respecting users' privacy

▶ Protecting kids

▶ Avoiding legal traps

*E*very Web site in cyberspace also exists in a real-world matrix of legal constraints. As a businessperson, you need to understand the legal environment to protect yourself and your company online, just as you protect it offline. Because legal concerns might affect your costs, audience definition, and profitability, issues of cyberlaw become marketing concerns.

As commercial uses and other applications of the Web expand, Congress creates new laws, such as the CAN-SPAM Act that I discuss in Chapter 8, or the Children's Online Privacy Protection Act. Congress can also decide to inhibit online activity, such as temporarily prohibiting the imposition of sales taxes on goods sold online to out-of-state destinations (though local taxes might still be collected) or forbidding online gambling, using servers in the U.S.

In other cases, courts and regulatory agencies apply existing laws to the online environment. Their activity generally encompasses intellectual property (IP) laws for copyright, trademark and patents, and basic business laws, such as fraud, warranties, disclaimers, and sweepstakes. If you sell internationally, you might need to research the laws and regulations of your target countries.

An activity that is illegal offline is illegal online.

There's nothing like running afoul of the law to bring your Web site and marketing efforts to a sudden and possibly expensive halt. In this chapter, I review generally accepted best practices in terms of U.S. laws that affect your Web site. In Chapter 16, I alert you to legislative and regulatory changes that might affect you in the future.

Besides consulting your business lawyer or an intellectual property attorney, you might want to check the resource sites in Table 15-1 for more information on the legal aspects of cyberspace.

Table 15-1	Legal Resource Sites	
Name	*URL*	*What You'll Find*
American Bar Association	`www.abanet.org/intelprop/sites.html`	Intellectual property resource list
American Bar Association	`www.abanet.org/intelprop/probono_nationwide.html`	Pro bono organizations dealing with intellectual property and cyberlaw
Electronic Frontier Foundation	`www.eff.org`	Not-for-profit organization defending free speech, privacy, and consumer rights online
FindLaw	`http://smallbusiness.findlaw.com/business-operations/internet.html`	Free legal information and forms for small businesses
International Technology Law Association	`www.itechlaw.org`	Professional legal association for computer lawyers

Protecting Copyright on the Web

Copyright protects creative work in any medium — text, photos, graphics, audio, video, multimedia, software — from being used by others without permission. Your work becomes your intellectual property as soon as you've created it in a fixed form. The rules for copyright are simple: Protect your own work and don't use other people's work without permission.

Whenever you sign an agreement with a Web developer, writer, graphic designer, or hosting company, be sure to read the fine print that says who is going to own the copyright on the material they create. A *work for hire* is when a person creates a copyrightable work but does not own it. How can this be? The Copyright Act allows for the copyright to go not to the creator but to the person who hired the creator to make the work. The law treats the creator as if he did not even participate. The employer owns the copyright, and it is as if they created the work themselves without any help from the actual creator.

You might need to ask that the work belong to you as a work for hire (when the copyright for a creative work is held by the person who hired the creator). Some creative contractors, especially photographers, might give you only a limited license to use the creative work in one application or will insist on holding the copyright. If you can't negotiate a change in the agreement, find another provider. What if the developer goes out of business? Or sells his or her company and you don't like the next owner? In the worst case, you could lose your site and/or its content if you get into a dispute with the provider. At the very least, insist on a non-exclusive right to use the programming on the site or other creative work in perpetuity on any server for no additional cost. Your agreement with employees should clearly state that you or your business retains ownership of any intellectual property they create for you.

Put a copyright notice on your Web site. The standard format includes the word `copyright`, `copr.`, or symbol © followed by the year, name of copyright holder, and usually the term `All Rights Reserved`. For example, on my Web site, I might include the following notice:

```
© 2000-2006 Watermelon Mountain Web Marketing All rights reserved.
```

Sometimes, the copyright notice specifies that the copyright applies to only a certain portion of the creative material, such as `Content ©`, or indicates that certain elements have been used with permission. Some companies supplement the copyright notice with a page of legal information, as ThirdAge does in Figure 15-1.

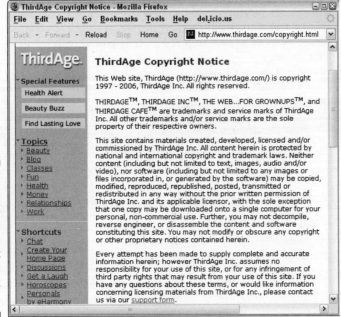

Figure 15-1:
The ThirdAge site displays both copyright and trademark information.

© *Third Age, Inc.* http:www.thirdage.com

Have your developer put the copyright notice in the footer so it appears on every page of your site.

This copyright notice gives you basic copyright protection. In most cases, this is enough. However, if you're a graphic designer or photographer with images to protect or if you think some of your material is at risk of being used without permission, file a copyright with the Library of Congress. Filing gives you better legal standing and a larger damage award if you win after suing someone for copyright infringement.

Carefully follow the directions at www.copyright.gov and send in $45 with your application form from www.copyright.gov/forms along with copies of your material. You can usually file copyright yourself, but call the copyright office or your attorney if you have any questions.

You can't (legally) take content from someone else's Web site and use it on your own site, even though you can physically right-click and save it or download it. Nope, not even if you include a credit line saying where it came from. Not even if you use only a portion of the content and link to the rest. Not text, not graphics, not compiled data, not photos. Nothing. Nada. Nil. Zilch. The copyright concept of fair use is designated for individuals, not for sharing with the world on the Web. Without permission, you can be sued for copyright infringement. Best case, you could be asked to cease and desist. Worst case, your site could be shut down, and you might face other damages.

If you want to use someone else's work, send her a permission request like the one in the nearby sidebar "Sample copyright permission." Don't use *inlining,* which links to graphics on someone else's site to display their images on your site. You certainly can't mirror or duplicate someone's site on your server even as a favor to a site overwhelmed with traffic — without written permission.

If you can't get permission for an image you'd like to use and can't afford to hire a photographer, take advantage of other sources, such as images on a federal government site. Unless otherwise specified, federal images are copyright free — your tax dollars at work. The manufacturers of products you're authorized to sell might provide free Web graphics as part of your online resale or distribution license.

Many Web sites offer free or low-cost images. A royalty-free arrangement gives you non-exclusive use of an image for a one-time flat fee, which can range in price. Table 15-2 lists a few sites to try.

Sample copyright permission

Dear Xxxxx:

Watermelon Mountain Web Marketing would like permission to use your *(information, article, screenshot, art, data, photograph)* on our Web site, WatermelonWeb.com. We have attached a copy of the information we would like to use. If this meets with your approval, please sign the release below and indicate the credit line that you would like to have appear. You may mail or fax back the signed form. Thank you for your prompt response.

The undersigned authorizes Watermelon Mountain Web Marketing to use the attached material on WatermelonWeb.com in perpetuity.

Signature:

Printed Name:

Title:

Company Name:

Company Address:

Telephone/Fax/E-mail:

Credit Line:

Table 15-2	Sources for Images	
Name	*URL*	*What You'll Find*
FreeStockPhotos.com	`http://freestockphotos.com`	Free images for members
Freerange Stock	`www.freerangestock.com`	Free images for members
Stock Exchange	`www.sxc.hu`	Free images for members
iStockphoto.com	`www.istockphoto.com/index.php`	Low-cost Web images
Getty Images	`http://creative.gettyimages.com`	Royalty-free images
Corbis	`http://pro.corbis.com`	Royalty-free images

Reserving Trademarks on the Web

Trademarks (for goods) or *service marks* (for services) give you the exclusive right to use a particular name or logotype within specific commercial categories. You can trademark your own name, if you want, and you must acknowledge the trademarks and service marks of others.

Trademark rights apply online. For instance, only the trademark holder can register a domain name with that trademark. The same constraint applies to celebrity names. You shouldn't use a trademarked name in your keyword meta tags or pay per click ads unless you're authorized by the manufacturer to sell or distribute the trademarked item. If you think a competitor is infringing one of your trademarks, see your IP or business attorney.

The first time you use a trademarked name (including your own) in text on your site, follow it with the superscript ® for a registered mark or (tm) for a pending mark that has not yet issued. Provide a notice of trademark ownership somewhere on your site. You can specify who owns which trademark or use a blanket statement, such as `All trademarks are the property of their respective owners`. (Refer to Figure 15-1.)

Filing a trademark is more complicated than filing a copyright application. After studying the Where to Start section on the USPTO (United States Patent and Trademark Office) site, `www.uspto.gov/web/trademarks/workflow/start.htm`, check the USPTO database (go to `www.uspto.gov/main/trademarks.htm` and click on *search*) for availability within your class of goods or services. Filing online costs $325. While you can legally submit a trademark application yourself, you might want to call an IP attorney for help.

Issues related to patent infringement and filing patents are more complex than I can cover in this book. See the USPTO site and your IP attorney.

A domain name might be available in the domain registration database, but still be trademarked. Check the U.S. Patent and Trademark Office (USPTO) database before you buy it.

Avoiding Litigation: From Disclaimers to Terms of Use

Sites that receive a lot of traffic from a wide range of users often include disclaimers limiting the site owners' exposure to liability and establishing terms of use. Like those ubiquitous agreements that require you to click Agree before downloading or enrolling in a service, these disclaimers and terms of use agreements serve primarily to protect companies from suit. However, in an age of concerns about privacy, pornography, and child access, the presence of these statements online might also keep you out of legal hot water.

Legislators, investors, or advertisers might become unhappy about content that pushes the envelope on sites that aren't identified as "adult." If you're building an online community with public postings, your business needs might soon conflict with users' desires for Internet freedom. For instance, networking sites like Tribe.net, MySpace.com, and YouTube.com are under pressure to keep out obscene material. In addition to terms of use agreements, these sites use a variety of techniques to enforce changing standards of acceptability:

- In December 2005, Tribe.net introduced a Terms of Use Guy to remove nude photos or inform authors of offensive posts.

- YouTube.com, where users post their own videos, asks users to report offensive videos in an online variant of community policing.

- Another user video site, vMix.com, hires reviewers to scan photos and text before posting.

- MySpace.com, perhaps the most popular social networking site with some 75 million members, uses filtering software to screen images for nudity, as well as human reviewers.

Decide whether you need to post disclaimers or terms of use on your site based on perceived risk and the types of information that your site includes. A *disclaimer* is a statement that waives liability or denies endorsement if users conduct unauthorized activity.

U.S. law requires that firms provide product warranties on request, if they exist, on consumer products that cost more than $15. Of course, this is a best practice technique, as I mention in Chapter 5.

You can find legal samples at business libraries, consult your business attorney, or purchase them at sites like FindLegalForms.com (www.findlegalforms.com) or AllBusiness.com (www.allbusiness.com/forms/internet/24/index.html). Or look at online disclaimers used by large corporations for inspiration (don't copy them!). There's a simple disclaimer form in Figure 15-2; you find other examples at the sites in Table 15-3.

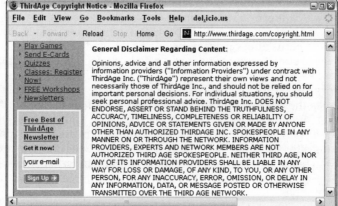

© Third Age, Inc. http:/www.thirdage.com

Figure 15-2:
The same
legal page
on the
ThirdAge
site includes
a succinct
disclaimer.

Table 15-3	Examples of Copyright and Legal Notices Online
Name	*URL*
Europa	http://europa.eu/geninfo/legal_notices_en.htm
MapQuest	www.mapquest.com/about/copyright.adp
Microsoft	www.microsoft.com/info/cpyright.mspx
Unilever United States, Inc.	www.unileverus.com/terms/termsofuse.html

If you're building a community with user-posted material, you need to consider what content you'll allow. State your requirements clearly in a Terms of Use agreement and decide how you'll enforce those standards. Include the costs of review in your site maintenance budget.

Linking Legally

Until the invention of the Web, legal issues involving hyperlinks between two sites didn't exist. On the one hand, some site owners want to link freely to any site of their choosing. Other sites want to control inbound links, deciding whether the referring site is acceptable. Some site owners have challenged links in court on the basis of trademark or copyright infringement, defamation, invasion of privacy, and other laws.

The courts have held that text links are legal without permission, even to pages other than the home page, a practice called *deep linking*. However, you'll find that some sites, such as Forbes.com, still want you to request permission to link to their site.

Here are some additional guidelines for linking to other sites:

✔ Stick with highlighted text links as much as possible.

✔ Ask permission for a link that pulls only certain information from a site, such as a picture, and redisplays it.

✔ Seek permission to use graphic links, such as someone's trademarked logo or anything else that seems questionable.

✔ On your Legal or Links page, post a disclaimer that you aren't responsible for the content on third-party sites and that these sites aren't necessarily associated with yours.

✔ Don't display content from another site in a frame on your site. It's misleading, even if you include the header graphic for the other site. Instead, use an external link, opening the other site in a new window.

These are best practice techniques, anyhow. Search engines don't like frames, which are an old technology. If you display another site in a new window, your site remains open in the browser, allowing visitors to return easily.

For more information on legal issues related to links and the Internet, visit Links & Law (www.linksandlaw.com/news.htm) or FindLaw (http://smallbusiness.findlaw.com/business-operations/internet/internet-linking.html).

Reviewing Privacy Policies

Users might provide information ranging from an e-mail address when signing up for a newsletter to a credit card number when making a purchase. Intentionally, or unintentionally, your statistical software or advertising software might track visitors' paths through your Web site. Or you might monitor their shopping preferences through *cookies* (small identification files that your site saves to visitors' computers) and reflect back those preferences through personalization techniques. You might ask for demographic data, including age, or company information and job title to prequalify visitors as prospects.

In these days of identity theft, you need to protect user information carefully. Users are increasingly aware of the risks of invasion of their online privacy, risks that go far beyond receiving junk mail in the post or porno messages in their e-mail inbox.

Start by reviewing what data you collect and why. Stop collecting information you don't need and never, ever, ask for a Social Security number. Of course, follow the basic security practices, always using a secure server when taking credit cards online and encrypting stored data. Decide not to sell or exchange users' e-mail addresses or other data and follow the best practices for e-mail I discuss in Chapter 8.

By all means, tell people how their data will and won't be used and how long it will be kept. Create an easily accessible privacy policy, perhaps following the guidelines set forth in the Privacy Statement Generator of the Organisation for Economic Co-operation and Development (www.oecd.org/document/39/0,2340,en_2649_201185_28863271_1_1_1_1,00.html).

For additional information about protecting user privacy, visit some of the sites listed in Table 15-4.

Table 15-4	Electronic Privacy Resources
Name	*URL*
Electronic Privacy Information Center	www.epic.org
Federal Trade Commission	www.ftc.gov/privacy/index.html
Center for Democracy and Technology	www.cdt.org
Privacy.org	www.privacy.org
W3C Platform for Privacy Preferences Project	www.w3.org/p3p

Establishing Kid-Safe Zones

If your site collects information from children under the age of 13, you must comply with the Children's Online Privacy Protection Act (COPPA) at www.ftc.gov/privacy/privacyinitiatives/childrens.html.

You can find specific directions on how to comply at www.ftc.gov/bcp/ conline/pubs/buspubs/coppa.htm. Basically, you're required to get parental consent before collecting information. Law or no law, it's good business to protect children online; you'll earn parental gratitude and loyalty for providing a safe and entertaining site.

The Keith Haring Foundation, dedicated to the work of the late artist, resolved the kid-safe issue with two separate sites, as I discuss in the nearby sidebar and show in Figure 15-3.

If you allow chat rooms and message boards on your child-oriented site, monitor responses before posting them, watching constantly to ensure that no predators are lurking or luring in the background. If you have any doubts, contact law enforcement authorities. Child-oriented sites should meet conservative standards for explicit imagery or text. Otherwise, you'll find that parental controls or filtering software might shut out your target audience.

Selling to children is tricky and subject to state laws. You should state clearly if children are targeted for sales and that a buyer must be at least 16 or 18. (Age limits are 21 for products like cigarettes and wine.) Make it easy for the credit card holder — usually the parent — to cancel the purchase and receive full credit. Asking for date of birth or for the verification number on the back of the card might reduce the number of unapproved transactions. Include a prominent note in the directions that children need parental permission to buy.

Keith Haring Kids

Keith Haring, an artist who lived from 1958–1990, was known for his bold lines and clever, almost cartoonlike figures. His work exudes vibrant energy, whimsy, and a bemused acceptance of a frantic world — all traits that make his art attractive to children. Grounded in a strong commitment to accessibility and public art, Haring incorporated trenchant social commentary in images he created for subways, murals, exhibits, and public spaces. Before his death from AIDS, Haring established the Foundation to continue his work with AIDS-related and children's charities and to maintain the archive of his work.

The Foundation has developed two separate sites, www.haring.com and www.haringkids.com, the former for adults and the latter for children. Both sites comply with COPPA. The adult site carries the following message, "IMPORTANT PARENTAL ADVISORY: Some of these exhibitions contain artwork of a sexually explicit nature that is not appropriate for children and that some people may find offensive. We recommend that children have restricted access to this site. Please click on the 'Kids' link above to visit www.haringkids.com, a website developed specifically for children." The children's site, which has age-appropriate material and lesson plans for teachers, doesn't sell or advertise products and doesn't link back to the adult site.

Advisory

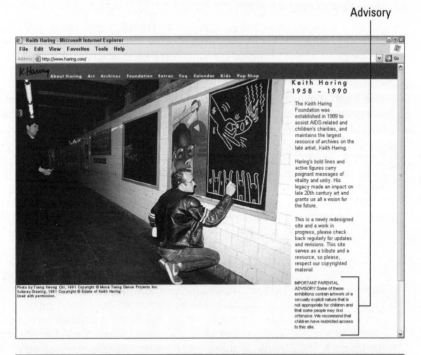

Figure 15-3:
The Keith
Haring
Foundation
maintains
two sites for
the late
artist: one
site with
adult
content and
a parental
advisory,
and another,
which is
child safe.

Both sites © Estate of Keith Haring. Design by Daniel Wiener.

An ounce of prevention

Here are some things you can do to protect your business from the dark side of cyberspace:

✔ **Buy cyberinsurance:** Most business insurance policies don't cover anything related to online activity, from denial of service attacks to Web content liability or business interruption losses due to server down time. These policies might be expensive, starting at around $5,000 for a small business, so you need to decide how much risk exposure you have. You'll find more information about cyberinsurance at

   www.microsoft.com/smallbusiness/resources/finance/business_insurance/how_cyber_
            insurance_might_ease_your_network_insecurity.mspx

✔ **Follow best practices:** CyberSource (http://cybersource.com/cgi-bin/resource_
   center/resources.cgi) and other companies offer white papers about best practices to prevent fraud. If you receive half a million dollars per year or more in business online, or have already been a victim of fraud, you'll find these sites worth researching.

✔ **Read up on Internet fraud:** Internet Fraud Watch (www.fraud.org/internet/
   intset.htm) details online scams against businesses and provides suggestions on how to protect yourself. Go to www.fraud.org/2005_Internet_Fraud_Report.pdf to read their report on 2005 fraud activity.

✔ **Report cybercrimes:** Have you been the victim of someone redirecting visitors from your Web site, illegally using your e-mail address, hacking into your Web site, abusing your intellectual property rights, stealing trade secrets, or any other cybercrime? Contact the Internet Crime Complaint Center (IC3) www.ic3.gov, which is a partnership between the FBI and the National White Collar Crime Center.

✔ **Report fraud incidents:** Call the National Fraud Information Center at 1-800-876-7060, fill out their online form (www.fraud.org/internet/intset.htm), or contact the Better Business Bureau (http://complaint.bbb.org). You might also contact econsumer.gov (www.econsumer.gov/English), a joint project of consumer protection agencies in 20 countries, including the U.S. Federal Trade Commission.

✔ **Try online escrow services:** For large transactions, such as selling a car online, try placing the transaction in an escrow account with a company such as Escrow.com (www.escrow.com/index.asp) to protect yourself against loss of payment. An escrow account also assures buyers that they'll receive their shipments in good condition. Another best practice to consider.

Safeguarding Your Business

With all the public concern about consumers being defrauded online, merchants receive little attention for the risks they face from fraud, theft of intellectual property, hacker activity, or denial of service attacks that shut down servers.

CyberSource estimates that online merchants in the U.S. and Canada lost $2.8 billion to online fraud in 2005, about 1.6 percent of overall online sales. Generally, as a merchant, you end up eating those losses. As described in Chapter 5, more merchants are taking advantage of online payment gateways with address and card code verification systems to validate credit card users, but these systems might lose effectiveness over time.

To reduce fraud, review (not cancel!) orders with different shipping and billing addresses, a foreign IP address, or multiple orders in a short time from the same customer.

This might not seem like a marketing issue, but online bad guys can affect your bottom line. Many of the ways you protect yourself also reassure your customers of your integrity and good will. The nearby sidebar, "An ounce of prevention," offers suggestions for things you can do to prevent and report losses.

Chapter 16

The Keys to Maintaining Your Web Presence

*I*n this final chapter, I return to marketing basics as the best way to maintain a vibrant, innovative, and profitable Web presence. Establishing a marketing-effective site and sustaining traffic are just the beginning. Good marketing dictates that you listen to your customers while adapting to changing trends in technology, competition, and legislation. You have to balance your natural desire to "stick to what works" with the need to accommodate an online world in constant flux. Oh, and you must still make money.

Luckily, this isn't too difficult — as long you neither hide nor hibernate. This chapter addresses some additional, best marketing practices that apply online, including letting your imagination roam free and having a good time. When your online business stops being fun, it's time to think about doing something else.

Marketing Begins with ABC

As I mention in Chapter 14, Web analytics can tell you when a site that has been perking along starts to slip, slide, or slump. After a while, your instinct will warn you, too. When tweaking your Web site doesn't work, circle back to the four Ps of Chapter 2: product, price, placement, and promotion. You'll probably find that the Web is the symptom, not the problem, more than 90 percent of the time.

The most critical measure is your bottom line! No other measure of Web success means anything if you're continuing to lose money after reaching your projected break-even point.

Whenever you're in doubt about the profitability of your site, reevaluate your business basics:

- ✔ **Review and revise your marketing plan.** Are your product mix and merchandising correct? Are your competitors carrying new products? Do you need more items, fresher items, different sizes or colors? Do you need to offer new services to accommodate changes in technology? Or conversely, have you overreached, trying to do a little bit of everything instead of focusing on your greatest (and most profitable) strengths?

- ✔ **Take another look at prices.** Are you still competitive? The Web tends to drive prices down because of price comparison sites and the increasing presence of major discounters online. If you can't make a profit matching a corporate giant's lowball prices, consider how to rephrase your *value proposition,* the statement that justifies your higher price with greater value. Your value could be 24/7 service, selection, warranty, online support, auxiliary products, or something else.

    Don't give in to the temptation to lower prices to the point that you lose money with every product you sell!

- ✔ **Revisit your decision about selling online versus offline, or both.** Have you accidentally cannibalized your sales? Are you competing with your own retailers?

- ✔ **Review your onsite, online, and offline promotional activities according to the principles in this book.** Are you driving the right people to your Web site?

    Promotional problems have an infinite number of right answers! No one answer works for everyone. In fact, more than one answer can work for you. Cast aside your Hamlet qualms, "to market or not to market?" Make an educated decision and try it. If it doesn't work, try something else.

Reaching Out to Your Customers

Feedback from your customers and prospects keeps your site, and your business, on track. They help you identify problems that need to be fixed immediately and garner ideas for new products, features, and services. I guarantee that listening beats apologizing any day! Let your customer know about your thoughtful changes in e-mail newsletters or on your site.

Some companies go even further, encouraging their customers to submit, and sometimes vote on, product designs for everything from shoes (www.fluevog.com/files_2/os-1.html) to soda labels (www.jonessoda.com/files_

new/yrlab.html) and T-shirts (http://threadless.com/submissions). Figure 16-1 shows the photo submission page for Jones Soda labels.

Your customers and prospects are the best experts at closing the marketing circle! There are lots of ways to gather information:

✔ Drop a business reply card into your shipment.

✔ Add a survey to your Web site.

✔ Ask callers what they think.

✔ If you have a bricks-&-clicks operation, ask people who come into the store what they might like to see on your site.

✔ Monitor complaints about your site that are sent to the Webmaster.

✔ Tally customer service requests for products or problems with order fulfillment.

✔ Drop into your blog, message board, or chat room at random times to see what's happening.

✔ Make it easy for customers to send you new product ideas or comments on current offerings.

✔ If you allow reviews on your own site, read them.

✔ Schedule time to check professional reviews or user ratings on sites like c|Net (www.cnet.com), Epinions.com, or Shopping.com.

Figure 16-1: Jones Soda invites users to submit photos for its soda labels and vote on the ones to be made — the ultimate in customer feedback.

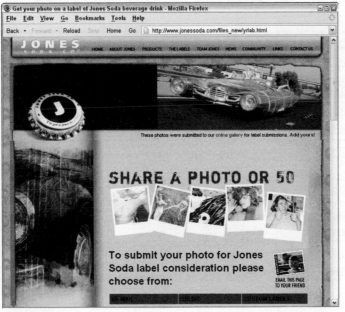

Courtesy Jones Soda Co.

Feedback can be viral, too, especially the negative kind. After bad corporate service is posted on the Web, you are exposed forever. Just ask AOL. Following AOL's call script, one of its customer service representatives made it nearly impossible for a subscriber to cancel in July 2006. The furious subscriber posted a five-minute audio clip of the interaction on his blog. The clip drove AOL into an apology, the Customer Hall of Infamy, and possible legal trouble. More than 300,000 people tried to reach the blog, the customer worked on his 15 minutes of fame with an appearance on the *Today* show, and YouTube.com posted the clip on its site. YouTube.com also hosted Comcast's moment of shame, a video of "A Comcast Technician Sleeping on My Couch." To their horror, both companies discovered viral marketing is a double-edged sword.

Rewriting Your Marketing Plan for the Future

Every company needs to pay attention to what's happening around it. Changes in competition, the business landscape, Internet technology, and legislation might all affect your bottom line. Every year, pull out your online marketing plan and adjust it to accommodate the changes you see around you.

Keep your antennae tuned to your own business sector and to the Internet overall. Table 16-1 lists some sites to review for current news about online business and technology. Scan these or other sites and sign up for a helpful newsletter, RSS feed, or subscription.

Table 16-1	Good Sites for Business News	
Title	*URL*	*Content*
B2B Online	http://btobonline.com	B2B marketing strategy
B2B Marketing Trends	www.b2bmarketing trends.com	B2B marketing techniques
ClickZ	www.clickz.com	Online marketing news and statistics
Internet Retailer	www.internetretailer.com	Industry news
Online Advertising	www.o-a.com/ acquisitions.html	Merger and acquisition deal flow
Practical eCommerce	www.practicale commerce.com	Online selling trends for small businesses
Wired Magazine	www.wired.com	News on technology and wired culture

Two-stepping with the competition

The corporate beat goes on, in spite of the dot-bomb financial bust of a few years ago. If you're a wedding planner, your site could be affected by TheKnot. com's acquisition of WeddingChannel.com. If you sell prints and posters, the merger of AllPosters.com and Art.com might affect your marketing strategy.

In addition to reading trade publications within your industry and local business news, try to subscribe to at least one Internet business newsletter to keep up with the latest activities.

For instance, you might discover that comScore Networks estimates that total, nontravel, e-commerce sales will pass $100 billion in 2006, a 22 percent growth over 2005. Or, you might find that people are buying bigger-ticket items online, shifting to broadband, and increasing their use of search engines and price comparison sites to find what they want.

Adapting to new technology

Internet technology never stays still. As more people switch to broadband connections, you can think about adding rich media (video, virtual reality, audio) to your site without alienating viewers who have slower Internet connections. This trend has already enhanced complementary marketing on TV and the Web, with commercials or entire infomercials now available online.

Take into account your target market when deciding to use rich media. While broadband use has expanded to more than half of U.S. households, it remains more widely available in urban areas and to households (generally nonminority) on the high side of the digital divide. Broadband access is actually higher in 11 other Asian and European countries than in the U.S., according to a 2005 study by CNNMoney.com.

New technologies have a way of popping up unexpectedly, offering creative new marketing opportunities but tagging your Web site as geriatric. Here are a few technologies to keep an eye on:

- ✔ **Satellite access cost and availability:** The cost of satellite broadband is dropping, allowing faster Internet access for rural and exurban communities. Slower and more expensive than cable or DSL, satellite runs about $50–$80 per month for 1.5 Mbps (megabits per second), with initial equipment costs of $300, from companies like WildBlue.com and its resellers. If you want to reach agricultural audiences, second-home owners in rural areas, or even high-income telecommuters who live along the urban/forest interface (or if you live there), this is important for you.

- ✔ **Data transmission speed:** The Web will get faster. National LambdaRail (www.nlr.net), a nationwide consortium of 20 research universities and corporations, has rolled out 15,000 miles of optical fiber across the country. Dedicated to advanced research into networking and online applications, LambdaRail's 10 Gbps (gigabits per second) network is 100 times faster than today's commercial Internet. Innovations on LambaRail eventually will affect the Internet that we use.

Watch for more video on demand, including IPTV (Internet Protocol TV), virtual reality, gaming, and other interactive applications, not to mention shared high-speed computing. This trend, of course, will affect customer expectations and the rich media content of your site.

✔ **Wireless devices:** Businesses that use the Web for local marketing already receive a boost from expanding wireless interconnections with cellphones and PDAs (personal digital assistants), as I discuss in Chapter 13. Take advantage of the coming integration of Web and global positioning systems to target local customers when they're ready for an impulse purchase or trying to find the closest service provider. This will be a great option for such sites as hospitality, tourism, entertainment, gas stations, plumbers, emergency vets, handyman services, and more.

✔ **Better interactive applications:** Ajax (Asynchronous JavaScript and XML, which is more than you wanted to know) is a suite of dynamic technologies that will make online shopping and other interactive activities faster and smoother than ever, giving the Web some of the capacity of desktop applications. Google Maps is an example of an Ajax application.

Keep an eye out for shopping cart software with capabilities that are currently available only at the high end. Within several years, you'll probably need to update your shopping site to keep up. For more information, see `http://adaptivepath.com/publications/essays/archives/00 0385.php`.

Adjusting to new rules

Chapter 15 addresses some of the ongoing legal and regulatory issues that surround online commerce. Net neutrality, one of the current issues, might affect your ability as the owner of a small site, perhaps using a small hosting company, to reach your potential customers cost-effectively. The issue pits telecommunications, wireless, and phone companies that provide broadband access against online businesses like Google, Microsoft, Yahoo!, and perhaps yours.

The telecoms want to charge a premium fee for faster Web access. Most of the Internet community (`www.savetheinternet.com`) worries that the telecom companies will put their own product offerings and sites that pay a premium in the "fast lane," leaving poorer-quality, slower service for everyone else, especially new, small businesses. Under *network neutrality,* all Internet sites would be treated equally.

Some Internet experts have proposed allowing higher rates for broader bandwidth users — for example, Voice Over Internet Protocol (VOIP) telephone, or video, versus standard data transmission — but keeping pricing neutral for all providers within a service category. As of this writing, a bill favoring the phone company position has passed the House Commerce Committee; a bill favoring the Internet company provision is in markup in the Senate Commerce Committee. Stay tuned!

Always keep your eye on taxes. While Internet access services are currently exempt from federal excise tax and state taxes, local and state governments, which depend on sales tax revenues, are interested in taxing goods and services sold online. They're seeking a simplified, automated way to collect and redistribute sales taxes for products sold out of state. Depending on the state, most online companies must already tax products delivered within the states in which their business is registered or has a physical presence.

Watch the news and get involved if this will affect your business. An outcry can make a difference. When a member of the European Parliament suggested taxing e-mail or mobile phone text messages in 2006, angry e-mails forced a retreat.

Also, watch for other forms of use differentiation that might affect your company. Already, AOL and Yahoo! have signed agreements with Goodmail, (www.goodmailsystems.com), which charges a fee to guarantee delivery of promotional, bulk e-mails. The result is higher costs for those who send promotional e-mails through these services.

The million-dollar home page

In August 2005, 21-year-old Alex Tew had a brainstorm. To pay for college, he would set up an all-advertising site with 1 million pixels and charge $1 per pixel as a gimmick. With a minimum price of $100 for a 10-x-10-pixel block, the site sold out in less than six months. Tew auctioned the final 1,000 pixels on eBay for $38,100, bringing his final take to $1,037,100, less $40,000–$50,000 in expenses.

Irreverent, self-deprecating, and clearly enjoying himself, Tew notes on his site that "business success is based on good, unique ideas that are well executed . . . I had to make key decisions at key times to keep the whole thing running and working. My success was unexpected, yes, but not accidental." He started with a single press release and word of mouth, which blossomed in a few chat rooms. Blogs and newspapers soon followed.

When he realized the site was generating sales and media attention, he says, "I actively promoted and ran the site as a business, because during its revenue-generating days, that's exactly what it was: a business. I gained over 3,000 customers and over $1 million in revenue, and that required some degree of planning and thought; it didn't just happen!" By mid-October, when he had sold more than $400,000 in ads, he hired a public relations professional to maximize media attention and increase the likelihood he'd reach his goal.

Dozens of copycat sites are trying to duplicate Alex's success. But none will. There can only be one first and he was it.

Having Fun

It's easy to feel overwhelmed by all the options for Web marketing and warnings about what can go wrong. Don't ever underestimate the power of a creative idea to trigger an avalanche of online and offline marketing attention. That's what happened with the Million Dollar Homepage (www.million dollarhomepage.com) described in the nearby sidebar. The founder, Alex Tew, not only made his million dollars (minus expenses), but also enjoyed the challenge of doing it.

Regardless of what the data says about trends or aggregate use, what matters is what's happening with your site, your business, your customers, your profits. Use your imagination and instincts to do what's best for you.

As you select marketing techniques, be sure to include ones that you enjoy doing. If you hate writing, don't do a blog; do PPC ads and follow the statistical results instead. If you love graphics, create banner ads. Delegate marketing tasks you dislike or hire a pro. Playing to your own creative strengths always produces the best results — customers will sense your passion.

If you enjoy discovering new techniques and overcoming challenges, you'll soon spin your Web marketing magic into gold. Good luck online!

Part VI
The Part of Tens

The 5th Wave   By Rich Tennant

"Yes, I think we should advertise with America Online. Besides, there is no Vladivostok Online."

In this part . . .

You'll find three quick wrap-ups of the principles in this book. Whether you're just initiating your Web site, re–designing an existing one, or somewhere in-between, it's always entertaining and educational to consider a list of things that can go wrong.

Free works when you market to others and *free* can work for your marketing. Chapter 17 runs down ten free techniques to bootstrap your Web marketing effort.

The list of the ten most common errors in Web marketing barely scratches the surface of mistakes that business owners make. The real list is endless, but if you avoid the ten described in Chapter 18, you're well on your way to success.

If your tired Web site has dried up as a source of leads or sales, try the ten methods listed in Chapter 19 to figure out the problem and solve it. This is must reading for anyone planning to redesign and relaunch a site.

Chapter 17

Ten Free Ways to Market Your Web Site

In This Chapter

▶ Kicking off your Web marketing with free techniques

▶ Using simple, free methods in e-mail and on your site

▶ Taking advantage of free search engine submissions and features

▶ Conducting a free link campaign

*F*ree. There's nothing like it. *Free* works when you market to others, and *free* can work for your marketing. Use these ten free techniques to bootstrap your Web marketing effort. As you make money from your Web investment, you'll have the funds for paid advertising and other techniques.

Even if you're one of those lucky ducks with money, you still need to start here. The first six techniques apply to every Web site. The only difference is whether you hire help or do it yourself.

Put Your URL on All Stationery and Packaging

There's no added cost to include your URL, *YourDomain.com,* on absolutely every public piece of paper that leaves your office: business cards, letterhead, invoices, packing slips, presentation folders, marketing collateral, spec sheets, and press releases.

Don't forget to include your URL on PowerPoint presentations and in the footer of white papers and proposals. Be sure your URL appears in all advertising, whether promotional items, print, radio, billboard, or TV. And of course, include it on all forms of packaging: cartons, labels, lids, bags, wrapping paper, ribbon, tissue, and any other containers.

Include Your URL in Your E-Mail Signature Block

E-mail programs allow you to create a signature block that appears on every e-mail you send. In addition to your name, title, company name, address, phone number, and fax number, include your five-to-seven word marketing tag and a link to your Web site. If you use the format `http://www.YourDomain.com`, the text automatically becomes a link in outgoing mail.

Use Calls to Action in Your Text

Calls to action are imperative verbs (such as *buy now*, *save*, *register to win*) that encourage your visitors to take a specific action on your Web site. The word *free*, as well as a textual link, is an implicit call to action. Use links and calls to action to help visitors navigate your site and to let them know what you'd like them to do. If you don't tell them, they won't know.

Collect Customer Testimonials

Recommendations from customers are golden! Whenever customers spontaneously offer praise, ask for permission to include their recommendations on your site. You don't have to identify the individuals in detail, but you need something more than "anonymous" as a source. You can collect testimonials from letters you receive, notes in a guestbook, or comments on a blog. Scatter the testimonials throughout your site on pages with related content rather than place them all on one page.

Submit to Four, Top Search Engines

Submit your Web site to the four, top search engines. It doesn't cost you a penny, and not even very much time. Submit to

- **Google** at `www.google.com/addurl/?continue=/addurl`
- **Yahoo!** at `http://search.yahoo.com/info/submit.html`
- **dmoz** (Open Directory Project) at `www.dmoz.org/add.html`
- **MSN** at `http://search.msn.com/docs/submit.aspx?FORM=WSDD2`

Conduct a Link Campaign

Inbound links from other Web sites not only bring you targeted traffic from other sites but also can improve your ranking in Google's search results. This is a time-consuming but free method of bringing high-quality visitors to your site.

Start by running a report at Google to find your own inbound links (type **link: http://www.yourdomain.com** in the search box) or those of your competitors. To identify your competitors, enter one of your keywords into Google search and review the inbound links of the top three or four sites that appear. Also, look for directories for your industry, award sites, professional associations, and vendors. Brainstorm other, related sites that might link to yours.

For the greatest benefits in Google's search results, ask for links from other sites that have a Google page rank of 5 or higher. Some sites have a page for adding your site online; others require an e-mail request for a link. Some require that you link back to them. Review the status of your requests after several months and make a second request if necessary. If you make a practice of looking for ten links each week, this won't seem as difficult a task.

Tell a Friend

The simplest of all viral marketing techniques, Tell a Friend, lets a Web visitor e-mail a friend or colleague a link to your site with a personal note of recommendation. Your developer can install free script (see Chapter 6) to handle this function. Be sure to include a link to Tell a Friend in your navigation so that visitors can quickly recommend your site, your products, or your services to someone they know is likely to be in the market for them. There's nothing like word of mouth!

Take Advantage of Free Google and Yahoo! Local Services and Coupons

Both Google and Yahoo! now offer free local listings tied to their map sites, allowing users to search for businesses within a specific geographical area. While hospitality, tourism, and entertainment sites are obvious beneficiaries of local search, local listings are valuable for every company. Many consumers like to buy locally because they think it will be easier to obtain post-purchase service or because they want to support local businesses.

Besides the listing (which is like a free ad), Google lets you offer a coupon and include your logo. Free is a great price for advertising, even if it brings in only a few customers.

Submit Your Shopping Site to Froogle

Most shopping sites are actually either pay per click, or pay per listing, search engines sites. Google's shopping search engine, called Froogle, is free to merchants. You can upload your inventory monthly (which is the minimum required frequency) or establish an RSS feed to update your online feed whenever your inventory changes. While you're at it, submit your print catalog to Google (`http://catalogs.google.com/intl/en/googlecatalogs/help_merchants.html`), also for free.

Deliver a Newsletter through Yahoo! Groups

If testimonials are gold, e-mail addresses are silver! Start collecting e-mail addresses even before your Web site is live. Be sure you ask permission to e-mail an occasional newsletter. If you can't afford the low-cost, template-based, newsletter services such as ConstantContact.com, start small with Yahoo! Groups.

After setting up your group at `http://groups.yahoo.com`, e-mail an invitation to your list of addresses to sign up. It's text-based news, but it's fast and it's easy and it's free.

Chapter 18

Ten Most Common Mistakes of Web Marketing

In This Chapter

▶ Recalling the importance of planning

▶ Reviewing the essence of implementation

▶ Remembering the value of review

Are you at your wit's end about your Web site? Worried about making irrecoverable mistakes when you start developing your site? (Not to worry. You can recover from most mistakes.) If you're thinking about a site redesign, check your current site against this list of problems and take advantage of the opportunity to fix them.

No matter what size or type of business, or how well financed, Web sites share common problems. Here are ten of those found most often. Not surprisingly, the problems start long before a Web site launches.

Not Setting Business Goals

Problem sites usually start with problem people, especially those who act before thinking. If you're not sure what your site is supposed to accomplish, it will end up as confused as you are. Start with clear business goals for the site, identify very specific target markets, and set quantifiable objectives so you can measure your success and enjoy your accomplishment.

If you already have a brick-and-mortar store, think about how to expand your market without cannibalizing it. If you're starting a new pure-play business, write a complete business plan first.

Not Planning

Site owners often think they can delegate everything to their developers and walk away from Web responsibility. Not so. No one knows your business and markets as well as you do. You need time to prepare content, write or review copy, obtain photographs, stock your store, and then maintain the site. Programming generally goes a lot faster than content.

Think ahead about everything: equipment, phone lines, staff, merchandising, measuring leads, shipping, wrapping, training, and so on. If you have problems offline, fix them before you go online. Nothing is ever simple — and that includes Web sites.

Underestimating the Time and Money It Will Take

If you're planning for Christmas sales, you can't go to a developer in August and expect to make money in December. Besides development time, you need to allow time for your site promotion to kick in.

Putting up something quick and dirty to start the clock ticking on a search engine listing is fine, but any serious Web site takes thought about how it will look, how it will function, what will be on it, and how it will be promoted. Allow at least three months for most sites, unless your company has deep pockets to pay multiple staffers or professionals to work on it.

Whatever you plan, your site will take twice as long and cost twice as much as you estimate!

Not Building a Search-Engine-Friendly Web Site

With all we know about search engines optimization, it's astonishing that companies and developers still build sites that are not only unfriendly, but also sometimes downright hostile to SEO. Huge corporations that buy enterprise-level solutions are among the worst offenders. If your developer or Web software doesn't support the following, consider a change:

✔ Search-engine-friendly URLs

✔ Site index

✔ Link page

✔ Linkable footers

✔ Contact information on every page

✔ A way to collect e-mail addresses

✔ XML feeds of site indexes to Google for large or database-driven sites

Thinking About "Me" Rather than "You"

From navigation to content, too many site owners tell their own stories rather than what site visitors want to know. A little imagination goes a long way. Put yourself in your customers' shoes. What do they want to know and how easily can they find it?

Like all other forms of advertising, Web sites are hostage to WIIFM (What's in it for me?). It's the question customers always ask and every site must answer from the first headline on the home page to the thank-you message at the end: "What's in it for me?"

Not Updating Your Site

A neglected site is a nonproductive one. If you abandon your site after it's built, you're wasting your investment. Update content, freshen merchandise, and counter what your competition is doing. Customers' expectations inexorably rise, conditioned by the best practices of sites such as Amazon.com.

You might get away with a poor site if you're the only supplier of hard-to-find products, but don't count on it. Remember: Your search engine rankings will slip if you don't update.

Waiting for Traffic to Click in the Door

So, you've built a better Web site, and the world is not beating a path to your domain. It can't, and it won't unless you actively promote your site. Search engines and an inbound link campaign are the two most essential components of Web marketing, yet many people don't do even that.

Onsite, online, and offline techniques must all be brought to bear in an active, continuous, and eternal marketing campaign. After all, Coca-Cola didn't stop marketing after it taught the world to sing.

Ignoring Statistics

Many site owners don't know they have statistics, let alone use them. They can't answer the simplest question about real trends in traffic. Instead of reviewing data, they react to someone's last impression.

While Web data of any sort is imprecise and shouldn't be trusted for absolute values, it's great for trends and relative evaluation. Plan to monitor statistics before you design your site. Confirm that your developer or host can provide the data you need.

Avoiding Problems with the Back Office

Web sites don't exist in a vacuum but in the context of your overall business operations. Many business owners blame their Web sites or Web marketing plans, when the real difficulty lies elsewhere. Is the right merchandise on the site? Is customer support available, either online or offline? Are there problems filling orders? With quality control on products? With staff maintaining the site? With your infrastructure, inventory, or accounting?

Being Unwilling to Change

Change is the only constant in the world. If you don't change with it, especially in the innovative environment of cyberspace, you will be left behind. It's easy to get attached to the past, to what's comfortable, to what you've always done. As soon as things start to look down, think about what you can change to improve. Better yet, keep an eye on trends and try to get ahead of your competition — as long as your changes track with your target market.

Chapter 19

Ten Tips for Tired Sites

In This Chapter

▶ Valuing the diagnostic information you can gather from site and sales statistics

▶ Refreshing content and site design

▶ Reinvigorating traffic

▶ Reviving sales

▶ Restoring profits

*W*oe is you! All of a sudden (or was it sudden?), your Web site has dried up as a source of leads or sales. The number of buyers flowing through the conversion funnel has been reduced to a trickle. What to do? Run around in circles and shriek to the skies? Blame your employees? Finger your developer? Take down your site? Ignore the whole mess until a temporary lack of sales turns into a real loss of money?

Instead, try these ten ways to figure out the problem and solve it. If you're planning to redesign and relaunch your site, read this section first. It's a must-read diagnostic list of problems to fix the next time around.

Diagnose the Problem Correctly

Before you begin solving any problem, investigate when the problem started and how long it's been going on. If it's sudden, make sure that your site has been running without problems. Check your daily site statistics. If there are hours or days without any traffic, contact your developer or host right away. You might have a serious issue with server reliability.

If you just launched your site, your expectations might be unrealistic or your fears might be well founded. If your site has been up for more than three years, it's probably due for tuneup, if not a complete redesign. If you haven't tended your site with loving care, your competition might have outdistanced you online.

Review your Web results to identify the starting point of the problem. Check Alexa.com to compare your site traffic to your competitors'. Search for your current competitors online and review their sites. Are you competitive with products, prices, Web site sophistication, and value? If not, you might find your problem right there. If you think you should still be near the top of the heap, sort your problems into one (or more) of these categories:

- User Appeal
- Site Traffic
- Sales Results and Conversion Rate
- The Bottom Line

Check Traffic Statistics for User Appeal

Here's where your Web analytics (see Chapter 14) really come into play. To check whether your site has lost its appeal, look at the following values in your traffic statistics:

- Number of Unique Users (a decline in this category alone is probably due to traffic)
- Number of Repeat Visitors
- Number of Sessions or Visits
- Number of Page Views per Visit
- Average Time per Page
- Average Time per Session

Go back at least three months before your site became anemic. A pattern of decline in any of the following categories is a sign that your site could use a makeover.

Review Your Design for User Appeal

Whether your site is old or new, take time to review your site with new eyes. Use the Web Site Assessment Form in Chapter 4 to rank your site for concept, content, navigation, decoration, and marketing efficacy. Have several people you don't know, but who fit the demographics of your target market, do the same.

Finally, ask several customers who have never used your site to accomplish a task or purchase something and give you feedback. Usually, a total of five people will give you enough feedback to get a good perspective on what's going on.

Every site must attract new viewers in the first few seconds on the home page, keep users on the site to see two or more pages, and bring them back for repeat visits. Where is your site falling down? If you see a slow, downward drift in time onsite, maybe your site is getting old. Post new content and see what happens.

Make Site Operation Easy for Users

Check all links to make sure they're working properly. Ask your developer to run a link verification program to check that all the internal and external (off-site) links on your site are working. You have to confirm by hand that those links are really going where you want them to and that external links all open in a new window. Make sure that all e-mail links function.

If you ask users to download PDF files, try them! Make sure they open properly and that there's a link for users to download Acrobat Reader. If you have forms, check that they work, too. Does the site have gracious error handling for phone numbers, e-mail address formats, or required fields that have been left blank? Does the site have a Thank You page to confirm that a request has been submitted? That's not only a matter of courtesy and usability, but essential for conversion tracking.

Review the following statistics for hints on identifying specific pages for repair:

- Most and least viewed pages
- Path through site
- Entry and exit pages
- Browsers and operating systems used
- Countries and languages
- Download time for key pages
- Page status reports, particularly Not Found and orphan pages

Most of all, make sure that essential calls to action are easy to follow. Is it simple to book a room, reserve a table, place tickets on will call, or buy online?

Check Page Statistics

People find your site in one of three ways: They type in your URL, they link from somewhere else, or they find you through search engines. Look at your traffic statistics for the past few months. If possible, compare them to use in comparable months from the prior year. Cyclical variations in traffic are normal for every site. Search engines look for recent updates; if you see a slow, downward drift in search engine position, try updating your site.

Look at the following data to detect changes from prior months that might indicate a problem:

✔ Comparable month use trends

✔ Variations in use by hour of day or day of the week

✔ Entry pages coded to ads

✔ Referrer URLs

✔ Search engines used

✔ Keywords used

✔ Search engine ranking (from Web Position or other tools)

Use Multiple Techniques to Build Traffic

Don't put all your marketing eggs in one basket. If overall traffic is down, you're not getting people into the top of the conversion funnel. Return to your Web Marketing Methods Checklist from Chapter 2. Make two copies. On one, check off all the techniques you're currently using. On the other, check off some new ones to try rather than, or in addition to, existing methods.

Use a combination of onsite, online, and offline marketing techniques to ensure that you have many ways to reach your audience. Choose from:

✔ **Free info tools:** Signature blocks, blurbs, FAQs, Yahoo! Groups

✔ **Onsite techniques:** Chat rooms, message boards, wikis, contents, games, coupons, surveys, free samples, event announcements, Tell a Friend

✔ **Word-of-Web online techniques:** Blogs, What's New, hot sites, award sites, online press releases, search engine optimization, inbound link campaigns, e-newsletters

✔ **Paid online advertising:** PPC campaigns, newsletter sponsorships, banner ads

✔ **Offline advertising:** Literature, stationery, packaging, promotional items, community events, direct mail, coordinated ads in other media

Check Statistics for Leads, Sales, and Conversions

Your *conversion rate* (the percentage of visitors who take a desired action, such as requesting a quote or making a purchase) is your single, most important statistic. Sales are easy to measure with store statistics. To track leads, you usually need to decide what you're going to measure in advance and set up a method for counting, such as a different phone extension for calls generated from your Web site.

For store statistics, see which products move and which ones don't. Are you losing too many people at checkout when they discover shipping costs? (Consider hiding some shipping and handling costs in the price or offering free shipping for orders over a certain amount.) Check out:

✔ Sales breakdown by product

✔ Shopping cart abandonment rate

✔ Shopping cart drop-off point (usually shipping!)

✔ Upsales rate

✔ Repeat sales

Optimize Your Site for Sales

Assuming your site fits the criteria for sales, review it to be sure you're doing everything needed to convert browsers to buyers. Here are some of the techniques you might use:

✔ Update merchandise regularly.

✔ Offer products that people want at a price they're willing to pay.

✔ Sell benefits, not features.

✔ Use marketing's three-letter word *(YOU!)*.

✔ Require only two clicks to order.

✔ Make the shopping process easy — for example, offering options to keep shopping, change the order, view a total, estimate shipping.

✔ Offer reasonably priced shipping.

✔ State customer policies clearly.

✔ Provide onsite product search capability.

- ✔ Include detailed product info.
- ✔ Use marketing's four-letter word *(FREE!)*.
- ✔ Increase your conversion rate with calls to action — for example, offering options to Add to Cart, Reserve Now, Register to Save.

Embrace the Worms

When you turn over the Web rock, the business worms crawl out. If you have *any* problems with your business — from short staffing to problems with a vendor to poor recordkeeping — going online will make them worse. Solve your problems first.

If you can't find the reason your Web site is losing money, the problem might be outside the site itself. Refocus on your target markets and business essentials. The following options might help you turn your Web site into a profit center:

- ✔ Improve the bottom line with back-office efficiency.
- ✔ Integrate your Web site with your real-world storefront and other marketing.
- ✔ Remember the 4 Ps of marketing: product, price, placement, promotion.
- ✔ Set a realistic budget.
- ✔ Set realistic expectations.

Never Stop Working on Your Site

Like your children, your Web site will be with you for the length of your (business) life. If you ignore your site, it will flag, sag, drag, and ultimately collapse from neglect. Recognize the commitment required before you start.

Index

• F •

• G •

• *H* •

• *I* •